Welcome to the EVERYTHING® series!

These handy, accessible books give you all you need to tackle a difficult project, gain a new hobby, comprehend a fascinating topic, prepare for an exam, or even brush up on something you learned back in school but have since forgotten.

You can read an *EVERYTHING*® book from cover-to-cover or just pick out the information you want from our four useful boxes: e-facts, e-ssentials, e-alerts, and e-questions. We literally give you everything you need to know on the subject, but throw in a lot of fun stuff along the way, too.

We now have well over 100 *EVERYTHING*® books in print, spanning such wide-ranging topics as weddings, pregnancy, wine, learning guitar, one-pot cooking, managing people, and so much more. When you're done reading them all, you can finally say you know *EVERYTHING*®!

FACTS

Important sound bytes of information

Quick handy tips

Urgent warnings

Solutions to common problems

THE
EVERYTHING®
Series

Dear Reader,
I bet you never thought that grammar could be entertaining—much less easy? Just you wait! As you jump in to *The Everything® Grammar and Style Book*, I hope you find an enjoyable introduction to the do's and don'ts of English grammar.

So whether you've been yearning to become an adjective authority, an adverb analyst, a capitalization kingpin, a cliché killer, a comma commander, a conjunction coordinator, an essay expert, a fragment finder, a grammar guru, a logic locator, a mechanics maestro, a noun namer, a pronoun professional, a punctuation potentate, a sentence specialist, a spelling sage, a verb verifier—or if you just want to be an all-around writing wizard—you've come to the right place. I hope you enjoy the book!

Sincerely,

Susan Thurman

Susan Thurman

THE
EVERYTHING®

GRAMMAR AND STYLE BOOK

All the rules you need to know to
master great writing

Susan Thurman

Adams Media Corporation
Avon, Massachusetts

EDITORIAL

Publishing Director: Gary M. Krebs

Managing Editor: Kate McBride

Copy Chief: Laura MacLaughlin

Acquisitions Editor: Bethany Brown

Development Editors: Lesley Bolton,
Michelle Coughlin

PRODUCTION

Production Director: Susan Beale

Production Manager: Michelle Roy Kelly

Series Designer: Daria Perreault

Layout and Graphics: Arlene Apone,
Paul Beatrice, Brooke Camfield,
Colleen Cunningham, Daria Perreault,
Frank Rivera

An Everything® Series Book.
Everything® and everything.com® are registered trademarks of F+W Publications, Inc.

Published by Adams Media, an F+W Publications Company
57 Littlefield Street, Avon, MA 02322 U.S.A.
www.adamsmedia.com

ISBN: 1-58062-573-8
Printed in the United States of America.

J I H G F E D C

Library of Congress Cataloging-in-Publication Data
Thurman, Susan (Susan Sommers)
The everything grammar and style book:
all the rules you need to know to master great writing /
by Susan Thurman
p.   cm.
Includes index.
ISBN 1-58062-573-8
1. English language–Rhetoric–Handbooks, manuals, etc. 2. English language–Grammar–Handbooks, manuals, etc.
3. English language–Style–Handbooks, manuals, etc. 4. Report writing–Handbooks, manuals, etc.
I. Title.
PE1408.T47   2002
808.042–dc21   2001055213

This publication is designed to provide accurate and authoritative information with regard to the subject matter covered. It is sold with the understanding that the publisher is not engaged in rendering legal, accounting, or other professional advice. If legal advice or other expert assistance is required, the services of a competent professional person should be sought.

—From a *Declaration of Principles* jointly adopted by a Committee of the
American Bar Association and a Committee of Publishers and Associations

Illustrations by Barry Littmann.

This book is available at quantity discounts for bulk purchases.
For information, call 1-800-872-5627.

Visit the entire Everything® series at everything.com

Contents

Introduction

ifyourhaveingdifficultyreadinthisthanmaybeitsgoodthatyouseenthisbo okyoucanrefertoittogetsomeinsightintogrammerspellingwritingstyleandlo tsofotherareasthatyouprobalyalwaysgroupdtogetherasjustenglish

Having a little trouble reading the previous paragraph? No wonder. It follows none of the conventions, or rules, of standard English. As you can see, it has no capitalization and no punctuation, and in some cases the spelling and grammar are wrong. In other words, it's a mess.

Of course, the paragraph is an extreme example of what can happen when standard rules aren't followed. If you had time—and if you had enough aspirin on hand—you could decipher the paragraph so you would finally understand it. But why should you have to? If it had been written in a way that's generally accepted, the paragraph would be simple to read and easy to understand.

If the writer had followed only the rules of capitalization, you'd have a small hint about what the paragraph is saying:

Ifyourhaveingdifficultyreadinthisthanmaybeitsgoodthatyouseenthisbo okYoucanrefertoittogetsomeinsightintogrammerspellingwritingstyleandlo tsofotherareasthatyouprobalyalwaysgroupdtogetherasjustEnglish

And if correct punctuation had been added, the message would have been almost clear:

If your having difficulty reading this, than maybe it's good that you seen this book. You can refer to it to get some insight into grammer, spelling, writing style, and lots of other areas that you probaly always groupd together as just "English."

With corrections in spelling and grammar—voilà!—you can whiz through the paragraph in no time:

If you're having difficulty reading this, then maybe it's good that you saw this book. You can refer to it to get some insight into grammar, spelling, writing style, and lots of other areas that you probably always grouped together as just "English."

The moral of the story? The rules—of grammar, spelling, punctuation, and capitalization—all have a purpose. When the writer and the readers understand—and use—the same rules (e.g., the difference between *its* and *it's*, or what a capital letter means, or how to spell *grammar*), then language becomes a code for easy, concise communication. This ability to communicate clearly through writing, which is important in so many areas of life, has been taking on new significance as people increasingly turn to e-mail for business and personal use.

But, you say, there are so many blasted rules. Yes, there are, but you use most of them already, especially if English is your native language. When was the last time you didn't capitalize the word *I?* Or when did you forget to put an apostrophe in a contraction like *can't?* You probably already know a lot more than you think you do and may just need a refresher in some areas.

Even though *The Everything® Grammar and Style Book* covers, well, everything, you don't have to read it cover to cover. It's designed so that you can refer to the specific sections you need, as you need them. If you don't understand how to use commas, for instance, all you have to do is turn to the section that explains them. Or if you've been given an assignment to write a précis, for example—and you don't even know what the word means—just look in the chapter on writing styles.

The goal here is to make your efforts to become a better writer as rewarding (and as painless) as possible. Maybe the poet Elizabeth Barrett Browning had *The Everything® Grammar and Style Book* in mind when she said, "At painful times, when composition is impossible and reading is not enough, grammars and dictionaries are excellent for distraction." (Okay, Browning died more than a hundred years ago, so maybe she just envisioned the need for *The Everything® Grammar and Style Book.*) Whether you're having trouble with composition or you just need to sort out some of the nuances of grammar, it's time to make *The Everything® Grammar and Style Book* your own "excellent . . . distraction."

CHAPTER 1
What's in a Word?

L et's begin our explorations into the wonderful world of grammar and style with the most elemental unit in which you can communicate meaning: the word. A single word can hold a world of meaning.

Spelling It All Out

You probably remember a few rules about spelling from your elementary school days. The poem that most students deem unforgettable is this one:

> *I before e,*
> *Except after c,*
> *Or when sounded as a,*
> *As in neighbor or weigh.*

That's certainly a helpful mnemonic—most of the time. It works for words such as *beige, ceiling, conceive, feign, field, inveigh, obeisance, priest, receive, shield, sleigh,* and *weight.*

But take a look at these words that don't follow the rule from the poem: *albeit, ancient, atheism, being, caffeine, codeine, conscience, cuneiform, deify, deign, deity, efficient, eiderdown, either, feisty, foreign, forfeit, heifer, height, heist, kaleidoscope, leisure, nonpareil, nucleic, protein, reimburse, reincarnation, science, seismic, seize, sleight, society, sovereign, species, sufficient, surfeit, vermeil,* and *weird.*

There are enough exceptions to make you wonder about the rule, aren't there?

Here are some of the rules that generally apply to English nouns. But note the word *generally.* English has adopted words from many languages, and those languages have differing ways of changing word forms. That means, unfortunately, that every rule will have an exception (and probably more than one exception, as you've seen). Although the whole thing can be pretty confusing, these rules will provide you with some useful guidelines for making your spelling decisions.

ESSENTIALS

You do know, of course, that you should not rely on the spell-check feature of your word processor to catch all of your spelling mistakes. Off coarse ewe due. Ewe no that the programme that ewe use two cheque mite look threw and threw and knot find awl your miss takes. An it wont tell ewe what ewe kneed too change the word two.

Making More: Forming Plurals of Nouns

1. To form the plural of most English words that don't end in -s, -z, -x, -sh, -ch, or -ss, add -s at the end:

   desk = desks, book = books, cup = cups

2. To form the plural of most English words that end in -s, -z, -x, -sh, -ch, and -ss, add -es at the end:

   bus = buses, buzz = buzzes, box = boxes, dish = dishes, church = churches, kiss = kisses

   There are some exceptions to this rule that include *quizzes, frizzes,* and *whizzes.* (Note that the -z is doubled.)

3. To form the plural of some English words that end in -o, add -es at the end:

   potato = potatoes, echo = echoes, hero = heroes, veto = vetoes

   To make things interesting, other words that end in -o, add only -s at the end:

   auto = autos, alto = altos, two = twos, zoo = zoos, piano = pianos, solo = solos

   And—just to keep you on your toes—some words ending in -o can form the plural in either way:

   buffalo = buffalo/buffaloes/buffalos, cargo = cargoes/cargos, ghetto = ghettos/ghettoes

   When in doubt about which form to use, consult the dictionary (you may want to see if your instructor or company prefers a particular dictionary) and use the plural form that is listed first.

4. To form the plural of most English words that end in a consonant plus -y, change the y to i and add -es:

   lady = ladies, candy = candies, penny = pennies

5. To form the plural of most English words that end in a vowel plus -y, add -s:

   joy = joys, Monday = Mondays, key = keys, buy = buys

6. To form the plural of most English words that end in *-f* or *-fe*, change the *f* to *v* and add *-es:*

   knife = knives, leaf = leaves, wife = wives, wolf = wolves

   Some exceptions to this rule include *oaf, chef, cliff, belief, tariff, bailiff, pontiff, plaintiff, roof,* and *chief.* All simply add *-s* to form their plural.

QUESTIONS?

Can you tell what's odd about these nouns: *ides, means, mathematics, outskirts, goods, economics, cattle, clothes, alms?* They're among the nouns that don't have a singular form.

7. Some words form their plurals in ways that defy categories:

   child = children, mouse = mice, foot = feet,
   person = people, tooth = teeth, ox = oxen

8. And—just to confuse matters further—some words are the same in both singular and plural:

   deer, offspring, crossroads, headquarters, cod, series

   You can find additional spelling rules concerning prefixes and suffixes at the end of this chapter.

FACTS

Many words that have come into English from other languages retain their original method of constructing plurals. Here are some of them:

one alumnus	two alumni
one analysis	two analyses
one cherub	two cherubim
one diagnosis	two diagnoses
one focus	two focuses or foci
one fungus	two fungi or funguses
one index	two indexes or indices
one radius	two radii

So Many Rules!

These are just some of the rules of spelling, but there are lots of others. You can find many Internet sites devoted to spelling rules. Just type in "English spelling rules" on a major search engine, and you'll get scores of hits. Some of the best sites are listed in Appendix A under "Spelling."

Make sure that any site you visit pertains to spelling rules for American English rather than British English; there can be quite a difference. Also, depending on your background, you may find it helpful to look at Internet sites that deal with English as a foreign language.

The English Way

You probably know that the meanings of some words are different in Britain than in the United States, such as the British usage of *chips* for what Americans call *French fries*, and *lorry* for what Americans call a *truck*. But are you aware that there are many variations in spelling as well? Here are a few of the variations between American English and British English:

AMERICAN ENGLISH	BRITISH ENGLISH
airplane	aeroplane
center	centre
check	cheque
color	colour
draft	draught
gray	grey
jail	gaol
labor	labour
plow	plough
program	programme
spelled	spelt
theater	theatre
tire	tyre

Mind-Blowing Mnemonics

Let's face it; spelling rules just don't sink in sometimes. There are just too many rules, and almost all of them have so many exceptions that learning them may not seem to be worth your time or trouble.

So how can you learn to spell properly? Many people create mnemonics (that is, a device, such as a rhyme, used to assist the memory) to help them spell correctly. Listed here are some commonly misspelled words and suggested mnemonic forms to help you remember the right spelling.

After looking at these mnemonics, try developing some of your own for words that you often misspell (of course, look up the words in the dictionary first to get the right spelling). For mnemonics for some commonly confused words, see Chapter 12.

- **abundance:** The problem with this word comes with not being sure of the ending. Is it *-ance* or *-ence?* Remember this mnemonic: "There is an abundance of people who can dance."
- **ache:** The middle letters cause the problem. Remember the first letter of each word of this sentence: "Aches Can Hurt Everywhere."
- **acquire:** Most misspellings omit the *c.* Remember: "I want to acquire air conditioning."
- **across:** One *c* or two? If you remember "walk across a crosswalk," you'll be sure of the spelling.
- **address:** One *d* or two? Remember: "I will add you to my address book."
- **aisle:** The beginning of this word usually poses the problem. Remember the first letter of each word of this sentence: "Athletics In Stadiums Looks Easy."
- **arctic:** The first *c* is often omitted. Remember the first letter of each word of this sentence: "A Really Cold Time Is Coming."
- **believe:** Is it spelled with an *-ie* or *-ei?* Remember: "Believe has a lie in it."
- **business:** The first part of the word is often misspelled. Remember: "I often take the bus in my business."

- **calendar:** The misspelling generally comes in the final vowel. Remember: "January is the first month of the calendar."
- **cemetery:** All of the vowels are *e*s. Remember: "Epitaphs are found in a cemetery."
- **defendant:** The last vowel is the problem. Remember: "At a picnic, it's hard to defend an ant."
- **dilemma:** One *m* or two? Remember: "Emma faced a dilemma."
- **doctor:** Is the ending *-er* or *-or?* Remember: "Get me to the doctor or else!"
- **escape:** The second letter is not an *x*. Remember: "It's essential to escape."
- **environment:** Watch that *n* in the middle. Remember: "There's lots of iron in the environment."
- **equivalent:** The problem usually comes with the last two syllables. Remember: "Is ale the equivalent of beer?"
- **especially:** The second letter is not an *x*. Remember: "I especially enjoy ESP."

FACTS

You might be as exasperated with spelling as was famous playwright George Bernard Shaw. Calling attention to various irregularities in spelling and pronunciation, Shaw once pointed out that *ghoti* was the correct spelling of "fish." How could that be? In the word *enough*, the letters *gh* make an *f* sound. In *women*, the *o* makes an *i* sound. In *fiction*, the *ti* makes an *sh* sound. Therefore, *ghoti* is how "fish" really should be spelled.

- **exceed:** Is it spelled *-eed* or *-ede?* Remember: "Don't exceed the speed limit."
- **expensive:** Is the fourth letter an *e* or an *i?* Remember: "Those pens were expensive."
- **familiar:** Sometimes people misspell the last four letters. Remember: "That liar is someone familiar."
- **February:** Even though the word is commonly mispronounced, there's an *r* after the *b*. Remember: "Brr, it's cold in February."

- **generally:** Sometimes the ending is misspelled. Remember: "The general is your ally."
- **grammar:** This word is spelled with an *-ar* on the end. Remember: "Bad grammar will mar your chances for a good job."
- **handkerchief:** There are problems with the beginning and the ending of the word. Remember: "Hand the chief a handkerchief."
- **hindrance:** There are several common misspellings of this word. Remember the first letter of each word of this sentence: "Hal Is Not Driving Right And Nobody Can Explain."
- **hoarse:** The middle of this word is the problem. Remember: "When you're hoarse, you feel as if you have oars in your throat."
- **indispensable:** Is the right ending *-ible* or *-able?* Remember: "That sable coat is indispensable."
- **knowledge:** Spellers often omit the *d.* Remember: "I know that ledge is dangerous."
- **loneliness:** The first *e* is often omitted. Remember: "Eli is known for his loneliness."
- **maintenance:** Problems arise with the middle syllable and with the *a* in the last syllable. Remember: "The main ten got an A in maintenance."
- **maneuver:** The *eu* in the middle of the sentence is often a problem. Remember that the word is spelled with the first letter of each word of this sentence: "Mary And Nancy Eat Ugly Vegetables—Even Radishes."
- **marriage:** Is it *-aige* or *-iage?* Remember: "You have to be a certain age for marriage."
- **mortgage:** There are often problems with both syllables. Remember: "Mort thought his mortgage rate was a gag."

FACTS

Haplography is the accidental omission of a letter or letter group that should be repeated in writing, as in *mispell* for *misspell.* Haplology is the spoken contraction of a word by omitting one or more letters or syllables (as in *libary* for *library*).

- **niece:** This is another word that goes against the *i* before *e* rule. Remember the first letter in each word of this sentence: "Niece Irma Expects Cute Earrings."
- **parallel:** Is it *-allel* or *-alel?* Remember: "There are two parallel lines in the middle of parallel."
- **peculiar:** The problem usually comes with the vowels at the end. Remember: "That peculiar fellow is a liar."
- **rhythm:** The two *h*s usually pose the problem. Remember: "Two syllables, two *h*s."
- **roommate:** This is often misspelled with only one *m*. Remember: "Two roommates, two *m*s."
- **separate:** The word is often misspelled by writing the second vowel as an *e*. Remember: "There's <u>a rat</u> in separate."
- **sincerely:** The second *e* is sometimes omitted. Remember: "Can I sincerely rely on you?"
- **skiing:** The problem comes with knowing to put two *i*s in the middle. Remember: "Skiing has two ski poles in the middle."
- **subtle:** The *b* is often omitted. Remember the first letter of each word of this sentence: "Some Ugly Boys Threw Logs Everywhere."
- **surprise:** The first *r* is sometimes omitted. Remember: "U R surprised when you receive a surprise." (Sound it out!)
- **villain:** The *a* is frequently omitted. Remember: "There's a villain in this villa."
- **Wednesday:** Because it's often mispronounced, this word is often misspelled when the *d* is omitted. Remember: "Try to wed on Wednesday."
- **weird:** This is another word that breaks the *i* before *e* rule. Remember the first letter in each word of this sentence: "Weird Eddie Is Really Daring."
- **wholly:** Unlike *whole*, there's no *e* but there are two *l*s. Remember: "There's holly in wholly."

Unlocking the Secrets of Root Words, Prefixes, and Suffixes

A number of the words we use today are shaped from prefixes, root words, and suffixes that originally came from many other languages, especially Latin, Greek, Old English, and French. By learning some of these roots, prefixes, and suffixes, you can analyze unfamiliar words, break them down into their component parts, and then apply their meanings to help you unlock the definition of the new words.

Root words (sometimes called base words) can add either prefixes or suffixes to create other words. Take, for instance, the root word *bene*, meaning "good." If you add various prefixes (letters that come at the beginning of a word) and suffixes (letters that come at the end of a word) to the Latin root word *bene*, you can create other words such as *benefit*, *benevolent*, *benediction*, and *unbeneficial*. Each prefix and suffix has a meaning of its own; so by adding one or the other—or both—to root words, you form new words. You can see the root word *bene* in each of the new words, and each of the new words still retains a meaning having to do with "good," but the prefix or suffix changes or expands on the meaning. (The prefix *un-*, for instance, means "not." That gives a whole new meaning to the word *unbeneficial*.)

In another example you can look at the root word *chron*, which comes from the Greek and means "time." Adding the prefix *syn-* (meaning "together with") and the suffix *-ize* (meaning "to cause to be") creates the modern word *synchronize*, which means "to set various timepieces at the same time." Use a different suffix, *-ology*, meaning "the study of," and you have *chronology*, which means "the study that deals with time divisions and that assigns events to their proper dates."

Interesting, too, is the way that ancient word forms have been used to create words in modern times. Two thousand years ago, for instance, no one knew that there would be a need for a word that meant *sending your voice far away*—but that's what the modern word *telephone* means. It's a combination of *tele*, meaning "distant or far away," and *phon*, meaning "voice or sound."

In Appendix C, you will find other common root words and some examples of modern English words that incorporate them, either with prefixes, suffixes, or both.

The Last Word on Spelling

Here are some rules for spelling words to which prefixes or suffixes have been added.

1. Words that end in -*x* don't change when a suffix is added to them:
   fax = faxing, hoax = hoaxed, mix = mixer

2. Words that end in -*c* don't change when a suffix is added to them if the letter before the *c* is *a*, *o*, *u*, or a consonant:
   talc = talcum, maniac = maniacal

3. Words that end in -*c* usually add *k* when a suffix is added to them if the letter before the *c* is *e* or *i* and the pronunciation of the *c* is hard:
   picnic = picnickers, colic = colicky, frolic = frolicking

4. Words that end in -*c* usually don't change when a suffix is added to them if the letter before the *c* is *e* or *i* and the pronunciation of the *c* is soft:
   critic = criticism, clinic = clinician, lyric = lyricist

5. Words that end in a single consonant that is immediately preceded by one or more unstressed vowels usually remain unchanged before any suffix:
   debit = debited, credit = creditor, felon = felony, travel = traveled, label = labeling
   Of course, to shake things up a bit, there are exceptions, such as:
   program = programmed, format = formatting, crystal = crystallize

6. When a prefix is added to form a new word, the root word usually remains unchanged:
   spell = misspell, cast = recast, approve = disapprove
   In some cases, however, the new word is hyphenated. These exceptions include when the last letter of the prefix and the first letter of

the word it is joining are the same vowel; when the prefix is being added to a proper noun; and when the new word formed by the prefix and the root must be distinguished from another word spelled in the same way but with a different meaning:

anti-institutional, mid-March, re-creation (versus recreation)

7. When adding a suffix to a word ending in *-y*, change the *y* to *i* when the *y* is preceded by a consonant:

   carry = carrier, irony = ironic, empty = emptied

   Note that this rule doesn't apply to words with an *-ing* ending:

   carry = carrying, empty = emptying

   This rule also doesn't apply to words in which the *-y* is preceded by a vowel:

   delay = delayed, enjoy = enjoyable

8. Two or more words that join to form a compound word usually keep the original spelling of each word:

   cufflink, billfold, bookcase, football, payday

9. If a word ends in *-ie*, change the *-ie* to *-y* before adding *-ing*:

   die = dying, lie = lying, tie = tying

10. When adding *-full* to the end of a word, change the ending to *-ful*:

    armful, grateful, careful, useful, colorful

CHAPTER 2

First Steps in Cracking "the Code" of Punctuation

Surely it has been a while since you were introduced to the rules of punctuation. In elementary school, you learned that each punctuation mark sends a certain message. By applying "the code" of punctuation and capitalization properly, your readers are able to understand your words in the way you intended.

Avoiding the Problem of Miscommunication

When readers and writers don't use the same format—the same code—for applying capital letters and punctuation marks, confusion is often the result. Using the rules of the code enables you and your reader to understand the same things. Take a look at the following:

> when the envelope arrived i opened it and screamed this is it i yelled in a voice that was loud enough to wake up the whole neighborhood running up from the basement my husband asked whats wrong nothings wrong i hastened to reply weve just become the latest winners in the state sweepstakes now well have enough money to go on that vacation weve dreamed about

There's more to the story, but at this point you've probably given up trying to decipher what's being said. Obviously, the words are jumbled together without any capitalization or punctuation, so reading them requires both time and trouble on your part.

However, if the story is rewritten and uses appropriate capital letters and punctuation marks, then reading it becomes a snap.

> When the envelope arrived, I opened it and screamed. "This is it!" I yelled in a voice that was loud enough to wake up the whole neighborhood.
> Running up from the basement, my husband asked, "What's wrong?"
> "Nothing's wrong," I hastened to reply. "We've just become the latest winners in the state sweepstakes. Now we'll have enough money to go on that vacation we've dreamed about."

Much better, wouldn't you say? The same words are used, but now you can easily read and understand the story because capital letters and punctuation marks have been correctly inserted.

The End of the Road

Let's begin at the end—of sentences, that is. There are three marks that signal that a sentence is over: a period, a question mark, and an exclamation point.

There shouldn't be a space between the last letter of the sentence and the end mark, although this is a mistake that's commonly made.

Points about Periods

A period is most often used to signal the end of a declarative sentence (one that states a fact) or an imperative sentence (one that gives a command or states a request). For example:

Declarative sentence: *The majority of the viewers stopped watching the program after the format was changed.*
Imperative sentence: *Hand me the pen that rolled near you.*

If a sentence reports a fact that contains a question, a period should be used at the end. Look at this sentence:

I wondered if you could join me tonight for a night on the town

The end punctuation should be a period because the sentence as a whole states a fact (that I'm wondering something) rather than asks a question. Periods are also used in abbreviations: *Dr.*, *Mr.*, *Ms.*, *Rev.*, *i.e.*, *etc.*, and *et al.*

If your declarative or imperative sentence ends with an abbreviation that takes a period, don't put an additional period at the end. Write:

I'll be at your apartment to pick you up at 8 P.M.

not

I'll be at your apartment to pick you up at 8 P.M..

Answering Your Questions about Question Marks

News flash: Question marks go at the end of direct questions and sentences that end in questions. But you knew that, didn't you? That wasn't really news, was it? Couldn't that information have been left out? You get the picture, don't you? Surely the point has sunk in by now, hasn't it?

A question mark is also used to show that there is doubt or uncertainty about something written in the sentence, such as a name, a date, or a word. In birth and death dates, such as (?–1565), the question mark means that the birth date has not been verified. Look at this example:

The police are searching for a fugitive known only as Richard-O (?) in connection with the crime.

Here, the question mark means that there is uncertainty about the person's name. But look at this example:

Paul said he would donate five thousand dollars (?) to the charity.

The question mark means that there's uncertainty about the exact amount of the donation.

Watch to see if a question mark is part of a title. If it is, be sure to include it:

I refuse to watch that new television program Can You Believe It?

Remember that question marks go inside quotation marks if the quoted material forms a question (see the section later in the chapter about quotation marks). Otherwise, question marks go outside quotation marks. Notice the difference in these examples:

Brendon asked, "Where in the world are those reports?"

Did Brendon say, "I thought I gave you the reports"?

If you have a series of questions that are not complete sentences, a question mark should be included after each fragment:

Can you believe that it's ten below zero? or that it's snowing? or that my electricity has gone off? or that the telephone has gone out? or that I'm completely out of snacks to get me through this weather?

They're Here! Exclamation Points

Another news flash: Exclamation points (exclamation marks) are used to express strong feelings! There's quite a difference between these two sentences:

Out of the blue, Marsha called Kyle last night.
Out of the blue, Marsha called Kyle last night!

The second sentence tells the reader that there was something extraordinary about the fact that Marsha called Kyle.

In formal writing, don't use an exclamation point (unless, of course, you're quoting a source or citing a title—or working for a tabloid magazine). In informal writing, you might include exclamation points after information that you find to be remarkable or information that you're excited about:

Paul said that he would donate five thousand dollars (!) to the charity.

or

Paul said that he would donate five thousand dollars to the charity!

Check to see if an exclamation point is part of a title. If it is, be sure to include it:

I refuse to watch that new television program I Can't Believe It!

Only in informal writing should you use more than one question mark or exclamation mark:

Is this picture of our former roommate for real?????
or
I can't believe that our former roommate is featured in Playboy!!!

May I Quote You on That?

Quotation marks ("/") are used at the beginning and ending of words, phrases, or sentences. They are used to show which words belong to you (the writer) and which belong to someone else.

The term *double quotes* is synonymous with "quotation marks." You'll learn about single quotes ('/') later.

The most common use of quotation marks is to show the reader the exact words a person said, in the exact order the person spoke them. This is called a direct quotation. Note the difference in the following sentences:

DIRECT QUOTATION

The bank robber said, "Hand over the money."

INDIRECT QUOTATION

The bank robber said to hand over the money.

DIRECT QUOTATION

The startled teller replied, "I don't have any money."

INDIRECT QUOTATION

The startled teller said that she didn't have any money.

Note that the same meaning is conveyed either way, but the use of quotation marks tells the reader that the words are being stated exactly as they were spoken.

One of the most common mistakes that is made about quotation marks is to use them immediately after a word such as *said* or *asked*. Quotation marks are used <u>correctly</u> in sentences like these:

Harry said, "Anna, will you pass me the butter?"
Anna said, "We don't have any butter."

The mistake comes in sentences that are indirect quotations (that is, the words after *said*, *asked*, and so on are not the exact words, in the exact order, that the speaker used).

Consider this sentence, which gives the same information about Harry and Anna:

Harry asked if Anna would pass him the butter.

The mistake often made is to punctuate that sentence this way:

Harry asked, "If Anna would pass him the butter."

But the words inside the quotation marks are not the exact words, in the exact order, that Harry used. Since these aren't the exact words, quotation marks cannot be used.

To Help You Along: Some Guidelines

Guideline #1. Every time you change speakers, indent and make a new paragraph, even if the person quoted is just saying one word. This is the signal for the reader to keep straight who's saying what. Take a look at this sequence:

When the telephone rang, Nick picked up the receiver and said, "Hello." Nora screamed into her end of the phone, "Who is this?" "Nick." "Nick who?" "Well, who is this?" "You know darned well who this is. You've sure called me often enough to know the sound of my voice!" "Huh?" "That's right. I'm hopping mad, and you know why."

Are you confused yet? Written that way, it is difficult for the reader to follow who is saying what. The dialogue should start a new paragraph each time the speaker changes. That way, the reader can identify the speaker. This is the way the passage should be written:

When the telephone rang, Nick picked up the receiver and said, "Hello." Nora screamed into her end of the phone, "Who is this?"

"Nick."

"Nick who?"

"Well, who is this?"

"You know darned well who this is. You've sure called me often enough to know the sound of my voice!"

"Huh?"

"That's right. I'm hopping mad, and you know why."

Guideline #2. If you're quoting more than one sentence from the same source (a person or a manuscript), put the closing quotation marks at the end of the speaker's last sentence of that paragraph *only*, not at the end of each sentence. This helps the reader know that the same person is speaking. For example:

At the diner, Geoff said, "I'll start with a cup of coffee and a large orange juice. Then I want scrambled eggs, bacon, and toast for breakfast. May I get home fries with that?"

Note that there are no quotation marks after *juice* or *breakfast*. That tells the reader that Geoff hasn't finished speaking.

Guideline #3. If you're quoting more than one paragraph from the same source (a person or a manuscript), put beginning quotation marks at the start of each paragraph of your quote and closing quotation marks at the end *only*. This lets the reader know that the words come from the same source, without any interruption. Take a look at this example:

The ransom letter read:

"We'll expect to receive the ransom money by this afternoon. You can get it from your Grandfather Perkins. We know he's loaded.

"Tell him not to try any funny stuff. We want the money in unmarked bills, and we don't want any police involved. We'll be in touch in ten hours to tell you where to deliver the dough. Just get it and keep your mouth shut."

Note that at the end of the first paragraph the word *loaded* doesn't have quotation marks after it, and there are quotation marks at the beginning and end of the second paragraph. This shows the reader that the same person is speaking or the same source is being quoted. The closing quotation marks designate when the quotation ends.

Guideline #4. Use quotation marks to enclose the titles of short works (short poems, short stories, titles of articles from magazines or newspapers, essays, chapters of books, songs, and episodes of television or radio programs):

To get the information I need for my book, I'm consulting a chapter called "The Art of Detection" from the book How Mysteries Are Written.

I've found a great deal of pleasure listening to the song "Love Letters," which is on the CD ABC and XYZ of Love.

Guideline #5. If you're using slang, technical terms, or other expressions outside the normal usage, enclose them in quotation marks:

My grandmother didn't know if it was a compliment or an insult when I described my best friend as being "phat."

In computer discussion groups, what does "start a new thread" mean?

Using the quotation marks lets the reader know which particular words or phrases you're emphasizing.

Guideline #6. Remember that periods and commas go *inside* closing quotation marks; colons and semicolons go *outside* closing quotation marks. If you examine a work closely, you'll see that following this rule doesn't really look right (and it's not adhered to in British English), but that is the way it is done in the United States. Look at this sentence:

I was reading the short story "Scared Out of My Wits," but I fell asleep in spite of myself.

See the comma after *Wits* and before the closing quotation marks? The actual title of the story is "Scared Out of My Wits" (notice that there is no comma in the title). However, the sentence continues and demands a comma, so American English requires a comma to be placed *inside* the closing quotation marks. Now look at this sentence:

I was reading the short story "Scared Out of My Wits"; I didn't find it to be scary at all.

The semicolon is *outside* the closing quotation marks after *Wits*.

Guideline #7. Deciding on the placement of the two other end marks of punctuation—the question mark and the exclamation mark—is tricky: These go either *inside* or *outside* the closing marks, depending on what's being quoted. Take, for instance, a question mark. It goes *inside* the closing quotation if what is being quoted is a question:

Martha said, "Did you fall asleep reading the story?"

The actual words that Martha said form the question, so the question mark goes *inside* the closing quotation mark to show the reader what she said. Look at this example:

Martha shouted, "I hope you know what you're doing!"

Again, the actual words that Martha said form the exclamation, so the exclamation mark goes inside the closing quotation mark. Now take a look at this example:

Did Martha say, "You must have fallen asleep"?

Note that the actual words that Martha said ("You must have fallen asleep") don't form a question; the sentence as a whole does. The question mark goes *outside* the closing quotation marks to show the reader that.

Martha actually said, "You must be right"!

Again, the actual words that Martha said don't form an exclamation; the sentence as a whole does. The exclamation mark goes *outside* the closing quotation marks to show the reader that.

What do you do when both the sentence as a whole *and* the words being quoted form a question or an exclamation? Use only *one* end mark (question mark or exclamation mark) and put it *inside* the closing quotation marks. Look at this example:

Did I hear Martha say, "Who called this afternoon?"

Quotes Within Quotes: Single Quotation Marks

In the United States, single quotation marks are used for a quotation within a quotation:

"Mark said, 'I'll be fine,' but then he collapsed," cried Shameka.

"I'm reading the story 'Plaid Blazers and Other Mysteries,'" said Laura.

Do you see that what Mark said ("I'll be fine") and the name of the short story ("Plaid Blazers and Other Mysteries") would normally be enclosed with double quotation marks? But since these phrases come inside material that already is in double marks, you let the reader know where the quotation (or title) begins by using a single quotation mark.

FACTS

Note that if you are reading a manuscript published in Britain, Canada, or many other countries, a number of the rules governing punctuation and spelling are different.

When not to use quotation marks with quotes: If you're writing using the Modern Language Association's (MLA) guidelines or the American Psychological Association's (APA) guidelines, keep in mind that there are specific rules for block quotations (passages of a certain length). In spite of the fact that you're quoting, you don't use quotation marks. You do, however, have a particular format for letting the reader know that the material you are citing is verbatim from the original text. Consult the particular guidelines for each format to see how to format this material.

CHAPTER 3
More Fun with Punctuation

N ow that you've mastered periods, question marks, exclamation points, and quotation marks, are you ready to take on a few more punctuation marks? The following shouldn't be too difficult to grasp, and we'll try and make the task as painless as possible.

The Dreaded Apostrophe

People often become confused about the purpose of apostrophes and end up using them in all sorts of creative ways! Perhaps you have done so yourself. If so, take heart, because you are certainly not alone. You can walk into almost any store and see signs like the following that feature the incorrect use of the apostrophe:

Special price's this week!   *Rent two movie's today!*   *Five can's for $4.00!*

None of these words needs an apostrophe. Each is a simple plural, and you almost never need to use an apostrophe to denote a plural. Using an apostrophe need not be so difficult. Let's start with the easiest use of the apostrophe, the contraction.

Cutting It Short: Contractions

An apostrophe often indicates that at least one letter has been omitted from a word. This is called a contraction. For example, the contraction *don't* stands for *do not*; the *o* in *not* has been omitted. *I'll* is a form of *I will*; in this case the *wi* of *will* has been omitted.

DO YOU KNOW THE CONTRACTIONS FORMED FROM THESE WORDS?	
is not	isn't
cannot	can't
she will	she'll
you have	you've
he is	he's

ESSENTIALS

Note that sometimes authors will use apostrophes in contractions to help the reader understand dialect. For instance, an author might write, "Alice is goin' swimmin' today." The reader understands that the final -gs are omitted from *going* and *swimming*, and that the author is trying to duplicate the type of speech (the dialect) that the character uses.

What's Mine Is Yours: Possession

Before using an apostrophe to show possession, first make sure that the phrase you're questioning actually denotes possession and is not simply a plural. For instance, in the phrase *the babies' rattles*, the babies possess rattles (so an apostrophe is used to indicate this to the reader); however, in the phrase *the babies in their cribs*, the babies are not possessing anything so an apostrophe is not needed.

ALERT

One of the most common mistakes with apostrophes comes with possessive pronouns (its, yours, his, hers, theirs, ours, whose). Remember that the only one of these words that ever takes an apostrophe is *its*, and only when the word means *it is*.

Here are some guidelines to help you make sense of it all.

Guideline #1. If a singular noun doesn't end in -*s*, its possessive ends in -*'s*. Say what? Take a look at this sentence:

The cars engine was still running.

The word *cars* needs an apostrophe to indicate possession, but where?

Use this mental trick to show where to place an apostrophe: Take the word that needs the apostrophe (*cars*) and the word that it's talking about (*engine*) and mentally turn the two words around so that the word you're wondering about is the object of a preposition. (This rule may be easier for you to understand this way: Turn the words around so that they form a phrase. Usually the phrase will use *of*, *from*, or *belonging to*.)

When you change *cars engine* around, you come up with *engine of the car*. Now look at the word *car*. *Car* is singular and doesn't end in -*s*, so the original should be punctuated -*'s*. You should have:

The car's engine was still running.

Try the trick again with this sentence:

Phils wallet was lying on the seat.

Mentally turn *Phils wallet* around so that you have *the wallet of (belonging to) Phil.*

After you've turned it around, you have the word *Phil*, which is singular and doesn't end in *-s*. That lets you know that you need to use *-'s*. It would read this way:

Phil's wallet was lying on the seat.

USE THE TRICK OF MENTALLY REARRANGING THE PHRASES, AND PLACE THE APOSTROPHE IN THE CORRECT PLACE IN THE FOLLOWING:

a mans suitcase	a man's suitcase
Shannons book	Shannon's book
the lions mane	the lion's mane
Mr. Browns car	Mr. Brown's car
a books pages	a book's pages

Guideline #2. When you have plural nouns that end in *-s* (and most do), add an apostrophe after the final *-s*. This tells the reader that you're talking about several people, places, or things. The same mental trick of turning the two words into a phrase applies.

Look at this sentence, which talks about two girls who had been reported missing:

The girls coats were found at the bus station.

Now just apply the trick. Take the phrase *girls coats*, and turn it around so that you have *coats of (belonging to) the girls.*

When you've turned the phrase around this time, the word *girls* ends in *-s*. This lets you know that you should add an apostrophe after the *-s* in *girls*, so the sentence should read this way:

The girls' coats were found at the bus station.

USE THE TRICK OF MENTALLY REARRANGING THE PHRASES, AND PLACE THE APOSTROPHE IN
THE CORRECT PLACE IN THE FOLLOWING:

five musicians instruments	five musicians' instruments
four cars fenders	four cars' fenders
twenty-four years worth	twenty-four years' worth
ten trees branches	ten trees' branches
twenty countries products	twenty countries' products

Although most English plurals end in -s or -es, there are a number of exceptions (and didn't you know there would be?), such as *children*, *women*, and *deer*. If a plural doesn't end in -s, the possessive is formed with an -'s (that is, treat it as if it were singular).

Again, the turnaround trick applies. Take the sentence:

The childrens coats were covered with mud.

Mentally turn *childrens coats* into the phrase *coats of the children*. Since *children* doesn't end in -s, its possessive would be -'s; so the correct punctuation would be:

The children's coats were covered with mud.

USE THE TRICK OF MENTALLY REARRANGING THE PHRASES, AND PLACE THE APOSTROPHE IN
THE CORRECT PLACE IN THE FOLLOWING:

the mens scores	the men's scores
the womens games	the women's games
the oxens yokes	the oxen's yokes

So far, so good? There is one tricky part left to consider. It concerns singular words that end in -s. There are two ways of punctuating these words. Guideline #3 is used more often than Guideline #4, but many people find that Guideline #4 is easier to grasp. You'll have to ask your instructor or employer if there is a preference as to which you should follow.

Guideline #3. If a singular word ends in -s, form its possessive by adding -'s (except in situations in which pronunciation would be difficult, such as *Moses* or *Achilles*). Look at this sentence:

Julie Jones information was invaluable in locating the missing girls.

Applying the turnaround trick would make the phrase that needs the apostrophe read this way: *information from Julie Jones.*

Guideline #3 would tell you that, since *Jones* is singular and ends in -*s*, you'd show its possessive by adding -*'s*. Therefore, the sentence would be punctuated this way:

Julie Jones's information was invaluable in locating the missing girls.

However, you may be told to use another rule:

Guideline #4. If a singular word ends in -*s*, form its possessive by adding an apostrophe after the -*s*. In this case, the sentence would be written this way:

Julie Jones' information was invaluable in locating the missing girls.

If using Guideline #4 is okay with your teacher or employer, then you only have to remember two rules about placing the apostrophe in possessives:

1. After you mentally turn the phrase around, if the word in question doesn't end in -*s*, add -*'s*.
2. After you mentally turn the phrase around, if the word in question ends in -*s*, add an apostrophe after the -*s*.

REARRANGE AND WRITE THE FOLLOWING PHRASES SO THAT THE POSSESSIVE IS USED. YOU CAN USE EITHER GUIDELINE **#3** OR GUIDELINE **#4**, DEPENDING ON YOUR INSTRUCTOR OR EMPLOYER'S PREFERENCE:

1. The computer belonging to Chris
2. The chair belonging to Lois
3. The hairstyle of Mrs. Williams
4. The house of Mr. Harris
5. The cards belonging to Katherine Mears

USING GUIDELINE #3, THE CORRECT ANSWERS WOULD BE:

1. Chris's computer
2. Lois's chair
3. Mrs. Williams's hairstyle
4. Mr. Harris's house
5. Katherine Mears's cards

USING GUIDELINE #4, THE CORRECT ANSWERS WOULD BE:

1. Chris' computer
2. Lois' chair
3. Mrs. Williams' hairstyle
4. Mr. Harris' house
5. Katherine Mears' cards

Joint Versus Individual Possession

There is a way to use apostrophes to show the reader whether the people you're talking about possess (own) something jointly or individually. Take a look at this sentence:

Jim and Allisons cars were stolen.

The question is, did Jim and Allison own the cars together or separately? If, say, Jim and Allison were a married couple and they had the misfortune of having two of their cars stolen, then the sentence would be punctuated this way:

Jim and Allison's cars were stolen.

The possessive is used after the last person's name *only*. This usage tells the reader that Jim and Allison had joint ownership of the cars.

But say Jim and Allison were neighbors, and there was a rash of car thefts on their block. The sentence would then be punctuated this way:

Jim's and Allison's cars were stolen.

The possessive is used after *both* names. This usage tells the reader that Jim and Allison had separate ownership of the cars.

USING THE RULES OF JOINT OR INDIVIDUAL OWNERSHIP, RELATE THAT INFORMATION TO THE READER IN THE FOLLOWING SENTENCES:

1. Barbara Hersh and Jack Porron own a hardware store together.
   a. Hersh's and Porron's Hardware Store
   b. Hersh and Porron's Hardware Store
2. Darla and Carla are talking about their babies.
   a. Darla's and Carla's babies
   b. Darla and Carla's babies
3. Mr. Conley and Mrs. Brown were comparing stories about their dentures.
   a. Mr. Conley's and Mrs. Brown's dentures
   b. Mr. Conley and Mrs. Brown's dentures
4. Phillip and his wife, Paula, are talking about their two children.
   a. Phillip's and Paula's two children
   b. Phillip and Paula's two children
5. Heidi and Harold are comparing the papers that each of them wrote.
   a. Heidi and Harold's papers
   b. Heidi's and Harold's papers

THE CORRECT ANSWERS ARE:

1. b. Hersh and Porron's Hardware Store
2. a. Darla's and Carla's babies
3. a. Mr. Conley's and Mrs. Brown's dentures
4. b. Phillip and Paula's two children
5. b. Heidi's and Harold's papers

A Rare Occasion: Using an Apostrophe to Form a Plural

Remember the store signs mentioned at the beginning of this section that incorrectly use an apostrophe:

Special price's this week!   *Rent two movie's today!*   *Five can's for $4.00!*

The words that have apostrophes are just plain ol' plurals; they don't show ownership in any way and so don't need apostrophes. (If you're unsure about whether you should use an apostrophe, ask yourself if the word in question owns or possesses anything.)

There are a few rare instances when you use apostrophes to form plurals. The first is when you're writing abbreviations that have more than one period.

M.D. = M.D.'s

Also, if you have proverbial expressions that involve individual letters or combinations of letters, use apostrophes to show their plurals.

Dot your i's and cross your t's.

In these instances, some style academic or company guides dictate that you shouldn't italicize the letter you're making plural; other guides take the opposite view. Be sure to consult the guide suggested by your instructor or company.

Another time that you should use an apostrophe to form a plural is when your reader would be confused by reading an *–s* alone (for instance, when an *–s* is added to an individual letter or letter combination, to hyphenated compounds, or to numbers used as nouns).

8 = 8's (instead of 8s)

Commendable Comma Comments

Like all other punctuation marks, a comma is used to avoid confusion in a sentence. When readers see a comma, they know that there is a slight pause, and they can tell how particular words or phrases relate to other parts of the sentence. Take a look at this sentence:

Will you call Mary Alice Lee and Jason or should I?

What's being said here? This sentence has entirely different meanings, depending on how commas are placed in it.

Will you call Mary, Alice, Lee, and Jason, or should I?
Will you call Mary Alice, Lee, and Jason, or should I?
Will you call Mary, Alice Lee, and Jason, or should I?

Using Commas with a Series

If you have a series of items, use a comma to separate the items. Take a look at this sentence:

The new convertible 2001 Ford and Chevy pickup were involved in a wreck.

How many vehicles were involved? With the following punctuation, you'd see that three vehicles were involved.

The new convertible, 2001 Ford, and Chevy pickup . . .

However, this punctuation shows that only two vehicles were involved.

The new convertible 2001 Ford and Chevy pickup . . .

FACTS

Commas are used more frequently than any other punctuation mark.

Use a comma between two or more adjectives (words that modify or describe or give more information about a noun or pronoun) that modify a noun (the name of a person, place, thing, or idea):

The man in the torn, tattered jacket moved quickly through the crowded, unlit street.

If the first adjective modifies the idea expressed by the combination of subsequent adjectives and the noun, then you don't need commas. Look at this sentence:

Many countries do not have stable central governments.

Since *central governments* would be considered a single unit, it is not necessary to separate it from the adjective modifying it *(stable)* with a comma.

If you're using *and*, *or*, or *nor* to connect the items in the series, don't use commas:

The flag is red and white and blue.
The flag might be red or white or blue.
The flag is neither red nor white nor blue.

ESSENTIALS

Some style guides mandate that the final comma in a series (also referred to as the "serial comma," "Harvard comma," or "Oxford comma") always be included; other guides dictate that it be eliminated, except in cases where the meaning would be misconstrued without it. You should find out which style your instructor or company prefers.

Using Commas with Compound Sentences

If you have two independent clauses (that is, two complete thoughts; two thoughts that could stand alone as sentences) and they're joined by *but*, *or*, *yet*, *so*, *for*, *and*, or *not* (remember the mnemonic *boysfan*), join them with a comma:

It was more than three hours past lunchtime, and everybody was grumbling about being hungry.

The exception: You may eliminate the comma if the two independent clauses are short and if there would be no danger of confusion with the comma not in the sentence. For example:

We filled up with gas and we went on our way.

If you have a simple sentence with a compound verb, don't put a comma between the verbs:

I wanted to get some rest [no comma] but needed to get more work done.

ALERT

Avoid using a comma with words that are generally thought of as pairs—even if they are in a series. For instance, you'd write:

I ate an apple, an orange, and peanut butter and jelly every day while I was in grade school.

Since peanut butter and jelly are often thought of as one food, you don't put a comma after *butter*.

Using Commas with Quoted Material

If a quoted sentence is interrupted by words such as *he said* or *she replied*, use commas in this way:

"For this contest," he said, "you need three pencils and two pieces of paper."

Note that the first comma goes before the closing quotation mark and the second comma goes before the beginning quotation mark.

If the words being quoted make up a question or an exclamation, don't include a comma:

"Put that down right now!" Barry cried.

Using Commas with Clauses, Phrases, Appositives, and Introductory Words

Use commas to set apart clauses (groups of words that have a subject and a predicate), participle phrases (see Chapter 8), and appositives (words or phrases that give information about a noun or pronoun) that aren't necessary to the meaning of the sentence.

Take a look at this sentence:

The handsome man over there, the only one who works in the deli department of the local supermarket, has black hair and brown eyes.

If you took out the clause *the only one who works in the deli department of the local supermarket*, you'd still have the same essential parts of the sentence. You don't need to know where the man works in order to learn his hair and eye color. (The nonessential part of this sentence is called a nonrestrictive clause. See Chapter 8 for more information.) Here's another way of looking at it: If you can take out the part in question (the part you're questioning for commas) and it still makes sense, then you should use the commas. Now look:

The only man who works in the deli department of the local supermarket was arrested for stealing four grapes and five apples.

In this case, if you removed *who works in the deli department of the local supermarket*, you'd have *The only man was arrested for stealing four grapes and five apples.* That isn't the meaning of the original sentence. *Remember:* If you need the extra words for the meaning, you don't need the commas.

Commas are also used after introductory words such as exclamations, common expressions, and names used in direct address that aren't necessary for the meaning of a sentence. If you have words that begin a sentence and you could understand the sentence without them, use a comma to separate them from the rest of the sentence. For example:

> *Why, don't you look nice tonight!*
> *Kayla, please help your brother find his tricycle.*
> *Now, what was I supposed to remember to do when I got home?*
> *No, I have no idea where you put the roll of stamps.*
> *If you must know, I have been dyeing my hair for the past ten years.*

A comma is also used before these same types of words and phrases when they appear at the end of a sentence, as long as they're not necessary for the meaning:

> *Don't you think that new CD really rocks, Jean Marie?*
> *You're not going to the party with the same person you went to the movies with, are you?*
> *Call me back at your convenience, if you please.*
> *You'll be coming with us to the company picnic on Sunday, I hope.*

Use commas around words that interrupt a sentence (called parenthetical expressions), as long as the words aren't necessary for the meaning:

> *The answer to the next question, Paula, can be found on page thirty-six.*
> *This textbook, unlike the one I had before, is written in a style I can understand.*

Use a comma after an introductory verbal (remember that a verbal is a participle, gerund, or infinitive) or verbal phrase:

> *Weeping at the sight of the destruction, the news reporter broke down on camera.*
> *To try to regain his composure, he took several deep breaths.*

Use a comma after an introductory adverb clause. (Remember that an adverb clause is a group of words that has a subject and a verb, and describes a verb, adjective, or other adverb.) For example:

Because I didn't stop at the red light, I got a ticket.

If Glenn comes in town tonight, the whole family is going to get together for a picnic.

Using Commas in Addresses

When writing out a mailing address as text (not on separate lines), put a comma between the person's last name and the start of the street address, then after the street address, then between the city and the state. It is not customary to put a comma between the state and the zip code. For example:

Please remit the payment to Abby Householder, 4238 Old Highway 41 North, Hebbardsville, KY 42309.

If you're putting address information on separate lines, use a comma only between the city and state:

Abby Householder
4238 Old Highway 41 North
Hebbardsville, KY 42309.

If you mention a city and state in text, put commas around the state:

I have to visit Clinton, Iowa, on my next sales trip.

The same is true if you mention a city and country; put commas around the country:

Using Commas in Dates

Put a comma after the day of the week (if you've stated it), the day of the month, and the year (if the sentence continues):

I'll be seeing you on Friday, February 23, 2001, at half past seven.

If you're writing only the day and month or the month and year, no comma is necessary:

I'll see you on February 23.
I'll see you in February 2002.

Using Commas in Letters

Put a comma after the greeting (salutation) of all friendly letters and the closing of all letters:

Dear Aunt Aggie,
Sincerely,

Using Commas with Titles or Degrees

If a person's title or degree follows his or her name, put commas around it:

Please call Robert Householder, Ph.D., at your convenience.
The deposition was given by Edward Butterworth, M.D.

Using Commas with Long Numbers

Using commas helps the reader understand the numbers more easily. If, for instance, you read the number 1376993, you'd have to stop and count how many numbers there are, and then group them in threes before you could understand the number. Using commas to divide the numbers makes for quicker interpretation:

Is it my imagination, or are there 1,376,993 rules for commas?

FACTS

A mistake that seems to be cropping up more and more is using a comma to separate a verb from its subject (as in "The flour in the container on top of the refrigerator, had been infested with bugs"). The comma after refrigerator should be eliminated.

CHAPTER 4
Punctuation Pairs

A few of the punctuation marks—in particular, colons and semicolons, hyphens and dashes, and parentheses and brackets—are closely linked in appearance, if not in actual function. This fact can cause confusion for the writer—and has even been known to strike fear into the heart of some. But fear no more! This chapter will clear up any ambiguity surrounding these punctuation pairs and will give you the tools you need to be able to use them with confidence.

Cleansing Your Colon

A colon is used to introduce particular information. One of the most common uses of a colon is to signal to the reader that a list will follow:

On the camping trip, please bring the following items: a flashlight, a sleeping bag, two boxes of matches, three changes of clothing, and food for six meals.

If you have a list that is the object of a verb or of a preposition, you don't need a colon:

On the camping trip, please bring a flashlight, a sleeping bag, two boxes of matches, three changes of clothing, and food for six meals.
(The list is the object of the verb *bring*.)

On the camping trip, please bring your supplies to Tom, Sally, Mykela, or Fernando.
(The list is the object of the preposition *to*.)

To be on the safe side, use an expression such as *the following* or *as follows* before the colon.

A colon is also used to explain or give more information about what has come before it in the sentence:

There are a number of complaints that I have against the tenant: she tore the plaster in the living room, her dog stained the carpet in every room, and she has not paid her rent in three months.

In formal papers, a colon usually precedes a lengthy quotation:

In his Gettysburg Address, Abraham Lincoln stated:
Four score and seven years ago, our forefathers brought forth on this continent a new nation, conceived in liberty and dedicated to the proposition that all men are created equal.

To determine what is meant by "lengthy," consult the style guide that has been designated by your instructor or employer.

There are other times when a colon is used:

- In the greeting of a business letter

  To Whom It May Concern:
- Between the hour and minutes in time

  a meeting at 4:15 P.M.
- In dividing a title from its subtitle

  My Favorite Punctuation Marks: Why I Love Colons
- In naming a chapter and verse of the Bible

  Genesis 2:10
- In naming the volume and number of a magazine

  Time 41: 14
- In naming the volume and page number of a magazine

  US News and World Report 166: 31
- Between the city and the publisher in a bibliographical entry

  London: Covent Garden Press

The Serviceable Semicolon

> *I have grown fond of semicolons in recent years. . . . It is almost always a greater pleasure to come across a semicolon than a period. The period tells you that that is that; if you didn't get all the meaning you wanted or expected, anyway you got all the writer intended to parcel out and now you have to move along. But with a semicolon there you get a pleasant little feeling of expectancy; there is more to come; read on; it will get clearer.* —Lewis Thomas, M.D., from *The Medusa and the Snail* (1979)

Although most people probably don't get as excited over semicolons as Mr. Thomas (an award-winning author and scientist), these punctuation marks can be very useful in their own way.

Semicolons signal a pause greater than one indicated by a comma but less than one indicated by a period. The most common use for a semicolon is joining two complete thoughts (independent clauses) into one sentence.

Look at the following sentences:

The bank teller determined the bill was counterfeit. There was no serial number on it.

Each of these sentences stands alone, but they could be joined by using a semicolon:

The bank teller determined the bill was counterfeit; there was no serial number on it.

 **E**SSENTIALS

Remember the mnemonic *boysfan* (the words *but, only, yet, so, for, and,* and *nor*)? If you join the complete thoughts with one of those words, you use a comma, not a semicolon.

Often semicolons are used with conjunctive adverbs and other transitional words or phrases, such as *on the other hand* or *therefore*. In this case, be sure that you put the semicolon at the point where the two thoughts are separated. For example:

Right: *There is more to this case than meets the eye; however, you'll have to wait to read about it in the newspapers.*
Wrong: *There is more to this case than meets the eye, you'll; however, have to read about it in the newspapers.*

Semicolons are sometimes used at the end of bulleted or numbered lists, depending on the style and the sentence construction. (Sometimes commas or periods are used, and sometimes there is no punctuation at all.) A list may appear like this:

In order to receive your award, you must do the following:

1. verify that you have been a member for at least three years;
2. submit copies of civic or charitable work done in the name of the club;
3. have at least three letters of recommendation.

There are many transitional words and phrases commonly used in English. Here are a few of them:

first	second	third
next	finally	then
moreover	likewise	similarly
for instance	nevertheless	consequently
otherwise	instead	as a result
that is	namely	in addition

Now, it's time to break a rule about semicolons. There are times when a semicolon is used when a comma would seem to be the correct punctuation mark. Look at this sentence:

The manhunt took place in Los Angeles, Nashville, Indiana, Stratford, Connecticut, Winnenan, Oklahoma, Dallas, and Olympia.

Notice that there are commas after the name of each city and each state (as the rule on commas says there should be). However, the reader will probably be confused about the true meaning of the sentence. Consider that a semicolon is a "notch above" a comma. By substituting a semicolon in places where you'd ordinarily use a comma, you make things clearer for the reader by showing him or her which cities go with which states. Look at how the sentence should be punctuated:

The manhunt took place in Los Angeles; Nashville, Indiana; Stratford, Connecticut; Winnenan, Oklahoma; Dallas; and Olympia.

Reading the sentence with semicolons used in this way, the reader can tell that the manhunt took place in Nashville, Indiana, as opposed to Nashville, Tennessee. Also, the reader can identify that Winnenan is located in Oklahoma.

When Semicolons Won't Work

Semicolons won't work if the two thoughts are not on the same playing field (that is, if they're not logically connected). Look at these two sentences:

The teller wore a blue suit. The police were called immediately.

Although both are sentences, there's no link between them. If a semicolon were used between these two sentences, readers would be scratching their heads, thinking they were missing something.

Semicolons also won't work if one of the thoughts is not a complete sentence. Look at this example:

The police were called immediately; screeching through the streets.

The first part of the sentence is a complete thought (*the police were called immediately*), but the second part is not (*screeching through the streets*).

The Power to Both Divide and Unite: The Hyphen

Hyphens and dashes are another tricky punctuation pair. A hyphen is a short horizontal line (next to a zero on a keyboard); a dash is longer. But the differences between them go much deeper than just a few fractions of an inch.

The most common use of the hyphen is to divide words at the ends of lines. The important rule to remember is to divide words only between syllables. Why is this important, you ask? Read the following lines:

Sarah was unhappy with her oldest child, her nineteen-year-old da-
ughter Lindsay. Lindsay was still relying on her mother to get her up wh-
en the alarm clock rang in the mornings, to see that her various deadli-
nes for typing papers for school were met, to take her side in the cons-
tant squabbles with her boyfriend, Harry.

See how difficult this is to read? That's because you've learned to read in syllables. When the words aren't divided correctly, you have to go back to the previous line and put the syllables together. So adhering to the rule of dividing words by syllables is important because it aids the reader.

The text should read:

Sarah was unhappy with her oldest child, her nineteen-year-old daughter Lindsay. Lindsay was still relying on her mother to get her up when the alarm clock rang in the mornings, to see that her various deadlines for typing papers for school were met, to take her side in the constant squabbles with her boyfriend, Harry.

If you're not sure of where the syllables occur, consult a dictionary. In addition, most word processing software contains automatic hyphenation tools that you may use. One-syllable words should not be divided.

No matter where the words are divided, be careful to leave more than one letter at the end of a line (or more than two at the beginning of a line) so that the reader's eyes can adjust quickly.

You would not write:

Beth wondered if the employment agency would call her back a-gain for another interview.

Nor would you write:

Beth killed her chances for another interview when she contact-ed the company president by telephone.

You should also avoid hyphenating acronyms (such as UNESCO or NAACP), numerals (such as 1,200 or 692), and contractions (such as haven't, didn't, couldn't). Keep in mind that some style guides may say that proper nouns (those that are capitalized) should not be hyphenated.

Also try to avoid dividing an Internet or e-mail address. Since these addresses often contain hyphens as part of the address, inserting an extra hyphen would certainly confuse the reader. If angle brackets are not used (see Chapter 5), extending the address to the second line without any extra punctuation would make the address clear for your reader. You should do that this way:

> When I tried to order, I was directed to this site:
> www.anglosaxon.com/rebates/year/1066/.

Hyphens with Numbers

Use a hyphen (not a dash) between two dates and between page numbers:

> Prohibition (1919–1933) came about as a result of the Eighteenth Amendment.
>
> See the section on the Roaring Twenties (pp. 31–35) for more information.

Technically, both of these instances use what's called an "en dash," which is longer than a hyphen and shorter than a normal dash, which is usually called an "em dash." Are you confused yet? Don't be. Most word processing programs have an INSERT icon or a character map that you can use to access en and em dashes, as well as other symbols.

Another common use of the hyphen comes when numbers are written as words instead of numerals. You probably do this already, but the rule says to hyphenate numbers from twenty-one to ninety-nine. If you look at words in which the hyphen isn't used (*sixtyfour*, *eightyseven*), you can see that they are difficult to read. The use of the hyphen makes reading easier.

Hyphens with Compound Adjectives

When a compound adjective (two or more adjectives that go together to form one thought or image) precedes the noun it modifies, it should be hyphenated. Look at these sentences:

> Charles Dickens was a nineteenth-century writer.

In this case, *nineteenth-century* is used as an adjective (it modifies the noun *writer*), and so it's hyphenated. Notice the difference:

> Charles Dickens was a writer who lived in the nineteenth century.

Here, *nineteenth century* is a noun, and so it's not hyphenated.

Some well-known scientists are studying the effects of global warming.

In this example, *well-known* is used as an adjective before the noun *scientists*, and so it is hyphenated.

Some scientists studying the effects of global warming are well known.

Since *well known* follows the noun here, it is not hyphenated.

Use a hyphen to join adjectives only if together they form the image. If they're separate words describing a noun (as *big, bulky package*), then don't use a hyphen. Take a look at this example:

loyal, long-time friend

Long and *time* go together to form the image that describes the friend, so they're hyphenated. If the hyphen were not there, then the reader would see *long time friend* and would wonder what a *long friend* was or what a *time friend* was.

If one of the modifiers before the noun is the word *very* or is an adverb that ends in *-ly*, you don't need a hyphen. You should write:

a very condescending attitude   *a strictly guarded secret*
a very little amount of money   *the highly publicized meeting*

Hyphens for Clarification

There are a few instances when a hyphen should be used to clarify the meaning of a sentence. For instance, look at this example:

Your favorite sports star resigned!

Should you be elated or upset? The way the sentence is punctuated now the star will no longer play, so his or her fans would be upset. If, however, what the writer intended to get across was that the star had signed another contract, the sentence should contain a hyphen and be written this way:

Your favorite sports star re-signed!

Now you understand the writer's intent. There aren't many words that have this idiosyncrasy (*recreation* and *recollect* are two others), but be careful of those that do.

FACTS

Hyphens are needed with three prefixes (*ex-*, *self-*, and *all-*) and with one suffix (*-elect*). Also, any time a prefix comes before a capitalized word, the prefix is hyphenated (such as *anti-American*). This is to avoid a capital letter in the middle of a word.

May I Interrupt? The Dash

The dash is a handy device, informal and essentially playful, telling you that you're about to take off on a different tack but still in some way connected with the present course—only you have to remember that the dash is there, and either put a second dash at the end of the notion to let the reader know that he's back on course, or else end the sentence, as here, with a period. —Lewis Thomas, M.D., from The Medusa and the Snail *(1979)*

Ah, the "playful" dash. As Mr. Thomas writes, a dash provides a window for some informality in writing, allowing the writer to introduce a sudden change in thought or tone. Look at this sentence:

The odometer has just reached thirty thousand miles, and I suppose it's time to call the garage to schedule a—oops! I just passed the street where we were supposed to turn.

The dash tells the reader that a sudden idea has interrupted the speaker's original thought.

SSENTIALS

If a dash is not available on the keyboard, type two hyphens (- -) in place of it. Remember that a dash should not be preceded or followed by an extra space.

A dash may also be used to give emphasis to something that's come before. Look at this sentence:

Elizabeth spent many hours carefully planning what she would pack in the van—the van that would be her home for the next three months.

Another time a dash may be used is in defining or giving more information about something in the sentence. Read this sentence:

Margaret knew that when she finally arrived at her sorority house, she would be warmly greeted by her sisters—Lillian, Bea, Kwila, and Arlene.

Note that the last example could also be punctuated by using parentheses or a colon in place of the dash. You might have written the same sentence this way:

Margaret knew that when she finally arrived at her sorority house, she would be warmly greeted by her sisters (Lillian, Bea, Kwila, and Arlene).

or this way:

Margaret knew that when she finally arrived at her sorority house, she would be warmly greeted by her sisters: Lillian, Bea, Kwila, and Arlene.

(You can see punctuating the sentence with colons is much stuffier than using a dash or parentheses. Generally speaking, save the colon for formal writing.)

ALERT

Be careful not to overuse dashes. If you do, they lose their effectiveness—and your writing looks too conversational or amateurish.

The Inside Scoop: Parentheses

You know what parentheses are (and—in case this comes up the next time you're on *Who Wants to Be a Millionaire?*—that the singular of the word is *parenthesis* and the plural is *parentheses*), but you may not be completely sure of when and how to use them. About square brackets, which, after all, are only used infrequently, you may know very little at all. Read on, in any case, and the following sections should help you master the two in a matter of minutes!

Using parentheses tells the reader that you're giving some extra information, something that isn't necessary to the meaning of the sentence but is helpful in understanding what's being read. For example:

For a complete study of Hitchcock's movies, consult Chapter 8 (pages 85–96).

Keep in mind that when a reader sees parentheses, he or she knows that the material enclosed is extraneous to the meaning of the sentence. If the information is necessary for the sentence to be read correctly, you shouldn't use parentheses. For instance, if you're comparing statistics about two floods that occurred in different years, you might have a sentence like this:

The high-water mark of the 1999 flood came in early April, as compared to the high-water mark of the 1956 flood, which occurred in late May.

You can't put *of the 1999 flood* or *of the 1956 flood* in parentheses because you need that information for the sentence. However, if you have a sentence written like this:

My latest (and, I hope, my last) adventure with blind dates was a month ago; I haven't recovered yet.

You could omit the material inside the parentheses and you'd still have the essence of the sentence. Granted, the sentence wouldn't be as cleverly worded, but the gist would be the same.

**SSENTIALS**

If punctuation is needed with the material inside the parentheses, be sure to place the punctuation marks inside the parentheses. Look at this sentence:

If someone wants to learn the punctuation rules (and who wouldn't?), this handbook is the place to go.

Only the words *and who wouldn't* form the question, and they're inside the parentheses, so the question mark also goes there.

Another time parentheses are commonly used is in giving dates, especially birth and death dates.

Dame Agatha Christie (1890–1976) wrote twelve novels that featured Miss Marple.

In addition, parentheses are used to enclose numbers or letters that name items in a series. Sometimes both the parentheses marks are used, and sometimes just the mark on the right-hand side is used:

Before checking the patient, you should (a) wash your hands; (b) make sure the patient's chart is nearby; (c) call for the attending nurse to supervise.

Before checking the patient, you should a) wash your hands; b) make sure the patient's chart is nearby; c) call for the attending nurse to supervise.

Whether you use both parentheses or just one, try to be consistent when you're naming items in a series. Also, be aware that if you use one parenthesis only, it's easy to get the letter mixed up with the preceding word.

In material that covers politics, you'll often see parentheses used to give a legislator's party affiliation and home state (in the case of national politics) or city or county (in the case of state politics).

Senator Abby Brackman (D-R.I.) met in her Washington office with a number of constituents, including Representative Mark Digery (R-Providence).

Another—though less common—use for parentheses is to show the reader that an alternate ending for a word may be read. Take a look at this sentence:

Please bring your child(ren) to the company picnic.

Keep in mind that parentheses would not be used this way in more formal writing; the sentence would be reworded to include both *child* and *children*.

Making a Rare Appearance: Square Brackets

Ordinarily, square brackets aren't used very often, except in dictionaries. If the dictionary is detailed enough, brackets are used to show the etymology, or the history, of the word being defined. (Now be honest— you've never noticed brackets in dictionaries, have you?)

One use of square brackets is in making certain that quoted material is clear or understandable for the reader. Suppose you're quoting a sentence that contains a pronoun without its antecedent, as in this example:

"He burst onto the party scene and began to take society by storm."

Just who is *he?* Unless the previous sentences had identified him, your readers wouldn't know. In that case, you'd use square brackets this way:

"He [Justin Lake] burst onto the scene and began to take society by storm."

Here's another example:

"It came as a big surprise to everyone at the party."

The reader would have no idea what *it* was. An announcement of retirement? an unexpected large check? a stripper popping out of a cake?

To explain the pronoun so that the reader understands the material more clearly, you might use brackets in this way:

"It [the fact that there was a thief in their midst] came as a big surprise to everyone at the party."

Along the same lines, you use brackets to alter the capitalization of something you're quoting so that it fits in your sentence or paragraph. For example:

"[T]he river's bank has eroded sufficiently to warrant major repair."

Use brackets for quoted material only if their use doesn't change the meaning of what's being quoted.

Remember! Just as with love and marriage and that horse and carriage, you can't have one side of parentheses or brackets without the other (except in display lists).

Another time that brackets are used occurs even less frequently. If you need to give information that you'd normally put in parentheses—but that information is already in parentheses—use brackets instead. This may sound confusing, but take a look at this and you'll see how the rule applies:

The man who was responsible for the arrest (James Bradson [1885–1940]) was never given credit.

Normally, you put a person's birth and death dates in parentheses, but since those dates would be placed in material that's already in parentheses, you use brackets instead.

Depending on the type of writing that you do, you might add the Latin word *sic* to the information that you're quoting. You don't know what *sic* means? It translates as "thus," or "so," or "in this manner." *Sic* is used to show that what you're quoting has a mistake that you are copying. By seeing the *sic* designation, the reader knows that the mistake was made by the original author and not you. Look at this sentence:

"This painting was donated to the museum on September 31 [sic]."

Now, you know and I know that "thirty days hath September"—not thirty-one, as stated in the example. By using [*sic*] the reader can tell that you copied the mistake as it was written in the original form. Note that *sic* is enclosed in brackets (and many handbooks or style guides dictate that it be italicized as well).

Most style guides allow you to use either brackets or parentheses to let the reader know that you've added italics to quoted material. The only rule is that you keep using the same device throughout the manuscript. Take your pick:

*The time of the accident is as **equally important** as is the date* [italics added].

*The time of the accident is as **equally important** as is the date* (italics added).

This lets the reader know that you—not the original speaker or writer—inserted the italics to emphasize specific material.

Generally speaking, you'll use brackets rarely—unless you're writing in a particular style. (For instance, in writing a script, stage directions are generally enclosed in brackets.). As with any writing, if you're told to use a particular style guide (say, for instance, *The Chicago Manual of Style*), be sure to consult it for the other infrequent times that brackets are used.

CHAPTER 5
Wrapping It All Up

Congratulations! You're almost done with the refresher course on punctuation. That wasn't so bad, was it? We'll wrap it up with some punctuation symbols that aren't used every day but that certainly come in handy on occasion: italics (underlining), angle brackets, ellipses, and slashes.

Getting Fancy: Italics and Underlining

What's the difference between underlining and italics? There isn't any. As a reader, you understand the same code when you see italics or underlining. With the use of computers, clicking a button and italicizing a word is just as easy as underlining it. But sometimes (when you're writing longhand or when you're using a typewriter), the option to italicize is not available. Just remember to use either underlining or italicizing consistently throughout your document rather than jumping from one to the other. A good idea is to ask if your instructor or company has a policy regarding a preference for italicizing or underlining. (Just so you know, the standard is normally to italicize, rather than to underline.)

So when is italicizing or underlining used? The most common use is in titles, but only titles of long works, such as books. For titles of short works—such as short stories, short poems, and essays—quotation marks are used. In the following example, the left-hand column shows the format for the name of a book; the right-hand column shows the name of a short story within that book:

The Complete Sherlock Holmes   "The Speckled Band"

or

<u>The Complete Sherlock Holmes</u>

Note that the titles of sacred books don't require any punctuation nor do books of the Bible.

I read the Bible for a half an hour today.
A copy of the Koran was on his bedside table.

Here's a more complete list of works that should be italicized (underlined):

- Book-length poems (note that most poems are not book-length): *Leaves of Grass*
- Plays: *A Raisin in the Sun*
- Operas: *Carmen*
- Movies: *Casablanca*
- Pamphlets: *What You Should Do Before You See the Doctor*

- Television programs (the title of an episode from a program would have quotation marks since it's shorter): *The X-Files*
- Works of art: *Mona Lisa*
- Long musical works (a CD would be underlined; a song from the CD would have quotation marks around it): *Greatest Love Songs of the Nineties*
- Magazines and newspapers (an article title from the magazine or newspaper would have quotation marks around it): *Time*
- Ships, aircraft, spacecraft, trains: *Titanic*, U.S.S. *Cole* (don't italicize the U.S.S.); *Spirit of St. Louis*; *Endeavor*; *Orient Express*

FACTS

In the Internet world, another common use for italics and underlining is in citing a URL, or Internet address; some style guides, however, require that angle brackets be used instead.

Keep in mind that articles (*a*, *an*, and *the*) are italicized (underlined) only when they're part of the actual title. For instance:

I read Sharyn McCrumb's book *The Rosewood Casket*.

The is part of the title of the book. On the other hand, you would write:

I spent time aboard the *Mir* spacecraft.

Mir is the name of the spacecraft; *the* is not part of its name.

Take Two: Emphasis—Another Use of Italics (Underlining)

Look at the following sentences and see if you can tell the difference:

"I'm *certain* I'm going to have to arrest you," the police chief said slyly.

"I'm certain *I'm* going to have to arrest you," the police chief said slyly.

"I'm certain I'm going to *have* to arrest you," the police chief said slyly.

"I'm certain I'm going to have to arrest *you*," the police chief said slyly.

"I'm certain I'm going to have to arrest you," the police chief said *slyly*.

Can you see that the only difference in the five sentences is the words that are italicized? This is another use of italics. In this case, the use of italics tells the reader where emphasis should be placed. This helps the writer let the reader know the speech patterns being used, and it also helps the reader understand those patterns.

Be careful not to overuse italics (underlining) for emphasis. If you use italics or underlining too frequently, you lose the emphasis you want to communicate, and (even worse) your reader soon loses interest. Look at this sentence and you'll see that the device is overdone:

"Chief, the *culprit* is *Mark*, not *me*. I wasn't *there* when the *wreck* happened," Bill cried *sullenly* to the policeman.

With so many words italicized, the emphasis has lost its effectiveness.

Take Three: Unusual Usage—Still Another Use of Italics (Underlining)

Read the following sentence and see if it makes sense to you:

The angry newspaper editor said to the young reporter, "You imbecile! You used robbery when you should have used burglary."

Say what? Is the editor telling the reporter that he or she committed the wrong crime? No, and if the writer had used the punctuation marks, then the sentence would make sense.

The rule is that when words, numbers, or letters are used outside of their normal context, they should be italicized (underlined). So the sentence really should be written this way:

The angry newspaper editor said to the reporter, "You imbecile! You used *robbery* when you should have used *burglary*."

Written this way, the reader understands that the reporter used the words *robbery* and *burglary* incorrectly in his or her story.

You'll also apply this rule if you're reproducing a sound through a word (if you're using a form of onomatopoeia), as in

Brrr! I didn't know it was this cold outside

or

When Jerri dropped her new calculator on the floor, she cringed as it went *kerplunk* when it landed.

The Final Take: Foreign Terms—One Last Use of Italics (Underlining)

The last use of italics (underlining) is related to the previous one. This rule says you should italicize (underline) a foreign word or phrase.

I was wavering about whether to go to the festival with my friends, but I decided *carpe diem*.

If a foreign word or phrase has become so widely used in English that there wouldn't be any question of its meaning (like per diem or summa cum laude), there's no need to italicize it.

Be careful to apply italics (underlining) only to punctuation (commas, periods, question marks, exclamation marks, and the like) if that punctuation is part of the title.

May screamed, "There's never been a better mystery than *The Murder of Roger Ackroyd!*"

The title of the book is *The Murder of Roger Ackroyd*; there is no exclamation point in the book's title, so it should not be italicized (underlined).

May screamed, "There's never been a better mystery than *The Murder of Roger Ackroyd*!"

The exclamation point and the ending quotation mark aren't italicized, since they aren't part of the title of the book.

SSENTIALS

Remember that you don't put two end marks of punctuation at the end of a sentence.

Angling for Some Attention: Angle Brackets

Before Internet usage became so commonplace, you'd see angle brackets used only in a mathematical context, with > being the symbol for "greater than" and < being the symbol for "less than."

Today, however, angle brackets are often used before and after URLs (Internet addresses). Everything within the angle brackets should be copied exactly as it is in order for the address to work.

Using angle brackets helps eliminate a problem that occurs with URLs. Many URLs contain miscellaneous marks of punctuation, including hyphens and periods, so determining whether a particular punctuation mark is part of the URL is not easy. Look at this sentence:

Be sure to check out the information about this book and lots of our other fine publications at <www.-i-love-angle-brackets.net/~angle.brackets>.

By putting the URL inside brackets this way, the reader can tell that the closing period is the end of the sentence and isn't part of the URL. If you've ever typed a URL incorrectly, you'll know how frustrating it can be to try to find one little mistake. Using angle brackets can help eliminate that.

FACTS

Some style guides will tell you to put e-mail addresses in angle brackets, too.

E-mail me at <anglebracketsRfun@newyork.net>.

What You're Not Saying . . . Ellipsis Points

When ellipsis points or marks (three spaced periods) are used, the reader knows that some material from a quotation has been omitted. Look at this sentence:

"Mary Jean left the game early because she felt that the team had no way of winning and she had a terrible headache," said Kathy Ann.

If you needed to quote that sentence, but the part about the team having no chance of winning had no relevance to what you were saying, you could use ellipsis points in this way:

"Mary Jean left the game early because . . . she had a terrible headache," said Kathy Ann.

Note that you should use ellipsis points only if the meaning of the sentence isn't changed by what you omit.

Suppose you have this sentence:

The policeman reported, "The car involved in the accident had been stolen and then driven by a woman whom friends called 'Honest Harriet.'"

You should not use ellipsis marks to shorten it this way:

The policeman reported, "The car involved in the accident had been . . . driven by a woman whom friends called 'Honest Harriet.'"

In doing so you would've left out some rather vital information.

If the material you are omitting occurs at the end of a sentence, or if you omit the last part of a quoted sentence but what is left remains grammatically complete, you would use four ellipsis points, with the first one functioning as a period. Take this original passage:

"A number of new people have joined the secret club. In fact, its membership has never been higher. Because the club is devoted to reading classical literature, however, its secret enrollment numbers have not been questioned by the public at large."

You could use ellipsis marks in these ways:

"A number of new people have joined the secret club. . . . Because the club is devoted to reading classical literature, however, its secret enrollment numbers have not been questioned by the public at large."

"A number of new people have joined. . . . [M]embership has never been higher. Because the club is devoted to reading classical literature, however, its secret enrollment numbers have not been questioned by the public at large."

Another use for ellipsis marks is in quoting someone and trying to show that there's a deliberate pause in what the person said. Read the following paragraph:

Jimmy thought to himself, "If I can just hold on to the ball long enough to get it over to Mike, I know he can get the shot off. . . . I have to pace myself and keep watching the clock. . . . Twenty-five seconds . . . Fifteen seconds . . . Eight seconds . . . Time for a pass."

The ellipsis marks tell your readers that they're reading all of Jimmy's thoughts and that Jimmy wasn't interrupted by anything, he just didn't have any conscious thoughts in the intervening time indicated by the ellipsis marks.

Slash It All! The Slash/Virgule/Solidus

What? You say you didn't know that a slash is also called a virgule and a solidus? Now, aren't you glad that you bought this book?

A virgule/slash/solidus is commonly used to mean *or*. Thus:

a slash/virgule/solidus = a slash or virgule or solidus
You may bring your spouse/significant other to the picnic. = You may bring your spouse or significant other to the picnic.

In mathematics, the slash is used to mean *per*, as in this sentence:

There are 5,280 feet/mile.

It is also used in fractions:

365/296 (meaning 365 divided by 296)

In literature, the slash separates lines of poetry that are written in a block style, as in this passage from Edgar Allan Poe's "The Raven":

Once upon a midnight dreary, while I pondered, weak and weary, / Over many a quaint and curious volume of forgotten lore— / While I nodded, nearly napping, suddenly there came a tapping, / As of some one gently rapping, rapping at my chamber door— / " 'Tis some visitor," I muttered, "tapping at my chamber door— / Only this and nothing more. . . ."

FACTS

In conjunction with modern efforts to be nonspecific about gender, the combinations he/she, s/he, him/her, and his/hers are often seen. Too many of these combinations can get awkward. To avoid them, rewrite the sentence, if possible. You can often eliminate the problem by using a plural (they) instead of the singular.

Since the popularity of the Internet, the most common use of a slash is in URLs. If you've ever inadvertently omitted a slash when you're typing an address, you know that getting the site to open is impossible.

CHAPTER 6

Parts of Speech— the Big Eight

You remember the parts of speech—your English teachers probably talked about them all the time. And why on earth would anyone other than an English teacher be interested in the parts of speech, you may be wondering—a valid question. The answer is that the parts of speech are basically the building blocks for good grammar and usage, and any writer who is not familiar with them will, sooner or later, run into problems.

Step Right Up and Name Your Noun

A noun simply gives the name of a person *(Sammy, man)*, place *(Philadelphia, city)*, or thing *(Toyota, car)*. Some definitions of *noun* also include a separate category: idea (e.g., *philosophy, warmth, love*). For purposes of capitalization and points of grammar, nouns are divided into various categories. Knowing the terms will come in handy when we get to the discussion of subject-verb agreement.

You'll notice that some of the nouns mentioned in the previous paragraph are capitalized and some are not. Proper nouns (particular persons, places, things, or ideas) are capitalized, whereas common nouns (everyday names of persons, places, things, or ideas) are not.

PROPER NOUN	COMMON NOUN
February	month
Egypt	country
Mrs. Davis	teacher

FACTS

Some nouns may act as either common or proper nouns, depending on how they are used. Take *senator*, for instance. When used alone, *senator* is a common noun:

The senator was elected to several terms in office.

When used in direct address or before a person's name, *senator* should be capitalized:

"Please, Senator, a moment of your time," the reporter begged.

Senator Johnson was elected to several terms in office.

Nouns are also divided into concrete and abstract nouns. Concrete nouns (which most nouns are) name things that can be seen, felt, heard, touched, or smelled *(star, water, album, television, flower)*. Abstract nouns name concepts, beliefs, or qualities *(freedom, capitalism, courage)*.

Some nouns are called compound nouns; these nouns consist of more than one word, but count as only one noun. Look at this name:

Franklin County Community and Technical College

It is a compound noun made up of six words, but it's only one noun (it's only one place). Here is another example:

John William Pearson III

Although John's name is made up of four words, he's only one person—so the name counts as only one noun.

Nouns are also classified as either count or noncount nouns. Count nouns are person, places, or things that can be (surprise!) counted (three *cars*, seventy-six *trombones*). Noncount nouns are persons, places, or things that cannot be counted *(unease, happiness)*. Noncount nouns are always singular.

Collective nouns are names of persons, places, or things that are sometimes counted as one unit (that is, they are considered to be singular) and sometimes counted separately (that is, they are considered to be plural). *Army*, *herd*, *pack*, and *family* are all collective nouns.

In a sentence, a noun will act either as a subject or some type of complement (predicate nominative, direct or indirect object of a verb, or object of a preposition).

The sunset was beautiful.
(The subject of this sentence is *sunset*.)

Cathy is a police officer.
(Here *police officer* is a predicate nominative, completing the verb *is*.)

Michael recently bought a new car.
(*Car* is the direct object of *bought*.)

I gave him my keys.
(*Him* is the indirect object of the verb *gave*; *keys* is its direct object.)

They went into the restaurant.
(*Restaurant* is the object of the preposition *into*.)

Pithy Pronouncements on Pronouns

The textbook definition of a pronoun is "a word that takes the place of a noun." Okay, just what does that mean? Read this paragraph:

When Mrs. Anne Marie Shreiner came into the room, Mrs. Anne Marie Shreiner thought to Mrs. Anne Marie Shreiner's self, "Is the situation just Mrs. Anne Marie Shreiner, or is the temperature really hot in here?" Mrs. Anne Marie Shreiner went to the window and opened the lower part of the window, only to have a number of mosquitoes quickly fly right at Mrs. Anne Marie Shreiner. Mrs. Anne Marie Shreiner said a few choice words, and then Mrs. Anne Marie Shreiner began swatting the pesky mosquitoes, managing to hit a few of the mosquitoes when the mosquitoes came to rest on Mrs. Anne Marie Shreiner's arm.

Isn't that the most boring paragraph you've ever read? That's because there are no pronouns used. Now read the same paragraph, but with pronouns inserted in the right places:

When Mrs. Anne Marie Shreiner came into the room, she thought to herself, "Is it just me, or is it really hot in here?" She went to the window and opened the lower part of it, only to have a number of mosquitoes quickly fly right at her. She said a few choice words, and then she began swatting the pesky mosquitoes, managing to hit a few of them when they came to rest on her arm.

What a difference a few pronouns make!

Pronouns are divided into different classifications. Notice that some pronouns fall into two classifications. To figure out which classification a pronoun falls into, you should follow a simple rule that will help you in general with the parts of speech: Look at the way the word is used in the sentence. Personal pronouns represent people or things: *I, me, you, he, him, she, her, it, we, us, they, them.*

I came to see you and him today.
We are carrying the load for them.

Possessive pronouns show ownership (possession): *mine, yours, hers, his, theirs, ours.*

"That purse is mine!" cried the woman to the would-be thief.

"These parking spaces are yours; ours are next to the door," the teachers explained to the students.

Demonstrative pronouns demonstrate or point out someone or something: *this, that, these, those.*

These are mine; those are yours.

This is his umbrella; that is your umbrella.

Relative pronouns relate one part of the sentence to another: *who, whom, which, that, whose.*

The man whom I almost hit last night was taken to the police station.
(*Whom* relates back to *man.*)

One country that I'd like to visit someday is France.
(*That* relates to *country.*)

Reflexive pronouns (sometimes called intensive pronouns) reflect back to someone or something else in the sentence: *myself, yourself, himself, herself, itself, ourselves, yourselves, themselves.*

I said I'd do it myself!
(*Myself* relates back to *I.*)

You must ask yourself what you would do in such a situation.
(*Yourself* relates back to *you.*)

One of the most pretentious mistakes writers and speakers make is using a reflexive pronoun when a simple personal pronoun (*I, me, you, he, him, she, her, it, we, us, they, them*) will do. A simple rule to follow is not to use a reflexive pronoun in a sentence if you haven't already specified whom or what you're talking about. Say what? For instance:

Please call Allan Contlesworth and myself at your earliest convenience.

You haven't said who "myself" is. The word *myself* should be replaced with *me* so that the sentence should be written:

Please call Allan Contlesworth and me at your earliest convenience.

Interrogative pronouns interrogate (ask a question): *who, whom, which, whose, what.*

Whom can I turn to in times of trouble?
What in the world was that politician talking about?

Indefinite pronouns, contrary to their label, sometimes refer to a definite (specific) person, place, or thing that has already been mentioned in the sentence. Indefinite pronouns include *all, another, any, anybody, anyone, anything, both, each, either, everybody, everyone, everything, few, many, most, much, neither, no one, nobody, none, nothing, one, other, others, several, some, somebody, someone,* and *something.*

Keep in mind that *all, any, more, most, none,* and *some* sometimes are singular and sometimes are plural.

FACTS

Pronouns are often incorrectly used in sentences like this:

Me and him are going out to get something to eat.

Me is? *Him* is? If a writer or speaker is over five years old, then he or she should never use pronouns in that way. See Chapter 8 for more discussion about subject and verb agreement.

Three Little Questions for Adjectives

The textbook definition of an adjective is "a word that modifies a noun or pronoun." It may help you define an adjective this way: an adjective describes, elaborates on, or gives more information about a person, place, or thing.

One way to determine if a word is an adjective is to ask yourself if the word in question gives you more information about a noun or pronoun.

The framed picture came crashing off the wall during the recent earthquake.

You think that the word *framed* is an adjective, and you ask yourself if it gives you more information about a noun. *Framed* does give you information about *picture*, and *picture* is a thing (a noun), so *framed* must be an adjective.

If that method of checking for an adjective doesn't work for you, try this one: Ask yourself if the word you wonder about answers one of these questions:

- Which one?
- What kind of?
- How many?

You can see that *framed* answers both *which one?* (which picture? the framed one) and *what kind?* (what kind of picture? the framed one), so it must be an adjective.

A special category of adjectives—articles—consists of just three words: *a*, *an*, and *the*. *A* and *an* are called indefinite articles because they do not indicate anyone or anything specific *(a house, an honor)*; *the* is called a definite article (actually, it's the only definite article) because it does name someone or something specific *(the owl, the transit system)*.

QUESTIONS?

When is it important to identify articles?
You should know articles when you're referring to capitalization rules. You should also know articles when you're deciding whether to use *a* or *an* before a word (such as—"a herb" or "an herb"?)

Another subcategory of adjectives is called determiners. These are adjectives that make specific the sense of a noun; they help determine to which particular units the nouns are referring (e.g., *the country*, *those apples*, *seven pencils*).

When trying to figure out if a word is an adjective, look at the way the word is used in the sentence. Take a look at these sentences:

I'll go to either game.
I'll go to either the basketball or the football game.

In the first sentence, *either* gives more information about (modifies) the noun (thing) *game*; so it's used as an adjective. In the second sentence, *either* is an indefinite pronoun (referring to the word *game*). Now look at these sentences:

The tense situation became much more relaxed when the little boy arrived.
What is the tense of that verb?

In the first sentence, *tense* describes *situation* (a thing), so it's an adjective. Looking at it another way, *tense* answers the question *what kind?* about *situation* (a thing), so it's an adjective. In the second sentence, *tense* is simply a thing, so it's a noun.

Show Me the Action (and the Being): Verbs

The Movers and the Shakers: Action Verbs

The textbook definition of a verb is "a word that expresses action or being." Verbs that express action are action verbs (not too difficult to understand, is it?). Action verbs are the most common verbs, and they are easy to spot. Look at these sentences:

Marilyn jumped for joy when Frank called her.
(*Jumped* and *called* both show action.)

The frog sits on top of the lily pad in the lake.

(*Sits* shows action—well, not much action, but you get the picture.)

Action verbs can be divided into two categories: transitive and intransitive. The textbook definition of a transitive verb is "a verb that takes an object." What does that mean? If you can answer *whom?* or *what?* to the verb in a sentence, then the verb is transitive.

I carried the injured boy to the waiting ambulance.

Carried whom or what? Since *boy* answers that question, the verb *carried* is transitive in that sentence.

Exhausted after a hard day's work, I sank into the sofa with great delight.

Sank whom or what? Nothing in the sentence answers that, so the verb *sank* is intransitive in that sentence. Looking at the way a word is used in a sentence will help you determine what part of speech it is.

Knowing about transitive and intransitive verbs can help you with some easily confused verbs, such as *lie* and *lay*, and *sit* and *set*. You'll be able to see that *lie* is intransitive (I lie down), *lay* is transitive (I lay the book on the table), *sit* is intransitive (I'll sit here for a while), and *set* is transitive (Mary Beth set the vase on the dresser).

Just "Being" Verbs

Granted, the action verb is easy to spot. But what in the world is meant by the part of the definition that says a verb "expresses . . . being"? That usually means that the word is a form of the verb *be*. But that's a problem because, except for *been* and *being*, most forms of *be* don't look remotely like *be*.

It would be nonstandard to say, for instance:

I be sitting on the dock of the bay.
You would say:
I am sitting on the dock of the bay.

In that case, *am* is a form of *be*. Looking at the past tense, it would be nonstandard to say:

Yesterday she be sitting on the dock of the bay.
Instead, you would write:
Yesterday she was sitting on the dock of the bay.
So *was* is a form of *be*.

Here are the forms of *be* (and, remember, that except for *been* and *being*, not one of them looks like *be*): *am, is, are, was, were, be, being, been*. These forms also include *has been, should have been, may be,* and *might be*.

Two More Players: Linking and Helping (Auxiliary) Verbs

Linking Verbs

Notice that the wording for defining "expresses . . . being" includes the word "usually." Just to complicate the situation, the words in the following list can sometimes be linking verbs (depending on when you went to school, you may know them as copulative verbs).

THE FOLLOWING VERBS CAN BE EITHER LINKING VERBS OR ACTION VERBS:		
appear	become	feel
grow	look	prove
remain	seem	smell
sound	stay	taste

So when are these twelve verbs action verbs, and when are they linking verbs? Use this test: If you can substitute a form of *be* (*am, is, was,* and so on) and the sentence still makes sense, by golly, you've got yourself a linking verb. Look at these examples:

The soup tasted too spicy for me.

Substitute *was* or *is* for *tasted* and you have this sentence:

The soup was (is) too spicy for me.

It makes perfect sense. Now look at this one:

I tasted the spicy soup.

Substitute *was* or *is* for *tasted* and you have this sentence:

I was (is) the spicy soup.

It doesn't make much sense the way it is written, does it? Since the substitution of a *be* verb doesn't make sense, you don't have a linking verb. You can try the same trick by substituting a form of *seem*:

The soup tasted too spicy for me.

Substitute *seemed* and you have the following:

The soup seemed too spicy for me.

It makes sense; therefore, *tasted* is a linking verb.

 Try the same trick with this sentence:

I tasted the spicy soup.

But you get:

I seemed the spicy soup.

It doesn't make sense; therefore, *tasted* is not a linking verb.

Helping (Auxiliary) Verbs

Another type of verb that may appear in a sentence is a helping verb or auxiliary verb. It can join the main verb (becoming the helper of the main verb) to express the tense, mood, and voice of the verb. Common helping verbs are *be, do, have, can, may,* and so on. (The first two sentences of this paragraph have helping verbs: *may* and *can.*)

Breaking It Down: The Principal Parts of Verbs

You may be familiar with the phrase "the principal parts of verbs." This refers to basic forms that verbs can take. In English there are four principal parts: the present infinitive (which you see as the main entry in a dictionary), the past tense, the past participle, and the present participle. (See Chapter 10 for more information about the principal parts of verbs.) Take a look at the principal parts of these verbs:

PRESENT INFINITIVE	PAST TENSE	PAST PARTICIPLE	PRESENT PARTICIPLE
turn	turned	turned	turning
scratch	scratched	scratched	scratching
hammer	hammered	hammered	hammering
bring	brought	brought	bringing
broadcast	broadcast	broadcast	broadcasting
rise	rose	risen	rising

You'll note that the first three examples all form their past and past participle by adding *-d* or *-ed* to the present infinitive. Most English verbs do this; they are called regular verbs. The last three examples, however, are not formed in the regular way; these are called (surprise!) irregular verbs. (There is more about verb forms in Chapter 10.) All verbs form the present participle by adding *-ing* to the present infinitive.

Admirable Advice about Adverbs

An adverb is a word that modifies (describes, gives more information about) a verb, adjective, or other adverb.

Yesterday the quite relieved soldier very quickly ran out of the woods when he saw his comrade frantically waving at him.

The adverbs in that sentence are *yesterday* (modifies the verb *ran*), *quite* (modifies the adjective *relieved*), *very* (modifies the adverb *quickly*), *quickly* (modifies the verb *ran*), and *frantically* (modifies the verb *waving*).

If you still need help finding adverbs, try this method: Ask yourself if the word you're wondering about answers one of these questions:

- How?
- When?
- Where?
- Why?
- Under what circumstances?
- How much?
- How often?
- To what extent?

In the example, *yesterday* answers the question *when?*; *quite* answers the question *to what extent?*; *very* answers the question *to what extent?* (or *how much?*); *quickly* answers the question *how?* (or *to what extent?*); and *frantically* answers the question *how?*

The Joiners: Conjunctive Adverbs

Conjunctive adverbs are in a category of their own. These words join independent clauses into one sentence. (You'll also see them in lists of transitional words and phrases.)

COMMON CONJUNCTIVE ADVERBS		
accordingly	however	nevertheless
also	incidentally	next
besides	indeed	otherwise
consequently	instead	still
finally	likewise	therefore
furthermore	meanwhile	thus
hence	moreover	

Use conjunctive adverbs to join short sentences into more complex thoughts; however, (did you notice the conjunctive adverb there?) be sure that:

1. You have a complete thought on either side of the conjunctive adverb.
2. You put a semicolon before it and a comma after it.

3. You're joining two closely related thoughts.
4. You've used the right conjunctive adverb.

There is a small group of adverbs known as intensifiers or qualifiers (*very* is the most common intensifier). These words increase the intensity of the adjectives and other adverbs they modify. Other common intensifiers are *awfully*, *extremely*, *kind of*, *more*, *most*, *pretty* (as in *pretty happy*), *quite*, *rather*, *really* (as in *really sad*), *somewhat*, *sort of*, and *too*.

Who Says Adverbs Can't Be Fun?

Tom Swifties are puns that use adverbs (usually adverbs that end in *-ly*). The adverbs create a "punny" description between how Tom asked or said something (the adverb) and the words he is quoted as saying. For example, here's a Tom Swifty: "Which way is the cemetery?" Tom asked gravely. (Get it? The word *gravely* is a play on the word *cemetery*.) Here are a number of Tom Swifties. See if you can fill in the adverbs that will make the Tom Swifties complete:

1. "Would you turn the light on?" Tom asked
2. "That's nothing; I've had a transplant," Tom's father countered
3. "I can't tell if that is sleet or hail," Tom said
4. "You're driving too fast!" Tom cried
5. "The florist has run out of flowers," Tom lamented
6. "This is the end of our relationship," Tom declared
7. "It's too warm in here!" Tom bellowed
8. "Because of my new job, I'll have to relocate," Tom remarked
9. "Play ball!" Tom shouted
10. "Let's go see a baseball game in Atlanta," Tom suggested
11. "I've had triple bypass surgery," Tom announced
12. "I'll walk around the block," Tom said
13. "Let's stop at McDonald's," Tom murmured
14. "I hate exams!" Tom thought
15. "Don't stick your finger out at me," Tom roared
16. "Let's not read this book; I hate Hemingway," Tom admitted

17. "May I put more spice in this pie mix?" Tom inquired _____

18. "That bird just flew in the chimney!" Tom cried _____

19. "Oh-oh. We need a spare tire," Tom proclaimed _____

20. "May I have some saccharine?" Tom requested _____

Answers to "Tom Swifties"

1. darkly.	11. heartily.
2. wholeheartedly.	12. squarely.
3. icily.	13. archly.
4. speedily.	14. testily.
5. lackadaisically.	15. pointedly.
6. finally.	16. earnestly.
7. hotly.	17. gingerly.
8. movingly.	18. swiftly.
9. gamely.	19. flatly.
10. bravely.	20. sweetly.

What's Your Position on Prepositions?

A preposition is a word that links a noun or pronoun to some other word in a sentence. Take, for example, these short sentences:

Jack and Jill went up the hill.
(*Up* is a preposition connecting *went* and *hill.*)

Little Jack Horner sat in a corner.
(*In* is a preposition connecting *sat* and *corner.*)

And he called for his fiddlers three.
(*For* is a preposition connecting *called* and *fiddlers.*)

Sing a song of sixpence.
(*Of* is a preposition connecting *song* and *sixpence.*)

THE MOST COMMON PREPOSITIONS				
about	behind	down	off	to
above	below	during	on	toward
across	beneath	except	onto	under
after	beside	for	out	underneath
against	between	from	outside	until
along	beyond	in	over	up
among	but	inside	past	upon
around	by	into	since	with
at	concerning	like	through	within
before	despite	of	throughout	without

Note that some prepositions (called compound prepositions) consist of more than one word: *in spite of*, *next to*, *on top of*, and *together with*.

FACTS

You may remember this definition from elementary school: A preposition tells any way a mouse can go (i.e., a mouse can go near, through, on, onto, above, along, and so forth). This definition works for most prepositions, though not all (how can a mouse go until? or despite?).

If you're trying to determine if a particular word is a preposition, here's a little trick that works for many prepositions: See if the word in question will fit in this sentence:

It went _____ the thing(s).

If the word in question makes sense in that sentence, it's a preposition. (Note that *of* is the most notable exception.)

Here's another way of remembering what a preposition is. Look at the last eight letters of the word *preposition*; they spell *position*. A preposition sometimes tells the position of something: *in*, *out*, *under*, *over*, *above*, and so forth.

Never end a sentence with a preposition. You've heard that one, haven't you? Well, sometimes that rule is right and sometimes it isn't. Generally, your writing sounds better if you can structure a sentence so that you don't end with a preposition. However, sometimes you want a more colloquial or conversational tone, and—let's face it—in speaking, we often end sentences with prepositions.

With whom are you going to the party?

That's the "no-preposition-at-the-end" construction.

Whom are you going to the party with?

That's almost the way the sentence normally is said (in fact, speakers usually use *who* instead of *whom* in a sentence like this, but you can read about that mistake in Chapter 9).

Who Put the *Junction* in *Conjunction?*

A conjunction joins words in a sentence; that is, it provides a junction between words. Conjunctions are divided into three categories: coordinating, correlative, and subordinating.

Coordinating conjunctions include *and, but, or, nor, for, so,* and *yet.* (Remember *boysfan?*)

Correlative conjunctions cannot stand alone; they must have a "relative" nearby, usually in the same sentence. The pairs include *both/and, either/or, neither/nor, not only/also,* and *not only/but also.*

Subordinating conjunctions are used in the beginning of dependent clauses (words that have a subject and verb but which cannot stand alone as sentences). You may remember that dependent clauses are sometimes called subordinate clauses.

COMMON SUBORDINATING CONJUNCTIONS		
after	how	than
although	if	that
as in	order that	though
as if	in that	unless
as long as	inasmuch as	until
as much as	now that	when
as soon as	once	where
assuming that	providing that	whenever
because	since	wherever
before	so long as	whether
even though	so that	while

Heavens to Betsy! and Other Interjections

Egad! You don't remember what an interjection is? It's a word that can either express surprise or some other kind of emotion, or it can be used as filler. It often stands alone. If an interjection is part of a sentence, it doesn't have a relation to the other words in the sentence; if it's taken out, the meaning must be unchanged. So *egad* and *oh* are interjections. Take a look at these sentences:

> *Hey, dude.*
> *Like, what's going on?*
> *Well, I don't know what to say.*
> *Ouch! Did you step on my toe?*

Hey, *like*, *well*, and *ouch* are interjections.

When you're expressing a strong emotion or surprise (as in *Stop!* or *Darn it all!*), use an exclamation point. If you're using milder emotion or merely using a filler (as in *like* or *well*), use a comma.

A note of caution about interjections: use them in moderation, if at all. In dialogue, interjections are used far more often than in more formal writing (where they are hardly ever used).

CHAPTER 7
Additional Pieces of the Puzzle

In addition to the eight main parts of speech, there are three other parts—participles, gerunds, and infinitives—called verbals. There are also three main parts of a sentence: a subject, a predicate (verb), and complements, or words that complete the meaning of the subject and predicate. Let's jump right in and see if we can tackle these not-so-tricky trios.

Here Come the Hybrids: Verbals

Verbals are called hybrids because they are part verb; but they don't act as verbs in a sentence, they act as other parts of speech. (Kind of sneaky of them, wouldn't you say?) Actually, this isn't as complicated as it sounds; in fact, you probably use verbals all the time without even realizing it!

Part This and Part That: Participles

A participle is part verb and part something else, but it's used as an adjective. (In the last chapter, remember, we talked about how adjectives answer one of three questions: *which one? what kind of?* or *how many?*) Some participles consist of a verb plus *-ing*, as in these sentences:

Just let sleeping dogs lie.

Sleeping consists of the verb *sleep* plus the ending *-ing*, and it acts as an adjective in the sentence. It describes *dogs*, and it answers the question *which ones?*

Shivering from the cold, Robert went immediately to the coffeepot and poured himself a large cup.

Shivering consists of the verb *shiver* plus the ending *-ing*, and it acts as an adjective in the sentence. It describes *Robert*, and it answers the question *what kind of?* or *which one?*

These are examples of present participles.

Other participles consist of a verb plus *-d* or *-ed*, as in these sentences:

The entire team, exhilarated from the unexpected victory, embraced the cheering fans.

Exhilarated consists of the verb *exhilarate* plus the ending *-ed*, and it acts as an adjective in the sentence. It describes *team*, and it answers the question *which ones?*

Stained with both mustard and ketchup, my new shirt went right into the washing machine.

Stained consists of the verb *stain* plus the ending *-ed*, and it acts as an adjective in the sentence. It describes *shirt*, and it answers the question *which one?*

In these examples, *exhilarated* and *stained* are past participles.

Just to make things complicated, there are a number of past participles that are formed irregularly (that is, without adding *-d* or *-ed*). Some examples are *arisen, begun, chosen, dealt, fled, frozen, gone, hurt, kept, lain, meant,* and *outgrown.*

So what's the big deal about a participle? Sometimes it's used in the wrong way, and that creates a dangling participle (also called a hanging participle or an unattached participle). Take a look at this sentence:

Babbling incoherently, the nurse quickly wrapped his arms around the child.

The way the sentence is written, it seems that the nurse was babbling (a participle) incoherently. What the writer means (at least, what we hope he or she means) is that the child was babbling incoherently. The sentence should be rewritten, perhaps this way:

The nurse quickly wrapped his arms around the babbling child.

Here's another example of a dangling participle:

Tired from the long day at the mall, the recliner looked like the perfect spot for Charlie.

How in the world did the recliner have such a tiring day at the mall? That participle (*tired*) and the rest of the words that go with it (its phrase: *tired from the long day at the mall*) should be moved. A better way to word that sentence would be:

The recliner looked like the perfect spot for Charlie, tired from the long day at the mall.

The Jolly Gerund

A gerund is a word that begins with a verb and ends in *-ing*. Wait a minute! Isn't that what a present participle is? Glad that you were paying attention. Now for the rest of the story. A gerund begins with a verb, ends in *-ing*, and acts like a noun (that is, it names a person, place, or thing) in a sentence.

Running up steep hills for the last six months has greatly increased my stamina.

Hector thought he could impress his boss by staying late at the office.

Running is a gerund. It is composed of a verb (*run*), ends in *-ing*, and is used as a noun in the sentence. *Staying* is another gerund. It is composed of a verb (*stay*), ends in *-ing*, and is used as a noun in the sentence.

ESSENTIALS

The "look at the way the word is used in the sentence" rule can be especially important with verbs, participles, and gerunds. Look at the different uses of *addressing* in these sentences:

Addressing the problem has made me realize what I must do.

Addressing the audience, Zelda became cold with sweat.

I'll put the invitations in the mail as soon I have finished addressing the envelopes.

In the first sentence, *addressing* is a gerund (a verb plus *-ing*, functioning as a noun). In the second sentence, *addressing* is a participle (a verb plus *-ing*, functioning as an adjective, describing Zelda). In the last sentence, *addressing* is a verb (showing action).

This rule is often ignored: Use a possessive noun or possessive pronoun *(my, your, his, her, its, our,* and *their)* before a gerund. Look at this sentence:

James continues to be amazed by (Barbara, Barbara's) singing.

You would use the possessive *Barbara's* before the gerund *singing*. The same is true for this sentence:

I was upset about (us, our) leaving so early in the morning.

The possessive pronoun *our* should be used before the gerund *leaving*.

To Be or Not to Be: Infinitives

The good news is that infinitives are easy to spot—usually. Infinitives are composed of *to* plus a verb (e.g., *to go, to carry, to drive*). Most of the time you will see infinitives used as nouns, but sometimes they crop up as adjectives or adverbs.

"I want to go home!" cried the youngster.
To go is an infinitive acting as a noun.

We come to bury Caesar.
To bury is an infinitive that acts as an adverb; it tells why we came.

Harry was the first guy in our crowd to marry.
To marry is an infinitive that acts as an adjective; it describes *guy*.

Now for the bad news. Sometimes the *to* part of an infinitive is omitted.

"Please help me make the bed before your parents get here," Arthur said to his wife.

That sentence means the same as

"Please help me to make the bed . . ."

Once you get used to looking at sentences in this way, you'll find that recognizing infinitives without the *to* will become automatic.

Many years ago grammarians decided that it was wrong to split an infinitive (that is, to insert a word—an adverb, to be exact—between *to* and the verb, as in *to plainly see* and *to hastily wed*). Thankfully, that rule has gone by the wayside for all but the stuffiest editors. So why was the "no split infinitive" rule created in the first place? In the days when the study of Latin was a mandatory part of the curriculum of many schools, rules of Latin grammar often affected rules of English grammar (now, why people didn't realize Latin and English were different languages is another story altogether). Since a Latin infinitive is written as one word, it cannot be split; ergo, grammarians said, the English infinitive should never be split either. To us, the enlightened ones of the twenty-first century, that dictum from days of old is an anachronism.

The purpose of language, after all, is to make meaning clear. Look at the following sentence:

Georgia needed to better understand the rules of English grammar.

Doesn't that read more clearly than the sentence written this way (with the infinitive not split):

Georgia needed to understand better the rules of English grammar.

or

Georgia needed better to understand the rules of English grammar.

Now look at this sentence:

To really understand split infinitives, look at their construction.

That sentence constructed without using a split infinitive would be worded like this:

To understand really split infinitives, look at their construction.

or

Really to understand split infinitives, look at their construction.

Those just don't do justice to the meaning of the sentence, do they? But now take a look at a sentence like this:

You're usually safe to make the split.

In that instance, if you split the infinitive, you'd end up with a sentence like this:

You're safe to usually make the split.

or

You're safe to make usually the split.

Neither of those sounds right either. Better to leave the infinitive whole in that case.

The moral of the story here is that you have to let your ear tell you whether a split infinitive works. If it does, then by all means use it; if not, leave the infinitive alone.

Breaking It Down and Clearing It Up

Now on to the parts of a sentence. As you probably know, a sentence can be very short or very long (but if it's very long, it's probably too confusing to be a good sentence). By definition, a sentence must have the following: (1) a predicate (usually called a verb) and (2) the subject of that verb, and (3) the words must contain a complete thought.

The Starring Roles: Subject and Predicate

The complete subject is the person, place, or thing that the sentence is about, along with all the words that modify it (describe it or give more information about it). The complete predicate (verb) is what the person, place, or thing is doing, or what condition the person, place, or thing is in.

COMPLETE SUBJECT	COMPLETE PREDICATE (VERB)
The aged, white-haired gentleman	walked slowly down the hallway.

The simple subject of a sentence is the fundamental part of the complete subject—the main noun(s) and pronoun(s) in the complete subject. In this example, the simple subject is *gentleman*.

The simple predicate (verb) of a sentence is the fundamental part of the complete predicate—the verb(s) that are in the complete predicate. In the example, the simple predicate is *walked*.

A sentence may also have compound subjects and predicates.

The aged, white-haired gentleman and his wife walked slowly down the hallway.

This sentence has a compound subject: *gentleman* and *wife*.

The aged, white-haired gentleman walked slowly and deliberately down the hallway and then paused to speak to me.

This sentence has a compound verb: *walked* and *paused.*

The aged, white-haired gentleman and his wife walked slowly down the hallway and then paused to speak to me.

This sentence has a compound subject—*gentleman* and *wife*—and a compound verb—*walked* and *paused.*

If you have trouble locating the subject of a sentence, find the verb and then ask *who* or *what* did the verb. Read this sentence:

After a tiring morning at the gym, the six young athletes fell onto the floor in exhaustion.

The verb is *fell.* If you ask, "Who or what fell?" you answer *athletes,* which is the subject.

FACTS

Some imperative sentences written in the second person are called "you understood" sentences. The reader or listener knows that the subject of the sentence is *you,* even though *you* is not spoken or written. For example, look at this sentence:

"Go get me some lemonade."

The reader, listener, or speaker understands that the meaning is "You go get me some lemonade."

Keep in mind that the subject of a sentence is never in a prepositional phrase. If the sentence is a question, the subject sometimes appears after the verb. To find the subject, turn the question around so that it resembles a declarative sentence. Then proceed in the normal way. Let's look at this sentence:

What is Amy going to do with that leftover sandwich?

Now, turn the wording around so that you have:

Amy is going to do what with that leftover sandwich?

Amy answers the *who?* or *what?* question about the verb *is going*. Being able to find the subject of a sentence will enable you to correctly use verbs and pronouns.

SSENTIALS

Some sentences begin with *there* or *here* (these words are sometimes called expletives). The inclination is to name the expletive as the subject. But neither *here* nor *there* is a subject when used in its normal manner. If you want a mnemonic for this, remember: "The subject is neither here nor there."

Making It Complete: Complements

Although some sentences are complete with only a subject and a predicate, many others need something else to complete their meaning. These additional parts of a sentence are called complements, and there are five types: direct object, object complement, indirect object, predicate adjective, and predicate nominative. Predicate adjectives and predicate nominatives are considered subject complements.

Direct Objects

One type of complement that is used with a transitive verb is a direct object: the word or words that receive the action of the verb. Direct objects are nouns (usually), pronouns (sometimes), or noun clauses (rarely). You can find the direct object by applying this formula:

1. First, find the subject of the sentence.
2. Second, find the transitive verb.
3. Third, say the subject and predicate, and then ask *whom?* or *what?* If a word answers either of those questions, it is a direct object.

All of this sounds more complicated than it is. Take a look at this sentence:

The little boy constantly dribbled the basketball in the outdoor playground.

You can find the subject *(boy)* and the verb *(dribbled)*, so all you do is say *boy dribbled whom or what?* The word that answers that question *(basketball)* is the direct object. Easy enough, huh?

Not all sentences that have direct objects will have an indirect object or an object complement. You have to apply the formula to see what is in the sentence. Another point to remember is that if a sentence doesn't have a direct object, it can't have an object complement or an indirect object.

Object Complements

Another kind of complement used with a transitive verb is an object complement (sometimes called an objective complement); it elaborates on or gives a fuller meaning to a direct object. Object complements can be nouns or adjectives. Take a look at this sentence:

Karen asked her friend Paulette for a ride home.

In this sentence the direct object is *Paulette* (Karen asked whom or what? *Paulette*), and the noun *friend* is the object complement (it helps to complete the information about the word *Paulette*). Object complements that act in this way—that is, they elaborate on the direct object—are nouns or pronouns.

Object complements can also be adjectives. Look at this sentence:

On a whim, Matthew painted his fingernails blue.

In this sentence the direct object is *fingernails* (Matthew painted whom or what? *fingernails*), and the adjective *blue* is the object complement (it elaborates on the information about the word *fingernails*).

Object complements that act in this way—that is, they describe the direct object—are adjectives.

Indirect Objects

The third type of complement used with a transitive verb is an indirect object. It comes before a direct object and answers the question *to whom?* or *for whom?* after the subject and verb. Here is a formula for finding an indirect object:

1. First, find the subject of the sentence.
2. Second, find the transitive verb.
3. Third, say the subject and the predicate, and then ask *to whom?* or *for whom?* If a word answers that question, it is an indirect object.

Look at this example:

Kyle reluctantly gave Linda the keys to his new car.

In this sentence, the subject is *Kyle* and the verb is *gave.* Using the formula of asking *to whom?* or *for whom?* after the subject and verb, you would say *Kyle gave to whom?* The answer is *Linda.*

FACTS

In order for a sentence to have an indirect object, *to* or *for* must be implied, not stated. If either of those words is stated, then you have a prepositional phrase, not an indirect object.

Mr. Hartfield made us a spaghetti dinner.

When you ask *Mr. Hartfield made for whom?* the answer is *us.* *Us* is an indirect object.

Mr. Hartfield made a spaghetti dinner for us.

Since *for* is in the sentence, *for us* is a prepositional phrase, not an indirect object.

Subject Complements

Other kinds of complements, called subject complements, are used with linking verbs only. (Linking verbs, you'll remember, are all forms of *be* and, in certain situations, *appear*, *become*, *feel*, *grow*, *look*, *remain*, *smell*, *sound*, *stay*, and *taste*.) Subject complements do just what their name implies—they complete (give you more information about) the subject. There are two types of subject complements: predicate adjectives and predicate nominatives.

Predicate Adjectives

A predicate adjective is an adjective that comes after a linking verb and describes the subject of the sentence. To find a predicate adjective, apply this formula:

1. First, make sure the sentence has a linking verb.
2. Second, find the subject of the sentence.
3. Third, say the subject, say the linking verb, and then ask *what?* If the word that answers the question *what?* is an adjective, then you have a predicate adjective.

Here is an example of a predicate adjective:

Crystal is certainly intelligent.

Apply the formula for this sentence: (1) you know that *is* is a linking verb; (2) you find *Crystal* as the subject of the sentence; (3) you say *Crystal is what?* Since *intelligent* answers that question, and *intelligent* is an adjective (it describes the noun *Crystal*), then you know that *intelligent* is a predicate adjective.

Predicate Nominatives

The other type of subject complement is the predicate nominative (sometimes called the predicate noun). It also comes after a linking verb and gives you more information about the subject. A predicate nominative must be a noun or pronoun. Here's the formula for finding a predicate nominative:

1. First, make sure the sentence has a linking verb.
2. Second, find the subject of the sentence.
3. Third, say the subject, say the linking verb, and then ask *who?* If the word that answers the question *who?* is a noun or pronoun, you have a predicate nominative.

Look at this sentence:

That man over there is DeShawn.

Apply the formula for this sentence: (1) you know that *is* is a linking verb; (2) you find *man* as the subject of the sentence; (3) you say *man is who?* Since *DeShawn* answers that question, and *DeShawn* is a noun (it names a person), then you know that *DeShawn* is a predicate nominative.

FACTS

Just like subjects and predicates, any kind of complement may be compound.

I played basketball and football in high school.
(compound direct objects)

Nora got her dogs Bow and Wow new engraved collars.
(compound object complements)

Tony brought Margaret and Todd a hamburger for lunch.
(compound indirect objects)

James felt elated and nervous about playing in his first game.
(compound predicate adjectives)

Laura is my aunt and my friend.
(compound predicate nominatives)

CHAPTER 8

Let's Have a Few Words

You have to crawl before you learn to walk. In the first few chapters, you were crawling through grammar—re-examining punctuation, parts of speech, and parts of a sentence. Now, you can progress to walking—putting punctuation and words together in more complex forms.

Finding Fundamental Phrases

A phrase is a group of words that acts as a particular part of speech or part of a sentence but doesn't have a verb and its subject. The most common type of phrase is the prepositional phrase.

A prepositional phrase is a group of words that begins with a preposition and ends with a noun or pronoun (the object of the preposition). Here are a few examples:

during the terrible storm
after our dinner
through the open doorway
for me

In a sentence, prepositional phrases act as adjectives (that is, they describe nouns or pronouns; they also answer the question *which one?* or *what kind of?*) or adverbs (that is, they describe verbs, adjectives, or other adverbs; they also answer the question *when? where? how? why? to what extent?* or *under what condition?*).

Adjective phrase: *Several friends from my job are getting together tonight.*

From my job is a prepositional phrase that acts as an adjective. You can determine that it's an adjective phrase because it modifies or describes the noun *friends.* If you look at it in another way, *from my job* is an adjective phrase because it answers the question *which ones?*

An adjective phrase is almost always placed right after the word or words it modifies.

Adverb phrase: *We'll meet at the restaurant at 8 P.M.*

At the restaurant is a prepositional phrase that acts as an adverb. You know it's an adverb phrase because it modifies or describes the verb *meet.* If you look at it in another way, *at the restaurant* is an adverb phrase because it answers the question *when?*

Another type of phrase is the participial phrase, which is made up of a participle and any words that modify it or are related to it. A participle, you remember, is a word that is formed from a verb plus an ending. A participle acts as an adjective; that is, it describes a noun or pronoun in your sentence. Present participles always end in -ing; past participles usually end in -d or –ed. But there are many exceptions. (See Chapter 7 for more discussion of participles.) For example:

Fleeing from the sudden storm, many picnickers sought refuge in the shelter house at the park.

Fleeing is a present participle; it is made up of a verb *flee* plus *-ing*, and it describes the noun *picnickers*. *Fleeing* and the words that go with it—*from the sudden storm*—make up the participial phrase.

A third type of phrase is the gerund phrase, which is made up of a gerund and any words that modify it or are related to it in your sentence. Remember that a gerund is a word that is formed from a verb plus *-ing*. Since a gerund acts as a noun, it can be a subject or an object. (See Chapter 7 for more discussion of gerunds.) Look at this sentence:

Singing the night away helped Joseph forget his troubles.

Singing is a gerund; it is made up of the verb *sing* plus *-ing*. In this sentence, it acts as the subject. *Singing* and the words that go with it—*the night away*—make up the gerund phrase.

A fourth type of phrase is the infinitive phrase, which is made up of an infinitive and any words that modify it in the sentence. An infinitive, you'll remember, is *to* plus a verb. An infinitive can act as several parts of speech, including a noun, an adjective, and an adverb. (See Chapter 7 for more discussion of infinitives.) For example:

"To go home is my only wish right now," sighed the tired mother after a long day of shopping with the children.

To go is an infinitive; it is made up of *to* plus the verb *go*. In this sentence, it acts as the subject of the sentence. The infinitive *To go* and the word that goes with it—*home*—make up the infinitive phrase.

The final type of phrase is an appositive phrase, which is made up of an appositive and any words that modify it or are related to it in the sentence. An appositive is a noun (usually) or pronoun (rarely) that gives details or identifies another noun or pronoun. Here is an example:

My favorite book, a dog-eared copy of To Kill a Mockingbird, has accompanied me on many vacations.

Copy is an appositive that refers to *book*. In this sentence, *copy* and the words that go with it—*a dog-eared*—make up the appositive phrase: *a dog-eared copy of* To Kill a Mockingbird.

Bringing It Up a Notch: Clauses

A clause is just a notch more complicated than a phrase. Like a phrase, a clause is used as a particular part of speech or part of a sentence; however, unlike a phrase, a clause has a verb and its subject. There are two main types of clauses: independent and subordinate.

The Declaration of Independent Clauses

An independent clause (sometimes called a main clause) is a group of words that has a verb and its subject. These words could stand alone as a sentence; that is, the words could make sense if they were by themselves. Here is an example:

The white index cards fell to the floor.

This is one independent clause. It has a subject *(cards)* and a verb *(fell)*, and it stands alone as a sentence. Now, look at this sentence:

The cards scattered on the floor, and I had to pick them all up.

This is made up of two independent clauses. The first—*the cards scattered on the floor*—has a subject *cards* and a verb *scattered*; it could stand alone as a sentence. The second—*I had to pick them all up*—has a subject *(I)* and a verb *(had)*; it also could stand alone as a sentence. Now look:

I had just alphabetized the cards when they fell on the floor and scattered everywhere.

The independent clause in this sentence is *I had just alphabetized the cards*. Although the rest of the sentence—*when they fell on the floor and scattered everywhere*—has a subject *(they)* and verbs *(fell* and *scattered)*, it can't stand alone as a complete thought, so it's not an independent clause.

 **SSENTIALS**

Remember that independent clauses joined by *and, but, for, or, so,* or *yet* are separated by a comma. Other independent clauses are separated by a semicolon.

In a State of Dependency: Subordinate Clauses

A subordinate clause (sometimes called a dependent clause) has a verb and its subject, but it can't stand alone as a sentence. If you read the words of a subordinate clause, you have a subject and a verb, but the words don't make sense by themselves. In order for a subordinate clause to make sense, it has to be attached to another part (to some independent clause) of the sentence. Look at the last example in the discussion about independent clauses:

I had just alphabetized the cards when they fell on the floor and scattered everywhere.

In this sentence, *when they fell on the floor and scattered everywhere* is a subordinate clause. It has a subject *they* and verbs *fell* and *scattered*. But read the words alone:

when they fell on the floor and scattered everywhere

So, what about them? What happened next? If the terminology seems complicated, think of the relationship this way: since a subordinate clause can't stand alone, it's secondary (subordinate) to the main clause of the sentence. Or, a subordinate clause relies (is dependent) on another clause (an independent clause) that's in the sentence.

There are three types of subordinate clauses, and each acts in a different way in the sentence.

A subordinate clause usually begins with a subordinating conjunction or a relative pronoun. See Chapter 6 for more information about pronouns.

An adjective clause is a subordinate clause that acts as an adjective; it modifies or describes a noun or pronoun. Looked at a different way, an adjective clause answers *which one?* or *what kind of?* An adjective clause is sometimes called a relative clause because relative pronouns *(who, whose, whom, which,* and *that)* often begin adjective clauses and relate the clause to the person, place, or thing that they describe.

That man, whom I went to high school with, walked right by as if he'd never met me.

Whom I went to high school with is an adjective clause. It has a verb *(went)* and its subject *(I)*, and it can't stand alone as a sentence. That's what makes it a subordinate clause. It's an adjective clause because it describes the noun *man*; in addition, it answers the question *which one?* about *man.*

Careful! Just to confuse you, sometimes an adjective clause has *that* deleted from it.

The new CD that I want has not yet been released.
The new CD I want has not yet been released.

Because an adjective clause modifies a noun, it can modify a subject, direct object, indirect object, predicate nominative, or object of a preposition in a sentence.

A noun clause is a subordinate clause that acts as a noun; it can be the subject, predicate nominative, appositive, object of a verb, or object of a preposition. A noun clause answers *who? whom?* or *what?*

Rocky couldn't believe what he heard at the water fountain.

What he heard at the water fountain is a noun clause. It has a subject (*he*) and a verb (*heard*) and it can't stand alone as a sentence, so it's some type of subordinate clause. Because it's the direct object of *couldn't believe* (and therefore functions in the sentence as a noun), it's a noun clause.

FACTS

> A noun clause is often introduced by *if, how, that, what, whatever, when, where, whether, which, who, whoever, whom, whomever, whose,* or *why*.

An adverb clause is a subordinate clause that acts as an adverb; it can modify or describe a verb, an adjective, or another adverb. Looked at in a different way, an adverb clause answers *when? where? how? why? to what extent? with what goal or result?* or *under what condition or circumstances?* An adverb clause is introduced by a subordinating conjunction, such as *after, although, as (if), because, once, until,* and *while.*

Mr. Sylvester came to visit because he needed some company for the evening.

Because he needed some company for the evening is an adverb clause. It has a subject (*he*) and a verb (*needed*). It can't stand alone as a sentence, so it's some type of subordinate clause. Because it modifies the verb *came*, it's an adverb clause.

Remember to use a comma after an introductory adverb clause, as in this example:

Whenever he came to visit, Mr. Sylvester always brought a box of candy for us.

QUESTIONS?

What's the difference between a phrase and a clause?
A clause has a verb and its subject; a phrase doesn't.

By eliminating the noun or pronoun and changing the verb, you can change clauses into phrases; in the same vein, you can add a subject and verb to a phrase and create a clause. Why would you want to change clauses into phrases (or vice versa)? After you've written a paragraph, you might notice that you've used the same format in several sentences, and because of that your writing seems monotonous or "singsongy." Reconstructing your sentences by changing clauses and phrases might help eliminate that effect and make your paragraph livelier. Notice the difference here:

Adjective clause: *That green van that is on the used car lot has caught my eye.*

Adjective phrase: *That new green van on the used car lot has caught my eye.*

By the same token, you can convert a subordinate clause into an independent clause by adding a few words:

The green van has caught my eye. The van is on the used car lot at the corner of Elm and Second.

A Matter of Necessity: Restrictive and Nonrestrictive Clauses

Clauses are also divided in another way, depending on whether they're necessary in a sentence. A restrictive clause (sometimes called an essential clause or a defining clause) is necessary to the basic meaning of the sentence; a nonrestrictive clause (sometimes called a nonessential clause or nondefining clause) can be eliminated from the sentence without changing its basic meaning.

The car that I was driving was stolen.
The car, which was stolen last Saturday, has been found.

In the first example, the clause *that I was driving* is necessary to complete the meaning of the sentence. In the second example, including the clause *which was stolen last Saturday* is not necessary in order to understand what the sentence says. In this instance, the clause is merely extra information.

Notice in the preceding examples that *that* is used to introduce restrictive clauses, while *which* is used to introduce nonrestrictive clauses. In general, take note of how particular words introduce different types of clauses. In determining parts of speech, look at the way the word was used in the sentence; in determining a type of clause, look at the way the clause is used in the sentence.

Putting It All Together: Constructing Sentences

Congratulations. Now that you've examined words, phrases, and clauses, you can put 'em all together and—voilà!—make sentences. Or can you? The truth is, there are a few additional things you should know. Grammarians get technical with sentences, just as they do with the parts that make up the sentences. Sentences are classified in both the way they're arranged (this is called sentence type) and in the way they function.

Surveying Sentence Types

You can determine the type of sentence by looking at *what kind* of clauses the sentence has and *how many* clauses the sentence has. There are four sentence types: simple, compound, complex, and compound-complex.

A simple sentence has one independent clause and no subordinate clause:

The man on the dapple gray horse confidently rode into town.

This sentence has one subject *(man)* and one verb *(rode)*.

In a simple sentence there may be compound subjects or verbs, but there may be only one complete thought (one independent or main clause).

A compound sentence has at least two independent clauses (two main clauses) but no subordinate clause (no dependent clause):

The man on the dapple gray horse confidently rode into town, and the townspeople began to fear for their lives.

This sentence has two independent clauses joined by *and*.

Remember that the independent clauses are joined by a comma plus one of the *boysfan* words (*but, or, yet, so, for, and,* or *not*) or by a semicolon.

A complex sentence has one independent clause (main clause) and one or more subordinate clauses (dependent clauses):

Although he had been warned not to come, the man on the dapple gray horse confidently rode into town.

This sentence has one independent clause *(the man on the dapple gray horse confidently rode into town)* and one subordinate clause *(although he had been warned not to come)*.

A compound-complex sentence has at least two independent clauses (main clauses) and one or more subordinate clauses (dependent clauses):

Although he had been warned not to come, the man on the dapple gray horse confidently rode into town, and the townspeople feared for their lives.

This sentence has one subordinate clause *(although he had been warned not to come)* and two independent clauses *(the man on the dapple gray horse confidently rode into town* and *the townspeople feared for their lives)*.

Using complex and compound-complex sentences keeps your writing style from becoming monotonous.

Fathoming Sentence Function

Sentences function in four different ways; they can be declarative, interrogative, imperative, and exclamatory.

A declarative sentence makes a statement:

I'll be seeing you tomorrow, and we can talk about our weekend plans.

An interrogative sentence asks a question:

Do you think we can talk about our weekend plans tomorrow?

An imperative sentence issues a command, makes a request, or gives instructions:

Come here so we can talk about our plans.

An exclamatory sentence expresses strong emotion:

How I hope we can be together this weekend!

FACTS

Sometimes you might have a combination of sentence types.

We will see you tonight, won't we?

The first part is a declarative sentence, and the second part is called a tag question.

Keeping the Harmony: Subject-Verb Agreement

Do you ever notice some kind of incompatibility in your sentences? When you read your sentences, do you hear a jarring ring that tells you that something's wrong? The problem may be that you have disagreement between your subjects and verbs. To smooth out the situation, all you need to do is be sure that you follow the rule about subject-verb agreement: You must make verbs agree with their subjects in number and in person.

Okay, that's the rule, but what does it mean? The first part *(make the verb agree with its subject in number)* is just this simple: If you use a singular subject, you have to use a singular verb; if you use a plural subject, you have to use a plural verb. Nothing hard about that, is there?

Well, as you probably suspect, a number of situations can arise to make the rule tricky.

The Problem of Prepositions

One problem comes with not using the right word as your subject. To keep from making this mistake, remember this hint: Mentally disregard any prepositional phrases that come after the subject. Prepositional phrases will just distract you. Take a look at these sentences:

*The tray of ice cubes (**has, have**) fallen on the kitchen floor.*

Since you know to disregard the prepositional phrase *of ice cubes*, you then have:

*The tray ~~of ice cubes~~ (**has, have**) fallen on the kitchen floor.*

Now, you're left with the subject of the sentence (*tray*). Of course, you would say,

"The tray has fallen on the kitchen floor."

Look at another example:

*Mr. Lilly, along with his dogs Pretzel and Popcorn, (was, **were**) walking down Hillcrest Boulevard.*

Again, mentally cross off the prepositional phrase—no matter how long it is—and you have:

*Mr. Lilly, ~~along with his dogs Pretzel and Popcorn,~~ (**was**, were) walking down Hillcrest Boulevard.*

You'd have no problem saying "Mr. Lilly was walking down Hillcrest Boulevard," so that lets you know the correct verb to use.

Pinpointing the Pronouns

When an indefinite pronoun is the subject of your sentence, you have to look at the individual pronoun. Sometimes this is a snap, as with the plural pronouns that take a plural verb *(both, few, many, others, several)*. Look at these sentences:

"Several scouts are [not is] in the stands at tonight's game," whispered the coach.

A few of us want [not wants] to go camping this weekend.

Just as some plural indefinite pronouns are easy to spot, so are some singular indefinite pronouns *(another, anybody, anyone, anything, each, either, everybody, everyone, everything, much, neither, no one, nobody, nothing, one, other, somebody, someone, something)*. The problem with indefinite pronouns is that a few of them are considered to be singular, even though they indicate a plural number (e.g., *each, everybody, everyone, everything*). For example:

Everybody is [not are] here, so we can get started on the trip.

No one is [not are] going to complain if you want to pick up the tab for tonight's meal.

Now comes a tricky rule: Five pronouns *(all, any, most, none,* and *some)* sometimes take a singular verb and sometimes take a plural verb. How do you know which one to use? This is the time—the only time— you break the rule about disregarding the prepositional phrases. Take a look at these sentences:

"Some of the money is [not are] missing!" cried the teller.

"Some of the people in the bank are [not is] the suspects," replied the policeman.

Most of my coworkers are [not is] cleared of any suspicion.

Most of my jewelry is [not are] still missing.

In each case, you have to look at the object of the preposition *(money, people, coworkers, jewelry)* to decide whether to use a singular or plural verb.

Seeking Solutions to Some Special Situations

Here are some more oddities of English grammar (as if you haven't seen enough of them already):

The phrase *the only one of those* uses a singular verb; however, the phrase *one of those* uses a plural verb. (Is your head spinning?) Maybe these examples will help:

The only one of those people I feel comfortable with is [not are] Gail Prince.

Gail is one of those people who always listen [not listens] when I have a problem.

If you have a sentence with *every* or *many a* before a word or group of words, then use a singular verb. For example:

Many a good man is [not are] trying to please his wife.
Every wife tries [not try] to help her husband understand.

When the phrase *the number* is part of the subject of a sentence, it takes a singular verb. When the phrase *a number* is part of the subject, it takes a plural verb. Look at these sentences:

The number of people who came to the concert is [not are] disappointing.
A number of people are [not is] at home watching the finals of the basketball tournament.

When the phrase *more than one* is part of the subject, it takes a singular verb:

More than one person is [not are] upset about the outcome of the election.

Another time that subjects may be singular or plural is with collective nouns. Collective nouns name groups, such as *cast, fleet,* or *gang.* Use a singular verb if you mean that the individual members of the group act or think together (they act as one unit). Use a plural verb if you mean that the individual members of the group act or think separately (they have different opinions or actions). For example:

The couple is renewing its donation of $50,000 for scholarships.
(The two people were donating as a unit.)

The couple were cleared of the charges of embezzlement of $50,000.
(The two were cleared separately.)

Still another problem with singular and plural verbs comes with expressions of amount. When the particular measurement or quantity (e.g., of time, money, weight, volume, food, or fractions) is considered as one unit or group, then use a singular verb:

Ten dollars to see this movie is [not are] highway robbery!
"Five hours is [not are] a long time to wait for this plane to take off,"
complained the angry passenger.
I would estimate that two thirds of the snow has [not have] melted.

Some nouns look plural but actually name one person, place, or thing, and so they are singular:

The United States is [not are] defending its title against the United Kingdom.
(Although there are fifty states in the United States, it is one country; therefore, you use a singular verb.)

The Everything® Grammar and Style Book is [not are] the best grammar book I've ever read!
(Even though there are six words in the title, *The Everything® Grammar and Style Book* is one book, so you use a singular verb.)

Because I think the subject is fascinating, I think it's odd that economics is [not are] called "the dismal science."
(*Economics* looks as if it's a plural word, but since it's one subject it needs a singular verb.)

Most *-ics* words (e.g., mathematics, mechanics, acrobatics, linguistics, and electronics) are singular.

Here's another special situation: When you use the words *pants*, *trousers*, *shears*, *spectacles*, *glasses*, *tongs*, and *scissors* alone, you use a plural verb:

These pants are [not is] too tight since I returned home from the cruise.
Do [not Does] these trousers come in any other color?
Those scissors are [not is] too sharp for a little boy to play with.

But put the words *a pair of* in front of *pants*, *trousers*, *shears*, *spectacles*, *glasses*, *tongs*, or *scissors*, and then you need a singular verb:

This pair of pants is [not are] too tight since I returned home from the cruise.
Does [not Do] this pair of trousers come in any other color?
That pair of scissors is [not are] too sharp for a little boy to play with.

If you think about it, the logic behind the usage is strange since *pair* means *two*, and *two* denotes a plural. Oh, well . . .

Compounding the Problem: Using Compound Subjects

The first rule in this part is easy. Compound subjects (subjects joined by *and*) take a plural verb:

Mary and Mark are [not is] here.
Mr. and Mrs. Clexton are [not is] joining us for an informal dinner tonight.

Here's an exception: If you have two or more subjects joined by *and*—and the subjects are thought of as one unit—then use a singular verb.

Peanut butter and jelly is my favorite kind of sandwich.
Is spaghetti and meatballs the special at Wolf's Restaurant today?

The second rule is *almost* as easy. Singular subjects joined by *or* or *nor* take a singular verb:

My teacher or my adviser is [not are] here to help me pick my new classes.

The butcher, the baker, or the candlestick maker is [not are] coming to tomorrow's career fair.

Rule number three is along the same lines as rule number two (and it's also *almost* as easy as the first rule). Plural subjects joined by *or* or *nor* take a plural verb:

The Smiths or the Joneses are [not is] visiting tonight.
The horses or the pigs are [not is] making too much noise tonight.

Did you notice the word *almost* in the second and third rules? The first rule was easy; all you had to do was look at subjects joined by *and*; then use a plural verb. The second and third rules require just a little more thought because you have to be sure that the subjects joined by *or* or *nor* are either *all* singular or *all* plural:

1. If all the subjects are singular, use a singular verb.
2. If all the subjects are plural, use a plural verb.

That covers all the examples in which the subjects are the same, but what if you have one singular subject and one plural subject joined by *or* or *nor*? Do you use a singular or plural verb? Simple: You go by the subject that's closer to the verb. So you would write:

My cat or my three dogs are [not is, since dogs is plural and is closer to the verb] coming with me on the trip.

Or, if you inverted the subjects, you would write:

My three dogs or my cat is [not are, since cat is singular and is closer to the verb] making me itch all the time.

Here, There, and Everywhere

Sometimes writers and speakers have a hard time with sentences that begin with *here* or *there*. Writing either

Here's the money I owe you.

or

There's plenty of time left.

is fine because if you changed the contractions into the two words each represents, you'd have "Here is the money I owe you" and "There is plenty of time left."

No problem, huh? Now look at these sentences:

Here's the books I told you I'd bring to you.
There's lots of sandwiches left, so help yourself.

In these examples if you change those contractions, you have "Here is the books I told you I'd bring to you" and "There is lots of sandwiches left, so help yourself." Obviously, you'd never say, "Here is the books" or "There is lots of sandwiches" (you wouldn't, would you?), so the verb form is wrong. Since each of those subjects is plural, you need the plural verb *(are)*.

So the rule is this: If you begin a sentence with *here* or *there* and you have a plural subject, be sure to use a plural verb (usually the verb *are*).

Inside Out

In order to provide originality to their sentence structure or to keep their paragraphs from being too monotonous, good writers often change the word order of their sentences from the normal subject-verb pattern. Instead of writing the sentence as in the first example, you might change the word order and present your sentence as it appears in the second example:

The soldiers came over the hill, determined to destroy the fortress
Over the hill came the soldiers, determined to destroy the fortress.

In both sentences, the subject (*soldiers*) and the verb (*came*) are the same, but the second sentence is written in what is called inverted order—the verb comes before the subject. The caution here is to be sure that the subject agrees with the verb, no matter in what order the sentence is written.

SSENTIALS

The same rule holds true for questions and for sentences that begin with *here* or *there*:

Here are all my friends gathered in one room.
There go two of my oldest friends!

In both sentences, the normal pattern of subject-verb is reversed. In the first sentence, the subject is *friends* and the verb is *are*. In the second sentence, the subject is *friends* and the verb is *go*.

Mixed Numbers

If you have a sentence with a plural subject and a singular predicate nominative (or vice versa), use the verb that agrees with the subject, not the predicate nominative. For example:

Although they're very expensive, Susie's favorite present is pink roses.
Although they're very expensive, pink roses are Susie's favorite present.

In the first sentence the subject (*present*) is singular, so the singular verb (*is*) is used. In the second sentence the subject (*roses*) is plural, so the plural verb (*are*) is used.

Do It! No, Don't Do It!

For some reason, *do*, *does*, *doesn't*, and *don't* are particular problems for certain speakers and writers. Repeat three times: *does* and *doesn't* are used only with singular subjects; *do* and *don't* are used only with plural subjects:

He doesn't [not don't] like the new supervisor anymore than I do.
It doesn't [not don't] matter if we like him or not; he's here to stay.

CHAPTER 9

Pertinent Points about Pesky Pronouns

D o you ever get confused about which pronoun to use? As handy as they are, pronouns sure can pose some problems for both speakers and writers. Yet using the proper pronoun is necessary to avoid both confusion and miscommunication.

Introducing the Pronoun

Consider the following:

Last night, the suspect was charged with hitting a fellow diner and knocking them to the floor. I spoke to E. J. and Pat earlier today, and I asked her if she had been there when it happened. She said that after the incident, the conversation between the other diners and she centered around thinking about whom would be questioned by the police. All the people who were discussing this they finally decided that if you were there, you probably were going to be questioned.

Can you point out what's wrong in this paragraph? The story has examples of several common pronoun problems:

- A plural pronoun that refers to a singular antecedent
- A pronoun that isn't clear about which antecedent it refers to
- Pronouns that shift points of view in the same sentence
- A pronoun that's not needed
- A pronoun that's in the wrong case
- Confusion about when to use *who* and *whom*

Maybe it's time to take a look at these pesky pronoun problems.

PRONOUNS ARE WORDS THAT TAKE THE PLACE OF NOUNS. THEY INCLUDE:		
I	herself	both
me	itself	each
you	ourselves	either
he	yourselves	everybody
him	themselves	everyone
she	this	everything
her	that	few
it	these	little
us	those	many
they	who	most
them	whom	much
mine	which	neither

yours	whose	no one
hers	what	nobody
his	all	none
theirs	another	nothing
ours	any	one
myself	anybody	other
yourself	anyone	others
himself	anything	several
some	somebody	someone

The Numbers Game: Problems with Agreement

Pronouns must agree in number with the words they refer to (their antecedents). Read these sentences:

After I saw whom the letters were from, I tossed it in the wastebasket.

After I saw whom the letters were from, I tossed them in the wastebasket.

The first sentence doesn't make sense because *it* is the wrong pronoun. The noun that *it* refers to is *letters*, and *letters* is a plural noun. The pronoun used to replace *it* should also be plural. In the second sentence, *it* has been replaced by *them*, which is plural. That's why the second sentence makes sense.

Put another way, the rule is this: If a pronoun is plural, the word it refers to (also known as its antecedent) must be plural; if a pronoun is singular, the word it refers to must be singular.

So what's the problem? No one would write a sentence like the first example, right? But complications do arise where some of the indefinite pronouns are concerned.

Definite Problems with Indefinite Pronouns

INDEFINITE PRONOUNS INCLUDE THE FOLLOWING:		
all	everyone	none
another	everything	nothing
any	few	one
anybody	little	other
anyone	many	others
anything	most	several
both	much	some
each	neither	somebody
either	no one	someone
everybody	nobody	something

Anyone, anybody, anything, each, either, everybody, everyone, everything, neither, nobody, none, no one, one, somebody, something, and *someone* are all considered to be singular words, so they all require a singular pronoun. But, if you think about it, the word *each* (for instance) implies more than one. If each person is doing something, that means more than one, right? The same can be said for *everybody, everything,* and *everyone.* This doesn't matter; all four words are considered singular. So you should write:

Everybody is seated, and each is waiting for the plane to take off.

Each of the dogs needs its personalized collar before it can be enrolled in dog obedience school.

Everyone must bring a list of her prenatal vitamins. (Using only her in this sentence is perfectly fine since there wouldn't be any men who would be taking prenatal vitamins.)

A common tendency in everyday speech is to use *they* or *their* in place of some singular pronouns. In the first example, you might hear the sentence spoken this way:

Everybody is seated, and they are waiting for the plane to take off.

This usage is called the "singular they" because *they* refers to an antecedent that's singular.

Even though using the "singular they" is becoming more commonplace, its usage is still frowned on in some circles. However, this may be one of the rules of grammar that eventually changes. The advocates of the "singular they" point out that using it helps prevent an overuse of *his or her* or *he or she.*

Now it's time to break a rule. Remember the one that says to disregard any prepositional phrase when you're looking for the subject of a sentence? Well, there are a few exceptions. (This is also discussed in Chapter 8 about subject-verb agreement.) Take a look at these two sentences:

All of the money is missing from the safe.
All of the cookies are missing from the jar.

In both sentences, the subject is *all.* But the first sentence has a singular verb and the second sentence has a plural verb—and both are correct.

With five pronouns *(all, any, most, none, and some),* the "disregard the prepositional phrase" rule is canceled out. For those five pronouns, look at the object of the preposition to determine which verb to use.

SSENTIALS

When you have compound antecedents that are joined by *or* or *nor* (or *either . . . or, neither . . . nor*), make the pronoun agree with the one that's closer to the verb. Here's an example:

Either the lion or the monkeys have already gotten their food.

Since *monkeys* is plural and it comes nearer to the pronoun, the plural pronoun *their* is used.

Either the monkeys or the lion has already gotten his food.

Since *lion* is singular and it comes nearer to the pronoun, the singular pronoun *his* is used.

So, do you think you can pinpoint the mistakes in the following paragraph? All of the pronouns and their antecedents should agree in number.

I didn't think anybody had remembered my birthday. When I came down to breakfast, everybody in the family was already eating their breakfast, but nobody offered as much as to give me a piece of toast. At work, everyone was already busy doing their different projects; they didn't even stop to look up when I came in. Each of them seemed to be in their own little world.

By changing the incorrect pronouns, you should have:

I didn't think anybody had remembered my birthday. When I came down to breakfast, everybody in the family was already eating his or her breakfast, but nobody offered as much as to give me a piece of toast. At work, everyone was already busy doing his or her different projects; they didn't even stop to look up when I came in. Each of them seemed to be in his or her own little world.

You can see, though, that there's a definite problem with that rewriting. While it may be grammatically correct, it sure doesn't read well. Contrary to rules of thirty or more years ago, using *his or her* rather than just *his* is now considered correct. But as you can see in the corrected paragraph, this can make for some rather awkward writing.

So what can you do to prevent this awkwardness? Rewriting the sentences to use plural nouns and pronouns instead of singular ones is far better. The paragraph could be rewritten this way:

I didn't think anybody had remembered my birthday. When I came down to breakfast, all of my family members were already eating their breakfast, but nobody offered as much as to give me a piece of toast. At work, all of my associates were already busy doing their different projects; they didn't even stop to look up when I came in. They seemed to be in their own little world.

Much better, isn't it?

When in Doubt: Vague Pronoun References

One of the most common writing problems occurs in sentences that have unclear antecedents of the pronouns.

Just what does that mean? As you recall, pronouns are words that take the place of nouns; antecedents are the nouns that the pronouns refer to. For example:

Shirley called to say she would be glad to help decorate for the party on Friday.

In this sentence, the pronoun *she* refers to *Shirley;* therefore, *Shirley* is the antecedent of *she.* Now, look at this example:

The movie's humor was rather sophomoric, and it didn't go over well with most of the audience.

The pronoun *it* refers to *humor; humor* is the antecedent of *it.*

In these examples, the antecedents are used correctly. They clearly refer to specific nouns (their antecedents). But take a look at this sentence:

Billy Joe invited Darrell to the ranch because he enjoyed horseback riding.

Well, now. Just whom does the word *he* in the second part of the sentence refer to—Billy Joe or Darrell? The antecedent of *he* isn't clear.

To make the sentence read clearly, it should be reworded:

Because Darrell enjoyed horseback riding, Billy Joe invited him to the ranch.

or

Billy Joe, who enjoyed horseback riding, invited Darrell to the ranch.

Now, look at these sentences:

Darlene called Georgia to report the unexpected news that she had gotten a raise. When Darlene told Janet the news, she said that they should celebrate.

Are you confused? Who got the raise—Darlene or Georgia? Who said that a celebration was in order—Darlene or Janet? Who was to be included in the celebration—Darlene, Georgia, and Janet? Georgia and

Janet? Darlene and Janet? The way the two sentences are now worded, the reader isn't sure.

There are several ways to correct the first sentence, depending on whom the author is referring to by the words *she* and *they.* Suppose Darlene is the one who has received the raise. One way to recast the sentence to express that meaning is this way:

Darlene, excited about the unexpected news that she had gotten a raise, called her friend Georgia.

Darlene, who had received the unexpected news that she had gotten a raise, called her friend Georgia.

Now, there's no doubt about who received the raise. If Georgia was the one who received the raise, then the sentence could be reworded this way:

Darlene called Georgia to report the unexpected news that Georgia had gotten a raise.

In the second sentence, who's going to celebrate? To make the meaning clearer, that sentence could be reworded this way:

Darlene told Janet the news, and she also said that the three of them should celebrate.

Now, it's clear who announced the celebration and who was to be included in it.

Sometimes a pronoun has no reference at all. Read this sentence:

Karen was afraid he would not remember to pick up the refreshments for the party.

Just who is *he?* Unless the man has been identified in an earlier sentence, the reader is left out in the cold about his identity.

Remember that an antecedent has to refer to a specific person, place, or thing. Look at this sentence:

The young recording star was elated, but he kept it hidden.

What did the star keep hidden? Was *it* supposed to refer to the fact that he felt elated? In that case, the sentence would read:

The young recording star was elated, but he kept elated hidden.

Doesn't make sense, does it? The word *elated* can't be the antecedent of *it* because *elated* isn't a person, place, or thing. The sentence needs to be reworded something like this:

The young recording star was elated with his hit record, but he kept his elation hidden.

Along the same lines, sometimes in a sentence there is a noun that the pronoun refers to, but it's not the right noun; the correct reference is missing from the sentence. Read this sentence:

After a successful fishing trip with his brothers, Steve let them all go.

The way the sentence is now worded, Steve let his brothers go. That's what *them* refers to in the sentence. But surely that's not what happened! What the writer means is that Steve let all the fish go. The sentence should be rewritten like this:

After a successful fishing trip with his brothers, Steve let all of their catch go.

Here's another example of a pronoun that doesn't refer to the right antecedent:

The new tax forms arrived today. They want me to fill out every line on the last three pages.

The way this sentence is worded, the tax forms want you to do the filling out. What the writer meant was that the Internal Revenue Service, or an accounting firm, or the office personnel at work—someone the writer had failed to name—wants the tax forms filled out. The sentence needs to be reworded to make it clear who *they* are.

The new tax forms arrived today. Our accountant wants me to fill out every line on the last three pages.

Be careful not to use *they* when you refer to unnamed persons; said another way, *they* must refer to people you specify. The same holds true for any pronoun, but *they, he, she,* and *it* are the ones most commonly misused in this way. If you think that you may have an unclear reference, one way to test the sentence is to do this:

1. Find the pronoun.
2. Replace the pronoun with its antecedent—the noun it refers to (remember, the noun must be the exact word).
3. If the sentence doesn't make sense, you need to reword your sentence.

When you're referring to people, use *who, whom,* or *whose,* not *which* or *that*. Here's an incorrect sentence:

> *I'm indebted to the people which helped me during the flood.*

Here's the sentence in the correct way:

> *I'm indebted to the people who helped me during the flood.*

One, Two, Three: What Person for Me?

Often you may have instructions that call for your material (for a paper, for a resume, for a memo, and so on) to be written in a particular person—first person, second person, or third person. That's fine, but what does it mean?

Both pronouns and point of view are expressed in first person, second person, and third person. You remember that first-person pronouns include *I, me, my, mine, we, our,* and *us* and the first-person point of view expresses the personal point of view of the speaker or author *(I will bring the book to Jack)*. Second-person pronouns include *you, your,* and *yours,* and material expressed in the second-person point of view directly addresses the listener or reader *(You will bring the book to Jack)*. Third-person pronouns include *he, she, him, her, his, hers, they, them, their,* and *theirs*. In the third-person point of view material is expressed from the point of view of a detached writer or other characters *(They will bring the book to Jack).*

Most instructors insist that academic writing be in the third person, although some now allow for first or second person, depending on the subject matter. If you're writing for a class, be sure to check with the instructor to determine if there is a requirement about using first, second, or third person. If you're writing for a company, check to see if there are particular guidelines about which person you should use. (If you're still in doubt, use third person.)

Just Leave Me Out of It! Shifts in Person

One of the most common problems in writing comes with a shift in person. The writer begins in either first or third person and then—without reason—shifts to second person. Take, for example, this paragraph:

Even in a casual atmosphere I can be embarrassed by someone else, and this causes you to become tense. For instance, somebody you know can embarrass you at a party or in a class. It's so simple for a stranger to embarrass you. This can be upsetting, depending on the kind of person you are; it can be hurtful even if you are mentally strong.

What's wrong with that paragraph? The writer begins in the first person (telling about himself or herself by using the pronoun *I*) and then shifts to second person. The constant use of *you* sounds as if the writer is preaching directly to the reader. That writer doesn't know the reader and doesn't know if he or she can easily be embarrassed by others, and so on. Except for the beginning sentence, the entire paragraph should be rewritten and put into first person. Here is one way of doing that:

Even in a casual atmosphere I can be embarrassed by someone else, and this causes me to become tense. For instance, somebody I know can embarrass me at a party or in a class. It's so simple for a stranger to embarrass me. This can be upsetting because of the kind of person I am, and it can be hurtful even if I am mentally strong.

Repeat three times: Consistency is the key. Consistency is the key. Consistency is the key. If you begin in third person (which is the most common way of writing), stay in third person. If you begin in first person (the second most common way of writing), stay in first person. If you begin in second person, stay in second person. Consistency is the key.

(You did notice that the preceding paragraph is written in second person, didn't you? Even the first four sentences are in second person. They're written in what's called a "you understood" form: even though the word *you* isn't included in the sentences, it is implied and the reader understands that *you* is the subject of each sentence.)

May I Talk to You? Using the Second Person

For various reasons, most instructors usually disapprove of second person in formal writing. So when is using second person acceptable? When you need an informal tone. Read something written in second person (remember, that means using *you* and *your*), and you'll find the tone is more conversational than if it had been written in first or third person. Use second person when you want your words to come across in a casual way. Take a look at this paragraph:

You'll need to watch the mixture carefully, and you may have to stir it quite often. When you get to the last step, make sure you add the final three ingredients slowly. If you add them too quickly, the combination will not blend and you'll have a mess on your hands.

You can easily read that paragraph. It's talking directly to you, telling you what to do in your cooking. But look at the same paragraph written in third person:

The mixture must be watched carefully, and it may have to be stirred quite often. At the last step, it is important that the final three ingredients be added slowly. If they are added too quickly, the combination will not blend and a mess will be created.

Now, that's pretty boring and stilted, isn't it? The directions are far better if you write them in the second person.

Another time that second-person writing is used with frequency is in advertising. Consider this sign:

Come see the friendly folks at Bradley's Used Car Lot!

That's more inviting than if it were written in the third person:

The reader of this sign is invited to come see the friendly folks at Bradley's Used Car Lot!

The friendly folks at Bradley's probably wouldn't have much business with a sign like that, would they?

Making a Case for Pronouns

Pronouns are also one of three cases: subjective, objective, and possessive. The way a pronoun is used in the sentence determines which case you should use.

1. Subjective pronouns include *I, you, he, she, it, we,* and *they.*
2. Objective pronouns include *me, you, him, her, it, us,* and *them.* (Note that *you* and *it* are included on both lists; you'll see why later.)
3. Possessive pronouns include *my, your, his, her, its, our,* and *their.* (Possessive pronouns are regarded as adjectives by some grammarians. These pronouns won't be discussed in this section because there's rarely a problem with using them correctly.)

SSENTIALS

Writers often have a problem deciding whether to use *we* or *us* when the pronoun comes before a noun, as in this example:

"(We, Us) seniors decided to play a prank on you," Matt told his instructors.

"You had better rethink a decision to play a prank on (we, us) teachers," came the sharp reply.

To decide which pronoun is correct, just delete the noun that the pronoun refers to (*seniors* in the first sentence, *teachers* in the second sentence) and see how you would actually say the sentence.

No-Brainer, Part One: Subjective Pronouns

Here's the first part of a no-brainer: Subjective pronouns are used as the subjects of sentences (whom or what you're talking about). You would say, for instance:

I am going to leave for my appointment.
She is late already.
They will never make it on time.

No problem seeing the right form in those sentences, is there? For some reason, though, a problem occasionally arises when subjects are compound. You might read, for instance:

His brothers and him are going to the ball game.
Margaret, Elizabeth, and me were at the mall for four hours yesterday.
Me and her see eye-to-eye on lots of things.

These pronouns are used incorrectly. Because the pronouns are used as subjects of the sentence, they should all be in the subjective case: *I,* *you, he, she, it, we,* or *they.* So, the sentences should read:

His brothers and he are going to the ball game.
Margaret, Elizabeth, and I were at the mall for four hours yesterday.
I and she see eye-to-eye on lots of things. (Actually, it's considered polite to put the other person first, so it's better to word this sentence like this: She and I see eye-to-eye on lots of things.)

If you're not sure if you've used the right pronoun, try writing or saying the sentence with only one subject. You'd never say:

Him is going to the ball game.
Me was at the mall for four hours yesterday.
Me sees eye-to-eye on lots of things.
Her sees eye-to-eye on lots of things.

Since those pronouns sound wrong when they're by themselves, you know that they're the wrong case. Change the pronouns to the ones you'd normally use when there's just one subject:

No-Brainer, Part Two: Objective Pronouns

Here's part two of the no-brainer: Objective pronouns are used as the objects in sentences. You would say, for instance:

Terry came to see her last night.
For the twins' birthday, Mother gave them several new CDs.
"Give me the money right now!" the robber demanded.

As with compound subjects, problems arise when there are compound objects. People will write or say sentences like this:

The argument arose last night between Carla and she.
Please buy a raffle ticket from Nonnie or I.
"The car sped by he and I, going 90 miles per hour," the witness testified.

Again, each pronoun is used incorrectly in these sentences. Because the pronouns are used as objects in the sentences, they should all be in the objective case: *me*, *you*, *him*, *her*, *it*, *us*, and *them*. So, the sentences should read:

The argument arose last night between Carla and her.
Please buy a raffle ticket from Nonnie or me.
"The car sped by him and me, going 90 miles per hour," the
witness testified.

The way to test yourself if you're not sure if you've used the right pronoun is to use the same trick that you used for the subjective pronoun problem, but substitute the objective form; that is, write or say the sentence with only one object. You'd never say:

The argument arose last night between she.
Please buy a raffle ticket from I.
"The car sped by he, going 90 miles per hour," the witness testified.
"The car sped by I, going 90 miles per hour," the witness testified.

Since those pronouns sound wrong when they're by themselves, you know that they're the wrong case. Change the pronouns to the ones you'd normally say when there is only one object.

So why were *you* and *it* on the lists of both subjective and objective pronouns? Because, unlike other pronouns on the lists (*I* and *me*, for example), English uses the same form for those two words.

It was nice to get a surprise in the mail.
(*It* is used as a subject.)
I got it in the mail.
(*It* is used as an object.)

You called me at four o'clock?
(*You* is used as a subject.)

I called you back at five o'clock.
(*You* is used as an object.)

Remember that pronouns that are predicate nominatives should be subject pronouns. Predicate nominatives, you recall, are nouns or pronouns that are used after linking verbs (usually forms of *be*, like *am, is, are, was,* and *were*).

Some Sticky Situations with *Than* and *As*

Another problem with pronouns sometimes arises in a sentence with words that are omitted following *than* or *as*.

Look at the following examples:

Greg said to Grace, "I always thought Mother liked you more than me."
Greg said to Grace, "I always thought Mother liked you more than I."

When the words that have been omitted after *than* are restored, the real meaning of the sentences becomes clear:

Greg said to Grace, "I always thought Mother liked you more than (she liked) me."

Greg said to Grace, "I always thought Mother liked you more than I (liked you)."

(Either way, Greg seems to be in quite a snit, doesn't he?)

The same type of confusion can result when words following *as* have been omitted. For example, someone might say or write something along the lines of:

My husband finds physics as interesting as me.

This implies that, to the husband, the subject of physics and his wife are of equal interest. Now, look at the correction:

My husband finds physics as interesting as I (do).

This signifies that both spouses are equally interested in physics—which, one hopes, is the intended meaning here.

By mentally adding the missing verb at the end of a sentence using *than* or *as* in this way, you'll be able to tell which pronoun to use.

Who and *Whom*: A Different Slant

For many people, deciding whether to use *who* or *whom* may be the most difficult of all the problems with pronouns. Do you say, "The man who I called this morning has already placed an order" or "The man whom I called this morning has already placed an order"? How can you make your mind up between "The student who is early will get the best seat" and "The student whom is early will get the best seat"?

If you have trouble deciding whether to use *who* or *whom* (or *whoever* or *whomever*), try the following method. It substitutes *he* and *him* for *who* and *whom* and provides a mnemonic for remembering when you should use which pronoun.

FACTS

The use of *whom* is gradually decreasing in casual speaking, although there are still many people who are conscientious about its use. Either way, its correct use is still enforced in writing.

First, remember to look only at the clause (a set of words with a subject and its verb) associated with *who* or *whom*. In some sentences, there is only one clause, and that makes finding the right word easy.

Often, though, there is more than one clause (an independent clause and one or more dependent clauses).

Next, scramble the words of the clause (if you have to) so that the words form a statement, not a question.

Now, substitute either *he* or *him* for *who* or *whom*. This will tell you whether to use *who* or *whom*. Use the mnemonic *he* = *who*, *hiM* = *whoM* (the final *m* helps you remember the association).

Be on the lookout for predicate nominatives. After you scramble the words, if you have a linking verb rather than an action verb, use *he* (*who*) instead of *him* (*whom*).

Ready to put all this to a test? Try this sentence:

(Who, Whom) telephoned so late last night?

Since there's only one clause in the sentence, all you need to do is see if it's necessary to scramble the words to make a statement. In this sentence, no scrambling is necessary. You can substitute *he* and have a perfectly good sentence: *He telephoned so late last night.* Since you substituted *he* instead of *him* (remember that *he* = *who*), you know to use *who* in the original question.

SSENTIALS An independent clause is a set of words with a subject and its verb that expresses a complete thought; it could stand alone as a sentence. A dependent clause—while having a subject and verb—makes no sense by itself; it cannot stand alone as a sentence.

Now, try this example:

(Who, Whom) were you telephoning so late at night?

There's still only one clause that you have to deal with. Scramble the words to make a statement; then substitute *he* or *him*, and you have the statement "You were telephoning him so late at night." Since you used *him* in the new sentence, you know to use *whom* in the original question.

Now, for a trickier example:

Eugene worried about (who, whom) Eddie would be teamed with in the competition.

As you can tell, this sentence has two clauses (you could tell that, couldn't you?). Remember that you're *only* concerned with the clause that contains the *who/whom* question. In this case, take the words after *about*, scramble them to make a statement, substitute *he* or *him*, and you have "Eddie would be teamed with him in the competition." Since you used *him*, you would know that the original sentence would use *whom* (remember the mnemonic *him* = *whom*). So the original sentence would read this way:

Eugene worried about whom Eddie would be teamed with in the competition.

Here's another example that you have to stop and think about:

Was that (who, whom) you thought it was?

When you look *only* at the clause the *who/whom* is concerned with and you substitute *he/him*, you have "it was he/him." A lightbulb goes off in your head because you recognize that *was* as being a linking verb. That tells you to use *he* (the predicate nominative).

CHAPTER 10

Figuring Out Some Finicky Forms

Y ou probably use certain tenses to express particular time periods without giving them a second thought. Perhaps, however, there are some verb forms that you've never fully understood. This chapter will iron out all the complexities of the different verb forms for you so that choosing different tenses will never again make you tense.

Let's Talk Tenses

English verbs are divided into three main tenses, which relate to time: present, past, and future. Each main tense is also subdivided into other categories: simple tense, progressive tense, perfect tense, and perfect progressive tense. These subcategories are used to differentiate when a particular action has been done (or is being done or will be done).

Are you confused yet? Take a look at this chart:

	Simple*	Progressive**	Perfect***	Perfect Progressive****
Present	hide	am/is/are hiding	have/has hidden	have/has been hiding
Past	hid	was/were hiding	had hidden	had been hiding
Future	will/shall hide	will be hiding	will have hidden	will have been hiding

*Indicates action that is usual or is repeated.
**Indicates action that is ongoing.
***Indicates action that is completed.
****Indicates ongoing action that will be completed at some definite time.

Each of these tenses signals the time something is done (or will be done or has been done) relative to when it's being written or spoken about. You still don't quite get the whole thing? Don't worry; it will all be cleared up for you in the next few pages, starting with explanations for each of the tenses. To lighten the mood, why don't we start with a little joke:

The teacher to the student: "Conjugate the verb 'to walk' in the simple present tense."
The student: "I walk. You walk. He . . ."
The teacher interrupts him: "Quicker, please."
The student: "I run. You run. . . ."

It's Elementary: The Simple Tense

The *simple present tense* tells an action that is usual or repeated:

I hide from the Mafia.

Looked at in a different way, the simple present tense relates actions that happen often or that state a fact or opinion.

To make sure they're using the correct verb form for the present tense, some writers find it helpful to begin the example sentence with the word *today*:

Today I hide from the Mafia.

The *simple past tense* tells an action that both began and ended in the past:

I hid from the Mafia.

To make sure they're using the correct verb form for the past tense, some writers find it helpful to mentally begin the example sentence with the word *yesterday*:

Yesterday I hid from the Mafia.

The *simple future tense* tells an upcoming action that will occur:

I will hide from the Mafia.

To make sure they're using the correct verb form for the future tense, some writers find it helpful to mentally begin the example sentence with the word *tomorrow*:

Tomorrow I will hide from the Mafia.

That's simple enough, isn't it? After this, though, the explanations of the other tenses get a little tricky—but I'm sure you're up to the challenge.

One Step Beyond: The Progressive Tense

Use the *present progressive tense* to show an action that's in progress at the time the statement is written:

I am hiding from the Mafia today.

Present progressive verbs are always formed by using *am, is,* or *are* and adding *-ing* to the verb.

Use the *past progressive tense* to show an action that was going on at some particular time in the past:

I was hiding from the Mafia yesterday.

Past progressive verbs are always formed by using *was* or *were* and adding *-ing* to the verb.

Use the *future progressive tense* to show an action that's continuous and that will occur in the future:

I will be hiding from the Mafia tomorrow.

Future progressive verbs are always formed by using *will be* or *shall be* and adding *-ing* to the verb.

No Room for Improvement: The Perfect Tense

Use the *present perfect tense* to convey action that happened sometime in the past or that started in the past but is ongoing in the present:

I have hidden from the Mafia for more than five years.

Present perfect verbs are always formed by using *has* or *have* and the past participle form of the verb.

Use the *past perfect tense* to indicate past action that occurred prior to another past action:

I had hidden from the Mafia for more than five years before I entered the Witness Protection Program.

Past perfect verbs are always formed by using *had* and the past participle form of the verb.

Use the *future perfect tense* to illustrate future action that will occur before some other action:

I will have hidden from the Mafia for more than five years before entering the Witness Protection Program.

Future perfect verbs are always formed by using *will have* and the past participle form of the verb.

Particulars of the Perfect Progressive Tense

Use the *present perfect progressive* to illustrate an action repeated over a period of time in the past, continuing in the present, and possibly carrying on in the future:

For the past five years, I have been hiding from the Mafia.

Present perfect progressive verbs are always formed by using *has been* or *have been* and the past participle form of the verb.

Use the *past perfect progressive* to illustrate a past continuous action that was completed before some other past action:

Before I entered the Witness Protection Program, I had been hiding from the Mafia for more than five years.

Past perfect progressive verbs are always formed by using *had been* and adding *-ing* to the verb.

Use the *future perfect progressive* to illustrate a future continuous action that will be completed before some future time:

Next month I will have been hiding from the Mafia for more than five years.

Future perfect progressive verbs are always formed by using *will have been* and adding *-ing* to the verb.

Those Irritating Irregular Verbs

The good news is that most English verbs form their past and past participle by adding *-d* or *-ed* to the base form of the verb (the form you'd find listed first in the dictionary). These are called regular verbs.

The bad news is that there are a number of verb forms that aren't formed in that way; some people call them "those %*#@^ verbs," but usually they're called irregular verbs (clever, huh?). Here is a list of irregular English verbs.

VERBS THAT TAKE AN IRREGULAR FORM

Base (Infinitive)	Simple Past	Past Participle
abide	abode/abided	abode/abided
arise	arose	arisen
awake	awoke/awaked	awaked/awoken
be	was, were	been
bear	bore	borne/born
beat	beat	beaten/beat
become	became	become
befall	befell	befallen
begin	began	begun
behold	beheld	beheld
bend	bent	bent
beseech	besought/beseeched	besought/beseeched
beset	beset	beset
bet	bet/betted	bet/betted
bid	bade/bid	bidden/bid
bind	bound	bound
bite	bit	bitten/bit
bleed	bled	bled
blow	blew	blown
break	broke	broken
breed	bred	bred
bring	brought	brought
broadcast	broadcast/broadcasted	broadcast/broadcasted
browbeat	browbeat	browbeaten
build	built	built
burn	burned/burnt	burned/burnt
burst	burst	burst
bust	busted	busted
buy	bought	bought
cast	cast	cast
catch	caught	caught

VERBS THAT TAKE AN IRREGULAR FORM		
BASE (INFINITIVE)	SIMPLE PAST	PAST PARTICIPLE
choose	chose	chosen
cling	clung	clung
come	came	come
cost	cost	cost
creep	crept	crept
cut	cut	cut
deal	dealt	dealt
dig	dug	dug
dive	dived/dove	dived
do	did	done
draw	drew	drawn
dream	dreamed/dreamt	dreamed/dreamt
drink	drank	drunk
drive	drove	driven
dwell	dwelt/dwelled	dwelt/dwelled
eat	ate	eaten
fall	fell	fallen
feed	fed	fed
feel	felt	felt
fight	fought	fought
find	found	found
fit	fitted/fit	fit
flee	fled	fled
fling	flung	flung
fly	flew	flown
forsake	forsook	forsaken
freeze	froze	frozen
get	got	gotten/got
gild	gilded/gilt	gilded/gilt
give	gave	given
go	went	gone
grind	ground	ground

VERBS THAT TAKE AN IRREGULAR FORM

BASE (INFINITIVE)	SIMPLE PAST	PAST PARTICIPLE
grow	grew	grown
hang (to suspend)	hung	hung
has	had	had
have	had	had
hear	heard	heard
hew	hewed	hewn/hewed
hide	hid	hidden/hid
hit	hit	hit
hold	held	held
hurt	hurt	hurt
input	input	input
inset	inset	inset
interbreed	interbred	interbred
keep	kept	kept
kneel	knelt/kneeled	knelt/kneeled
knit	knit/knitted	knit/knitted
know	knew	known
lay	laid	laid
lead	led	led
lean	leaned	leaned
leap	leaped/leapt	leaped/leapt
learn	learned/learnt	learned/learnt
leave	left	left
lend	lent	lent
lie (to rest or recline)	lay	lain
light	lighted/lit	lighted/lit
lose	lost	lost
make	made	made
mean	meant	meant
meet	met	met
mistake	mistook	mistaken
mow	mowed	mowed/mown
outbid	outbid	outbid

VERBS THAT TAKE AN IRREGULAR FORM

BASE (INFINITIVE)	SIMPLE PAST	PAST PARTICIPLE
outdo	outdid	outdone
outgrow	outgrew	outgrown
outrun	outran	outrun
outsell	outsold	outsold
partake	partook	partaken
pay	paid	paid
plead	pleaded/pled	pleaded/pled
proofread	proofread	proofread
prove	proved/proven	proved/proven
put	put	put
quit	quit/quitted	quit/quitted
read	read	read
rid	rid/ridded	rid/ridded
ride	rode	ridden
ring	rang	rung
rise	rose	risen
run	ran	run
saw (to cut)	sawed	sawed/sawn
say	said	said
see	saw	seen
seek	sought	sought
sell	sold	sold
send	sent	sent
set	set	set
sew	sewed	sewn/sewed
shake	shook	shaken
shave	shaved	shaved/shaven
shear	sheared	sheared/shorn
shed	shed	shed
shine	shone/shined	shone/shined
shoe	shod	shod/shodden
shoot	shot	shot
show	showed	shown/showed

VERBS THAT TAKE AN IRREGULAR FORM

BASE (INFINITIVE)	SIMPLE PAST	PAST PARTICIPLE
shrink	shrank/shrunk	shrunk/shrunken
shut	shut	shut
sing	sang/sung	sung
sink	sank/sunk	sunk
sit	sat	sat
slay	slew	slain
sleep	slept	slept
slide	slid	slid
sling	slung	slung
slit	slit	slit
smell	smelled/smelt	smelled/smelt
smite	smote	smitten/smote
sow	sowed	sown/sowed
speak	spoke	spoken
speed	sped/speeded	sped/speeded
spell	spelled/spelt	spelled/spelt
spend	spent	spent
spill	spilled/spilt	spilled/spilt
spin	spun	spun
spit	spat/spit	spat/spit
split	split	split
spoil	spoiled/spoilt	spoiled/spoilt
spoon-feed	spoon-fed	spoon-fed
spread	spread	spread
spring	sprang/sprung	sprung
stand	stood	stood
steal	stole	stolen
stick	stuck	stuck
sting	stung	stung
stink	stank/stunk	stunk
strew	strewed	strewn/strewed
stride	strode	stridden
strike	struck	struck/stricken

VERBS THAT TAKE AN IRREGULAR FORM

BASE (INFINITIVE)	SIMPLE PAST	PAST PARTICIPLE
string	strung	strung
strive	strove	striven/strived
swear	swore	sworn
sweep	swept	swept
swell	swelled	swelled/swollen
swim	swam	swum
swing	swung	swung
take	took	taken
teach	taught	taught
tear	tore	torn
tell	told	told
think	thought	thought
thrive	thrived/throve	thrived/thriven
throw	threw	thrown
tread	trod	trodden/trod
understand	understood	understood
uphold	upheld	upheld
upset	upset	upset
wake	woke/waked	waked/woken
wear	wore	worn
weave	wove	woven
wed	wedded	wed/wedded
weep	wept	wept
wet	wet/wetted	wet/wetted
win	won	won
wind	wound	wound
wring	wrung	wrung

Just to keep you on your toes, two verbs—hang and lie—may be regular or irregular, depending on their meaning in the sentence. If *hang* means *to use a noose*, it's a regular verb. If it means *to affix to a wall*, it's irregular. For example:

A picture of the hanged man's mother hung in his cell.

If *lie* is used to mean *to tell a falsehood,* it's a regular verb. If it means *to rest or recline*, it's irregular. Here's an example:

As he lay on the beach, Dave lied about where he had put the key.

What Kind of Mood Are You In?

In addition to tenses, English verbs are divided into moods, which show the writer's attitude toward what he or she is saying. The first two moods, indicative and imperative, are not confusing at all, and, fortunately, they're used far more frequently than the third mood, the subjunctive.

Almost all verbs are used in the indicative mood, which means that the verb's sentence states a fact or an actuality. All of these sentences are in the indicative mood:

I'll be seeing you later on tonight. We'll go to the movies with our friends and then get something to eat afterward. You may wear whatever you want. You look nice in whatever you wear. We are all casual dressers, so don't worry about your attire.

Verbs used in the imperative mood are in sentences that make requests or give a command. All of these sentences are in the imperative mood:

Please give me the phone.
Give it to me right now!
Give it to me—or else!

The subjunctive mood is the one that speakers and writers sometimes have problems with. Fortunately, it's used with only two verbs *(be* and *were)*, and in modern English, it's used in only two kinds of sentences:

1. Statements that are contrary to fact (providing they begin with *if* or *unless)*, improbable, or doubtful
2. Statements that express a wish, a request or recommendation, an urgent appeal, or a demand

The following are verb forms used in the subjunctive mood:

PRESENT SUBJUNCTIVE	
SINGULAR	**PLURAL**
(if) I be	(if) we be
(if) you be	(if) you be
(if) he/she/it be	(if)they be
PAST SUBJUNCTIVE	
SINGULAR	**PLURAL**
(if) I were	(if) we were
(if) you were	(if) you were
(if) he/she/it were	(if) they were

Here are several examples:

Mary Alice moved that the minutes be [not are] accepted.

This statement expresses a request.

If I were [not was] a millionaire, I would never have to think about saving money.

I am not a millionaire, so the idea that I am is contrary to fact.

If Barry were [not was] here, the problem could be solved in a snap.

Barry is not here, so the statement is contrary to the fact.

Long live [not lives] the queen!

This can be viewed as a wish, an urgent appeal, or a request.

"Far be it from me [not it is] to give you any advice," said the mother to her teenager.

This is a wish or demand.

It's important that everybody be [not is] at the meeting, or we will have to reschedule.

This is a wish or request—a strong request, at that.

FACTS

Some grammarians add a fourth category of mood—interrogative— but most include interrogative sentences (you do remember that interrogative sentences ask a question, don't you?) in the indicative group.

Comparatively Speaking

Sometimes you need to show how something compares with or measures up to something else. Say, for example, you and your friends enjoy watching horror movies. You may want to report back to them on a new scary movie you've seen, letting them know whether it's *scarier* than another one you've all recently watched together or perhaps even the *scariest* movie you've ever seen (in which case, you might have some serious nightmares!). A scary movie can become a *scarier* movie if it's compared to another one, or it can become the *scariest* movie if it's compared to several others. You get the picture?

In writing comparisons, you can use one of three different forms (called degrees) of adjectives and adverbs:

- The positive degree simply makes a statement about a person, place, or thing.
- The comparative degree compares two (but only two) people, places, or things.
- The superlative degree compares more than two people, places, or things.

POSITIVE	COMPARATIVE	SUPERLATIVE
blue	bluer	bluest
dirty	dirtier	dirtiest
happy	happier	happiest
tall	taller	tallest

Here are a couple of rules to help you in forming the comparative and superlative:

- **Rule #1.** One-syllable adjectives and adverbs usually form their comparative form by adding -*er* and their superlative form by adding -*est* (see the examples *tall* and *blue* in the table).
- **Rule #2.** Adjectives of more than two syllables and adverbs ending in -*ly* usually form comparative forms by using *more* (or *less*) and superlative forms by using *most* (or *least*)

POSITIVE	COMPARATIVE	SUPERLATIVE
awkwardly	more awkwardly	most awkwardly
comfortable	more comfortable	most comfortable
qualified	less qualified	least qualified

- **Rule #3.** Confusion sometimes takes place in forming comparisons of words of two syllables only. Here's the rub: Sometimes two-syllable words use the -*er*, *est* forms, and sometimes they use the *more*, *most* (or *less*, *least*) forms. (You knew there had to be some complications in there somewhere, didn't you?)

POSITIVE	COMPARATIVE	SUPERLATIVE
sleepy	sleepier	sleepiest
tiring	more tiring	most tiring

So how do you know whether to use the -*er*, *est* form or the *more*, *most* form? You have to use a dictionary (a large dictionary, not a paperback one) if you're not sure. If there are no comparative or superlative forms listed in the dictionary, then use the *more*, *most* form.

Did you happen to notice the word *usually* in the first two rules? It's there because there are a few exceptions to the rules. The good news is that there aren't many exceptions. Among them are:

POSITIVE	COMPARATIVE	SUPERLATIVE
bad	worse	worst
far	farther/further	farthest/furthest
good	better	best
well	better	best
ill	worse	worst
little	littler/less/lesser	littlest/least
many	more	most
much	more	most
old (persons)	elder	eldest
old (things)	older	oldest

ESSENTIALS

Remember that some adjectives can't be compared. Words like *round, unique, favorite*, and *true* are already absolutes (for example, something can't be rounder than something else).

Before we get to the use of double negatives, one of the most noticeable blunders that can be made in the English language (and which I'm sure you can spot a mile away), let's first touch on a couple of other errors to avoid with comparisons. For example, a common mistake in both writing and speaking is to use the superlative form when the comparative should be used. Remember that if you're comparing two persons, places, or things, you use only the comparative form (not the superlative). Look at these sentences:

Of my two dogs, the cocker spaniel is the friendliest.
Susannah has two sons; Charlie is the eldest and Herb is the youngest.

In both of those sentences, the comparison is between only two *(two dogs, two sons)*, so the sentences should be written with the comparative form *(friendlier, elder, younger)* instead of the superlative.

Another frequent mistake in comparisons is to use both the *-er* and *more* or *-est* and *most* forms with the same noun, as in *the most tallest statue* or *a more happier child*. Remember that one form is the limit (and, of course, it has to be the correct form). In the examples, *most* and *more* need to be eliminated.

Sometimes comparisons can be ambiguous. Because some comparisons can be interpreted more than one way, be sure that you include all the words necessary to give the meaning you intend.

Read this sentence:

In the long jump, Adele could beat her rival Fern more often than her teammate Sherry.

Constructed that way, it isn't clear if the meaning is the following:

In the long jump, Adele could beat her rival Fern more often than her teammate Sherry could.

or

In the long jump, Adele could beat her rival Fern more often than she could beat her teammate Sherry.

Avoiding Double Negatives

Okay, now for the double negatives; that is, two negative words that are used to stress denial or opposition. Examples of these include:

After he was laid off, Hal realized that he didn't need none of the luxuries he'd become accustomed to.
(*Didn't* and *none* are negatives.)

That man was not doing nothing but just standing there!
(*Not* and *nothing* are negatives.)

Jessica wondered why William didn't call nobody when he became sick.
(*Didn't* and *nobody* are negatives.)

Mr. Brown said he ain't got none of those apples that you want.

(*Ain't* and *none* are negatives—and you also know that *ain't* is considered nonstandard, don't you?)

FACTS

Although it's easy to see that *not* (or contractions that have *not* as part of them) and words with negative prefixes (e.g., uncommon) are negative, these words are also negative: *barely, hardly, neither, no, nobody, none, no one, nothing, nowhere, scarcely*.

You'll often hear or read double negatives in colloquial speech:

You ain't heard nothin' yet!
Bart says he hasn't seen Betty nowhere.

One exception to the rule of avoiding double negatives is when you intend a positive or lukewarm meaning. Read this sentence:

I was not unhappy with my recent raise.

The connotation in the double negatives *(not* and *unhappy)* tells the reader that, while the writer wasn't unhappy, he or she wasn't exactly over the moon either.

It's also fine to use double negatives if you're using a phrase or clause for emphasis, as in this example:

"I will not take a bribe, not today, not tomorrow, not any time in my life,"
the politician cried.

Since we began this chapter on a light note, let's end on one as well.

A linguistics professor was lecturing to his class one day. "In English," he said, "a double negative forms a positive. In some languages, such as Russian, a double negative is still a negative. However, there is no language wherein a double positive can form a negative."
A voice from the back of the room piped up in reply, "Yeah, right."

CHAPTER 11
Keeping It Coherent

Certain elements can either make or break a sentence. If a sentence contains a misplaced modifier or is essentially illogical, it becomes confusing at best and ludicrous at worst. This chapter will give you some pointers for looking critically at your sentence construction so that your writing (and your reputation!) remain solid.

Manglers of Meaning: Misplaced Modifiers

Simply put, misplaced modifiers are words or phrases that you've put in the wrong place. All of your words—whether they're single words, phrases, or clauses—should be as close as possible to whatever they modify (the words they describe or give more information about). Take a look at this sentence, written with a single word in the wrong place:

After her wreck, Joanna could comprehend what the ambulance driver was barely saying.

The way the sentence is written, the ambulance driver is barely speaking—but surely that's not what the writer meant. *Barely* is out of its correct place because it modifies the wrong word. It should be moved so that it modifies the verb *could comprehend*. The sentence should be written this way:

After her wreck, Joanna could barely comprehend what the ambulance driver was saying.

In addition to being single words, misplaced modifiers can also be phrases, as in this example:

Witnesses reported that the woman was driving the getaway car with flowing black hair.

How interesting, a car with flowing black hair. *With flowing black hair* is in the wrong place in the sentence (it's misplaced) and should be placed after *woman*. That way, the sentence would read:

Witnesses reported that the woman with flowing black hair was driving the getaway car.

Clauses, too, can be put in the wrong place, as in the following sentence:

Mrs. Anderson could not stop thinking about her sick baby running in the six-mile road race.

That's quite a baby who can run a six-mile road race (not to mention running while being sick). The clause *running in the six-mile road race* is out of place in the sentence; it should be closer to the noun it modifies *(Mrs. Anderson)*. The sentence should be reworded this way:

Running in the six-mile road race, Mrs. Anderson could not stop thinking about her sick baby.

One of the most common problems with misplaced modifiers comes with what are called limiting modifiers—words like *almost*, *even*, *hardly*, *just*, *merely*, *nearly*, *only* (*only* is the one misplaced most often), *scarcely*, and *simply*. To convey the correct meaning, limiting modifiers must be placed in front of the words they modify.

Take a look at these sentences:

Already, Mr. Goulooze has almost eaten four slabs of ribs!

How does a person almost eat something? Did he have great willpower four different times? Or should the sentence be reworded to say that Mr. Goulooze has eaten almost four slabs of ribs?

Richard has nearly wrecked every car he's had.

Has Richard nearly wrecked the cars—in which case, he should be grateful for his luck—or has he wrecked nearly every car?

Another problem often arises with the word *not*. In speaking, we often say something like this:

All these chairs in the office are not comfortable for the employees.

The problem with that blanket statement is that the word *not* may be in the wrong place. If the meaning was that some of the chairs were uncomfortable, then the sentence should be reworded this way:

Not all these chairs in the office are comfortable for the employees.

Dangling Modifiers

Dangling modifiers are another problem in writing and speaking. Dangling modifiers have no word or phrase to describe; they just dangle, or hang, in the sentence without something to hold on to. Take a look at these sentences:

Long ears drooping on the floor, Julie wondered how the dog could walk.

Is it time for Julie to consider plastic surgery?

While performing, the audience gasped as the singer forgot the words to the song.

Why was the audience performing?

After getting a new paint job, reupholstering was now needed for the car.

Why would reupholstering be painted?

Each of the sentences needs to be reworded so that the modifiers have something to attach to.

Julie wondered how the dog could walk with its long ears drooping on the floor.

The audience gasped as the singer forgot the words to the song while he was performing.

After getting a new paint job, the car needed to be reupholstered.

Squinting Modifiers

Another problem comes with squinting modifiers (sometimes called two-way modifiers). These are words that can logically modify or describe something on either side of them, but the reader can't tell if the words modify what's on their left or right. Take a look at this sentence:

The instructor said after the semester ended that Mark was eligible to retake the test.

What does the phrase *after the semester ended* apply to? Did the instructor *tell* Mark this after the semester ended, or was Mark *eligible* to retake the test after the semester ended? The way this sentence is worded, the meaning is not clear. To correct this sentence, change the placement of the modifier.

After the semester ended, the instructor said that Mark was eligible to retake the test.

The instructor said that Mark was eligible to retake the test after the semester ended.

Parallelism in Writing

For your work to be easily read—and, in some cases, for it to be coherent—using parallelism is important. Parallelism helps you give equality and balance to separate points that you make.

Confused? Not to worry. Understanding parallelism isn't as difficult as it may seem. In using parallelism, you simply write all the similar parts of a sentence in the same way. If you've used two nouns, you don't suddenly switch to a gerund. If you've used verbs that have a certain tense, you don't suddenly change tenses. If you begin in one voice, you don't suddenly switch to another voice.

Take a look at some of the examples that follow, and you'll get a clearer understanding of what parallelism is and how important it is in your writing.

FACTS

Here are some famous lines that use parallelism effectively:

With this faith we will be able to work together, to pray together, to struggle together, to go to jail together, to stand up for freedom together, knowing that we will be free one day.
— *Rev. Martin Luther King Jr.*

I came, I saw, I conquered. — *Julius Caesar*

Parallelism Problem #1: Items in Pairs or in a Series

When naming items, you should present them all in the same way. Look at this problem sentence:

This afternoon I washed, waxed, and then I was vacuuming the car.

Here is the problem viewed one way:

This afternoon I washed (past tense verb), waxed (past tense verb), and then I was vacuuming (past progressive tense verb) the car.

Here is the problem viewed another way:

This afternoon I washed (-ed word), waxed (-ed word), and then I was vacuuming (-ing word) the car.

Here is the repaired sentence that's now parallel:

This afternoon I washed, waxed, and vacuumed the car.

All the verbs are now in the same tense; all verbs are now *–ed* words.

The following example shows the incorrect use of parallel items in a series when a colon is used:

Compared to a typewriter, a word processor has three helpful features that save time: you can quickly edit material you don't want, you can save drafts and revise them, and it can automatically correct words that you frequently misspell.

Here is the problem viewed one way:

Compared to a typewriter, a word processor has three helpful features that save time: you [second person] can quickly edit material you don't want, you [second person] can save drafts and revise them, and it [third person] can automatically correct words that you frequently misspell.

Here is the problem viewed another way:

Compared to a typewriter, a word processor has three helpful features that save time: you [you as subject] can quickly edit material you don't want, you [*you* as subject] can save drafts and revise them, and it [*it* as subject] can automatically correct words that you frequently misspell.

Here is the repaired sentence that's now parallel:

Compared to a typewriter, a word processor has three helpful features that save time: you can quickly edit material you don't want, you can save drafts and revise them, and you can automatically correct words that you frequently misspell.

Parallelism Problem #2: Clauses

When using more than one clause, you should keep the same voice and use the same type of introduction in each. Here is the problem sentence:

I was worried that Bill would drive too fast, that the road would be too slippery, and that the car would be stopped by the police.

Here is the problem viewed one way:

I was worried that Bill would drive too fast [active voice], that the road would be too slippery [active voice], and that the car would be stopped by the police [passive voice].

Here is the repaired sentence that's now parallel:

I was worried that Bill would drive too fast, that the road would be too slippery, and that the police would stop the car.

Here is another problem sentence:

You promised that you would bring everything for the picnic, that you would be on time, and not to forget the bug repellent.

This is one way to look at the problem:

You promised that you would bring everything for the picnic [clause introduced with a subordinating conjunction], that you would be on time [clause introduced with a subordinating conjunction], and not to forget the bug repellent [clause introduced with an adverb and infinitive].

Or you can look at it this way:

You promised that you would bring everything for the picnic [clause introduced with that], that you would be on time [clause introduced with that], and not to forget the bug repellent [clause introduced with not to forget].

Here's the repaired sentence that's now parallel:

You promised that you would bring everything for the picnic, that you would be on time, and that you would not forget the bug repellent.

Parallelism Problem #3: Placement

Items in a series should be placed in similar locations. Take a look at this problem sentence:

Mike is not only very kind but also is very good-looking.

Let's look at the problem:

Mike is not only [first part of a correlative conjunction not only comes after the verb] very kind but also [second part of a correlative conjunction but also comes before the verb] is very good-looking.

Here's the repaired sentence that's now parallel:

Mike is not only very kind but also very good-looking.

Parallelism Problem #4:
Placement of Emphasis or Chronology

If the items have different degrees of importance or if they occur at different times, you should order them according to their emphasis or chronology. Look at this problem sentence:

Misuse of the drug can result in fever, death, or dizziness.

Now, identify the problem:

Misuse of the drug can result in fever [something that's bad], death [something that's the worst of the three], or dizziness [something that's bad].

Here's the repaired sentence that's now parallel:

Misuse of the drug can result in fever, dizziness, or death.

In writing your sentence this way you've built up to the climax; the worst problem—death. Note that you could also include a word or phrase before the last element to add to the buildup; you could word the sentence like this:

Misuse of the drug can result in fever, dizziness, or even death.

Parallelism Problem #5: Missing Words

You should be sure to include all the words you need for each item. Look at this problem sentence:

The telephone is either ringing off the wall and sometimes it's silent for several days.

Identify the problem:

The telephone is either [first part of a correlative conjunction] ringing off the wall and [the second—and necessary—part of the correlative conjunction is missing] sometimes it's silent for several days.

Here's the repaired sentence that's now parallel:

The telephone is either ringing off the wall or it's silent for several days.

Parallelism Problem #6: Unclear Meaning

You should include all the words that are necessary to indicate the items you're referring to. Look at this problem sentence:

In conducting my interview, I talked with the college senior and candidate for the job.

Identify the problem:

In conducting my interview, I talked with the college senior and candidate for the job.

Did the speaker talk with one person who was a senior and who was interviewing for the job, or with two people—one of whom was a senior and one of whom was interviewing for the job?

Here's the repaired sentence that's now parallel:

In conducting my interview, I talked with both the college senior and the candidate for the job.

Parallelism Problem #7: Too Many Words

You don't need to repeat the same introductory word if it applies to all of the items. Let's look at this problem sentence:

I hope to see you on November 20, December 13, and on January 7.

Identify the problem:

I hope to see you on [preposition before noun] November 20, [preposition missing] December 13, and on [preposition appears again] January 7.

Here's the repaired sentence that's now parallel:

I hope to see you on November 20, December 13, and January 7.

Note that the same preposition *(on)* relates to each date, so there is no need to repeat it.

Parallelism Problem #8: Too Few Words

If different prepositions apply to items in a series, be sure to include all the prepositions. Look at this problem sentence:

The invading ants are on the living room floor, the dining room table, and the sink. (Yikes! Better get out the bug spray!)

Identify the problem:

The invading ants are on [the preposition on is used with this phrase] the floor, [the preposition on is used with this phrase] the kitchen table, and [the preposition on is used with this phrase, but the preposition should be in] the sink.

Here's the repaired sentence that's now parallel:

The invading ants are on the living room floor, on the dining room table, and in the sink.

Note that the beginning preposition *(on)* does not relate to each area, so you need to repeat it in the second phrase and change it to *in* for the third phrase.

Sometimes you may deliberately choose to repeat certain elements of your sentence. Take a look at this sentence:

I promise to cut taxes, spending, and exorbitant salary raises.

That sentence is fine the way it is, but to add emphasis to the cuts, you might choose to write the sentence this way:

I promise to cut taxes, to cut spending, and to cut exorbitant raises in salary.

Parallelism Problem #9: Parallel Sentences

To add emphasis or smoothness, you should construct your sentences in a parallel way. Look at this example:

I was nervous and frightened, but I hid my emotions. My sister showed the world that she felt confident and carefree.

Identify the problem: Actually, there's no grammatical problem with the sentences, but they can certainly be improved by being written in a parallel manner.

Here are the repaired sentences that are now parallel:

I was nervous and frightened, but I hid my emotions. My sister was confident and carefree, but she showed the world how she felt.

Tips for Parallelism

If a lack of parallelism is often a problem in your writing, try the following tips:

- Look for *-ing* or *-ed* constructions.
- Look for constructions beginning with *it*, *that*, *to*, and *you*.
- Look for constructions beginning with the same preposition.
- Look at the voice (active or passive) used in the constructions.
- Check to see if one of the constructions is more important than the others; if so, place it last.
- If you've used a correlative conjunction, check to see if you have its partner (e.g., *either . . . or*).

SSENTIALS   Sometimes your ear is more reliable than your eye. Good writers read their material aloud and listen for words and phrases that are not parallel.

If you have items in a series, write them down in a column. Look for common elements in two parts of the series, and then convert the other items so they'll be formed in the same way.

Logically Speaking

Making sure that your sentences are inherently logical is one of the most important steps in becoming a good writer. In fact, no matter how meticulous you are in crafting the grammar and punctuation of your sentences, and regardless of how careful you are with your spelling and word usage, if your material has errors in logic, all your hard work will have been for nothing. Lapses in logic can take several different forms. Some are instantly recognizable in a sentence, while others are a little more subtle and, thus, a little more insidious. Don't let these errors sneak up on you! As you write, keep the following common mistakes in mind.

Asking the Impossible: Faulty Predication

Faulty predication (sometimes called illogical predication or—are you ready for this one?—selectional restriction violation) is one type of illogical writing. Don't worry, I won't make you get out your dictionary; the definition of *predication* is the way the subject and verb interact. When your subject and verb don't make sense together (that is, the subject can't "be" or "do" the verb), then you have faulty predication.

Take a look at these sentences:

Martha is a tooth that is bothering her.

The new breath mint assures customers that it will last all day.

An economics class is when you study monetary and fiscal policy.

In tennis, the term "playing the net" is where you place yourself close to the net in order to hit balls before they bounce.

The reason Avonda was late was because she had a flat tire.

Asking the right questions helps understand the new material.

Each of these sentences has an example of faulty predication. Obviously, Martha isn't a tooth; a breath mint is incapable of assuring anybody of anything; a class isn't *when* anything; playing the net isn't *where* anything; a reason isn't *because* anything; and asking doesn't help understand. Each of these sentences needs to be reworded, perhaps like this:

Martha has a tooth that is bothering her.

The makers of the new breath mint assure customers that the mint will last all day.

In an economics class you study monetary and fiscal policy.

When "playing the net" in tennis, you place yourself close to the net in order to hit balls before they bounce.

The reason Avonda was late was that she had a flat tire.

Asking the right questions helps you understand the new material.

To check for faulty predication, ask yourself if it's possible for each subject to "do" or "be" the verb. If it's not possible, then change the wording.

The illogical uses of *when* and *where* are two of the most common examples of faulty predication. Don't describe a noun or pronoun by using *when* or *where*. Be sure to check your sentence every time (that is, whenever and wherever) you use *when* or *where*.

When *A* Doesn't Follow *B*: Faulty Coordination

Faulty coordination occurs if you join (combine or coordinate) two clauses in an illogical way:

I made my way to the head of the checkout line, yet I realized I had forgotten my wallet.

The word *yet* (the word that joins, combines, or coordinates the two clauses) is used incorrectly. The sentence should read:

I made my way to the head of the checkout line, but then I realized I had forgotten my wallet.

Another example of faulty coordination comes in sentences that contain independent clauses of unequal importance. The sentences are written in a way that makes the clauses seem equal, as in the following sentence:

I paid $50,000 for my new car, and it has tinted glass.

The cost of the car is much more important than the fact that it has tinted glass (at least, it certainly is to most people). To correct the problem, you could make the second clause subordinate to the first (making the second clause an adjective clause).

I paid $50,000 for my new car, which has tinted glass.

Absolutely—Not!

One common problem with comparison occurs when you use absolute adjectives, which are words that—by their definition—cannot be compared. *Round*, for instance, is one of those words. Something is either round or it's not. Since one thing cannot be rounder than something else, *round* is an absolute adjective.

OTHER ABSOLUTE ADJECTIVES INCLUDE THE FOLLOWING:	
blank	pure
complete	square
dead	straight
empty	true
eternal	unanimous
favorite	unique
permanent	vacant

Look at these examples:

I hadn't studied for the test; the paper I turned in was somewhat blank.

You can't have a paper that is somewhat blank; either it has something on it or it doesn't.

This is my most favorite restaurant.

Because *favorite* means "at the top of my list," one place can't be more favorite than someplace else.

Since these are words that can't be compared, be sure not to use *more*, *most*, *quite*, *rather*, *somewhat*, *very*, and other qualifiers in front of them.

Putting Apples with Oranges: Faulty Comparisons

Another problem with faulty comparison occurs if you compare two unlike people, places, or things:

The traffic mishaps in April were more numerous than May.

This sentence compares mishaps to May, which makes no sense. The sentence should be rewritten like this:

The traffic mishaps in April were more numerous than the mishaps in May.

Take a look at this one:

I've come to the conclusion that the people in Crydonville are friendlier than Park City.

Here people are being compared to a city—obviously, an illogical comparison. The sentence needs to be reworded, perhaps like this:

I've come to the conclusion that the people in Crydonville are friendlier than the people in Park City.

QUESTIONS?

Have you ever noticed how often incomplete comparisons are used in radio and television commercials and printed advertisements?
Name recognition is the goal of many companies, so having the name in print or on the air is of utmost importance. Following through with incomplete comparisons doesn't matter to advertisers as long as the customer sees—and remembers—the name of the product.

Still another problem is an ambiguous comparison, which occurs if you write a statement that could be interpreted two different ways. Look at this sentence:

Dawn dislikes traveling alone more than Dave.

It has an ambiguous comparison because the reader isn't sure what the word *more* applies to. Does Dawn dislike traveling alone more than she dislikes Dave, or does she dislike it more than Dave does?

Let's Not Be Hasty! Sweeping Generalizations

Sweeping (or hasty) generalizations use all-encompassing words like *anyone, everyone, always, never, everything, all, only,* and *none,* and superlatives like *best, greatest, most, least.*

The country never recovers from an economic downturn in just one week.

Be careful with sentences with generalizations like this one. What happens to the writer's credibility if the country does, in fact, recover from a downturn in one week? You're far better off to write in terms of what happens *most of the time* than in terms of what *always* or *never* happens (not to mention that you're protected when you make a mistake). One rewording of the example is this:

The country almost never recovers from an economic downturn in one week.

Here's another example of a sweeping generalization:

Everyone should strenuously exercise at least thirty minutes a day.

Everyone? Surely a newborn baby or someone who's recovering from surgery shouldn't strenuously exercise. If you reword the sentence, you can leave some room for exceptions or for debate. Here's a rewording that is more reasonable:

Everyone who is able should exercise at least thirty minutes a day.

I Don't Follow You: Non Sequiturs

A non sequitur is a problem in logic that states an effect that doesn't follow its cause. Put another way, with a non sequitur, the inference or conclusion that you assert doesn't logically follow from what you previously stated.

I turned in a paper; therefore, I'll pass the class.

As any teacher can tell you, the fact that you turned in a paper doesn't necessarily mean that you will pass the class. What if the paper is (a) not on the assigned topic? (b) too short or too long? (c) plagiarized? (d) three weeks late? (e) written on a kindergarten level? In other words, just because one thing happened, the other does not necessarily follow. Here are other examples of non sequiturs:

I've bought products made by Commonwealth Foods for years. Their new product, Dog Biscuits for Humans, is bound to be tasty.

Jack stole a box of paper clips from the office. He probably cheats on his taxes, too.

Whitson is our representative in Congress. Certainly we can trust her.

The Missing Link: Omitted Words

Another frequent mistake in logic is to omit *else* or *other* in sentences with comparisons. Read this sentence:

Aunt Lucy likes Cousin Louise more than she likes anyone in the family.

The way the sentence is written, Cousin Louise isn't in the family. The sentence needs to be reworded this way:

Aunt Lucy likes Cousin Louise more than she likes anyone else in the family.

Sometimes sentences need the word *than* or *as* in order for them to be logical:

Steve said he could play the guitar as well, if not better than, Jack.

Taking out the phrase *if not better than* leaves *Steve said he could play the guitar as well Jack*, a sentence that's obviously incomplete. The sentence should be written with the extra *as* to complete the phrase:

Steve said he could play the guitar as well as, if not better than, Jack.

Without Rhyme or Reason: Additional Lapses in Logic

Another type of illogical writing to check for is commonly called *post hoc, ergo propter hoc*, which translates as *after this, so because of this*. (This is also called coincidental correlation.) Here the assumption is that because one thing follows another, the first caused the second.

Terry washed her car in the morning, and it began to rain in the afternoon.

The second event was not caused by the first: the rain was not caused by the car being washed (although, come to think of it, it does seem to rain every time you wash your car, doesn't it?).

If you use a false dilemma (sometimes called an either/or fallacy), you state that only two alternatives exist, when there are actually more than two.

Mrs. Robertson can get to her appointment in one of two ways: she can either drive her car or she can walk.

Mrs. Robertson has other choices: she could call a cab, take the bus, or ask a friend for a ride, so she is not limited to only two ways of getting to her appointment. If your argument has a red herring, then it dodges the real issue by citing an irrelevant concern as evidence.

The driver in front of me ran the red light and was speeding, so it's not right that I get a ticket for going 100 mph in a 50 mph zone.

The writer or speaker did something wrong; the fact that the driver ahead did something worse is irrelevant.

FACTS

Originally, the term red herring was used in hunting. Red (preserved) herring has a strong odor, and hunters used it to create a trail when training their dogs to follow a scent. However, others, such as fox lovers, used it for their own purposes—to throw dogs off a scent.

If you're guilty of circular reasoning, then your writing has what its name implies—reasoning that goes around in a circle, with nothing substantial in the middle. Here's an example:

The epidemic was dangerous because everyone in town felt unsafe and at risk.

That sentence has no insight because the writer gives no clarification in the second part of the sentence about why the epidemic was dangerous; the fact that everyone felt unsafe and at risk doesn't explain the danger.

CHAPTER 12

Shaping Strong Sentences

Fragments and run-ons can significantly weaken your writing, confusing the reader and preventing you from getting your point across. But don't let them scare you; by this time you've already mastered so many points of grammar and style that you'll probably find gaining the upper hand over fragments and run-ons to be a piece of cake!

A Few Words about Fragments

You've been told time and again not to use sentence fragments. Right? (Notice that fragment?) Generally speaking, you shouldn't use fragments because they can be confusing for your reader and they sometimes don't get your point across.

How can you recognize fragments? The textbook definition says that a fragment is "a group of words that is not a sentence." Okay, so what constitutes a sentence? Again, the textbook definition says a sentence is a group of words that (1) has a subject, (2) has a predicate (verb), and (3) expresses a complete thought.

FACTS

Depending on when and where you went to school, you might be more familiar with the definition that says that a sentence must form an independent clause. Actually, an independent clause must have a subject, predicate, and complete thought, so the definitions are the same.

If a string of words doesn't have all three of the qualifications (a subject, a verb, and an expression of a complete thought), then you have a fragment rather than a sentence. That's pretty straightforward, don't you think? Take a look at these two words:

Spot ran.

You have a subject *(Spot)*, a verb *(ran)*, and the words express a complete thought; in other words, you don't get confused when you read the two words by themselves. Since you have all the requirements (subject, verb, complete thought), you have a sentence.

Now, look at this group of words:

Although she had a new job in a modern office building.

This example is a subordinate clause that's punctuated as if it were a sentence. You have a subject *(she)* and a verb *(had)*, but what you don't have is a complete thought. The words serve only to introduce you to the main idea of the sentence. If someone said only those words to you, you'd be left hanging because you wouldn't know what the main idea was. (Although she had a new job—what? She took off for the Far East? She called in sick on her first day? She decided to elope with a billionaire and never had to work again?) The *although* that introduces the sentence means that there should be something else to explain the first group of words.

A participial phrase often creates another common sentence fragment. Look at these examples:

Scared stiff by the intense wind and storm.
Going to the beach with her family and friends.

Neither of these groups of words has a main clause to identify who or what is being talked about. Who was scared stiff? Who was going to the beach? Obviously, something's missing.

If you're not sure if the words you've used constitute a sentence, first write them by themselves and then ask yourself if they could be understood without something else being added. If you're still not sure, let them get cold for a while and then reread them. If you're *still* not sure, call a friend and say those particular words and nothing else. You know you have a fragment if your friend says something along the lines of, "And then what?"

Another good way to see if you have a fragment is to take the word group and turn it into a yes-or-no question. If you answer yes to the question, you have a sentence; if you answer no (or if the question makes no sense), you have a fragment. Look at these examples:

She ran quickly back to the shelter of the mansion.

Did she run quickly back to the shelter of the mansion? Yes, she did. Therefore, you have a sentence.

Scared stiff by the intense wind and storm.

Did scared stiff by the intense wind and storm? No, that doesn't make sense. You have a fragment.

Read the following paragraph and see if you can spot the fragments:

The lone woman trudged up the muddy riverbank. Determined that she would make the best of a bad situation. Because of her family's recent run of bad luck. She knew that she had to contribute to the family's finances. That's why she had accepted a teaching position. In this town that was new to her. Impatiently waiting for someone to show her where she was to live. She surveyed the streets and rundown buildings of the little village. Little did she know the problems that she would face in the "wilderness," as she had mentally thought of her new home. First, the schoolhouse was not ready. Even though she had written that she wanted to begin classes on the 24th. The day after her arrival.

Did you spot all the fragments? Take a look at:

Determined that she would make the best of a bad situation.
Because of her family's recent run of bad luck.
In this town that was new to her.
Impatiently waiting for someone to show her where she was to live.
Even though she had written that she wanted to begin classes on the 24th.
The day after her arrival.

If you had those words alone on a piece of paper, would anybody know what you meant? No—those words don't form complete thoughts.

Now, how can you correct these fragments? Usually the fragment should be connected to the sentence immediately before or after it—whichever sentence the fragment refers to. (A word of caution: Just be sure that the newly created sentence makes sense.)

The first fragment *(Determined that she would make the best of a bad situation)* can be corrected by hooking it on to the sentence right before it. The corrected sentence should read:

The lone woman trudged up the muddy riverbank, determined that she would make the best of a bad situation.

You could also put the fragment at the beginning of a sentence:

Determined that she would make the best of a bad situation, the lone woman trudged up the muddy riverbank.

Or you could put the fragment inside the sentence:

The lone woman, determined that she would make the best of a bad situation, trudged up the muddy riverbank.

Each of these three new sentences makes sense.

Now, look at the second fragment: *Because of her family's recent run of bad luck.* What about their run of bad luck? Again, if you said those words—and only those words—to someone, he or she would give you a blank stare. You hadn't given the reason behind the *because.* To correct this fragment, you could tack the fragment onto the beginning or middle of the sentence that follows it in the original paragraph:

Because of her family's recent run of bad luck, she knew that she had to contribute to the family's finances.

She knew that, because of her family's recent run of bad luck, she had to contribute to the family's finances.

By slightly changing some wording (without changing the meaning), you could also add this fragment to the end of the sentence:

She knew that she had to contribute to her family's finances because of their recent run of bad luck.

Here's another example of possibilities for rewording a sentence when you incorporate a fragment. Take this fragment and its related sentence:

Impatiently waiting for someone to show her where she was to live. She surveyed the village.

You might reword the fragment and sentence and combine them this way:

She surveyed the village as she waited impatiently for someone to show her where she was to live.

Another way you might revise is to create an appositive. Take this combination of a sentence and two fragments:

First, the schoolhouse was not ready. Even though she had written that she wanted to begin classes on the 24th. The day after her arrival.

It can be rewritten to read:

First, the schoolhouse was not ready even though she had written that she wanted to begin classes on the 24th, the day after her arrival.

Here, *the day after her arrival* functions as an appositive.

Acceptable Uses of Fragments

Formal writing generally doesn't permit you to use fragments; however, using them occasionally is okay for a casual writing style if they don't confuse your reader. Also, keep in mind that using fragments (even sparingly) depends on your audience, the restrictions of your instructor or company, and your personal writing style.

You might use fragments in short stories or novels (you have begun writing your Great American Novel, haven't you?). A rule of thumb is that you shouldn't use them too often and you certainly shouldn't use them in any way that would puzzle your readers.

Rarely—if ever—should you use a fragment in a news story in a magazine or newspaper. If, however, you're writing an editorial, a fragment might be just what you need to get your point across.

Do we need the new tax that's on the ballot? Without a doubt. Will it pass? Probably not.

Both *Without a doubt* and *Probably not* are fragments. But consider how the same passage would be worded if the fragments were turned into complete sentences.

Do we need the new tax that's on the ballot? Without a doubt we do. Will it pass? No, it probably will not.

ESSENTIALS

Remember that you may use fragments if you're quoting someone; in fact, you must use fragments if that's what the speaker used.

Fragments are also acceptable in bulleted or numbered lists. Take a look at the following example:

Acceptable uses of a fragment include the following:

- When you're quoting someone
- In a bulleted or numbered list
- To make a quick point—but only when the construction isn't confusing to the reader

Taken individually, each of the bullets is a fragment, but its meaning is clear. In the type of writing that you do, if you're permitted (or even encouraged) to include bulleted lists, then using fragments is fine.

Sometimes you'll see a fragment intentionally used for emphasis or wry humor. Look at the title of this section and you'll see words that were deliberately constructed as fragments. Also, take a look at this example:

Marcy quickly told the prospective employer she would never accept a job in a city more than a hundred miles from her hometown. Never. Under no circumstances. For no amount of money. Well, maybe for a new car, an expense account, and double her current salary.

FACTS

Using fragments as titles, captions, or headings is generally acceptable. Space restrictions will not usually allow complete sentences. You'll also frequently see fragments used in advertising. Since they're shorter, readers probably remember fragments more easily than they would complete sentences.

Reining In Run-on Sentences

Another type of mistake of sentence construction is a run-on sentence. The term *run-on* simply means that your sentence has at least two complete thoughts (two independent clauses, if your mind thinks that way), but it lacks the necessary punctuation between the thoughts. This punctuation is needed for your reader to know when one thought stops and another begins. Consider the following sentence:

The punctuation code gives your readers a signal about where one thought stops and another begins if you don't use some code your readers will be confused.

Say what? Instead of having the needed punctuation between *begins* and *if*, the sentence, well, "runs on" and its meaning is unclear. (A fairly simple concept, wouldn't you say?)

It's Time to Take a Break: Fused Sentences and Comma Splices

One type of run-on, called a fused sentence, occurs when two (or more) sentences are fused together without a punctuation mark to show the reader where the break occurs. Take a look at this sentence:

For our annual picnic, Tom and Jill brought hamburgers we brought potato salad.

In the sentence, there are two separate thoughts:

For our annual picnic, Tom and Jill brought hamburgers
and
we brought potato salad.

This sentence needs some punctuation to tell the reader where one thought ends and another begins. You may do this in one of three ways:

- By creating two separate sentences *(For our annual picnic, Tom and Jill brought hamburgers. We brought potato salad.)*
- By inserting a semicolon *(For our annual picnic, Tom and Jill brought hamburgers; we brought potato salad.)*
- By inserting a comma and one of seven conjunctions—*but, or, yet, so, for, and, nor* (remember *boysfan?*) *(For our annual picnic, Tom and Jill brought hamburgers, and we brought potato salad.)*

ESSENTIALS Remember that you must have two (or more) complete thoughts in order to correct a run-on sentence. Ask yourself if each group of words could stand alone (could be a sentence by itself). If one group of words doesn't make sense as a sentence, then you don't have a complete thought and you don't have a run-on sentence.

Another type of run-on is a comma splice (sometimes known as a comma fault), a sentence that has two complete thoughts that are spliced together by just a comma. The problem with a comma splice is that the comma should be replaced by something different—a different punctuation mark, additional words, or both. Take a look at this sentence:

Jamal wanted to go to the ball game, his friend Jason wanted to see the new movie.

On either side of the comma, you have a complete thought. The punctuation code says that you need something stronger than just a comma to help the reader understand that a thought has been completed.

You have several choices to correct the sentence. You may create two separate sentences by using a period:

Jamal wanted to go to the ball game. His friend Jason wanted to see the new movie.

Or you may separate the two complete thoughts with a semicolon:

Jamal wanted to go to the ball game; his friend Jason wanted to see the new movie.

Or you may separate the two complete thoughts with a semicolon and a connecting word or phrase:

Jamal wanted to go to the ball game; however, his friend Jason wanted to see the new movie.

Or you may join the two sentences by leaving in the comma but adding one of seven conjunctions (*but, or, yet, so, for, and, nor*).

Of course, you may use the conjunctions only if the sentence makes sense. You may have:

Jamal wanted to go to the ball game, but his friend Jason wanted to see the new movie.

FACTS

A frequent comma splice occurs with two quoted sentences, as in this example:

"We're going to the theater at seven," Paula said, "I'd better get dressed right now."

Paula stated two separate sentences, so you should use either a period (preferable in this case) or a semicolon after *said*.

There is another way you can correct either a fused sentence or a comma splice: you can reword the sentence so that one part becomes subordinate (that is, it can't stand alone as a complete thought). Let's look at the first example:

For our annual picnic, Tom and Jill brought hamburgers we brought potato salad.

You might reword this in a number of ways:

While Tom and Jill brought hamburgers for our annual picnic, we brought potato salad.

or

Whereas Tom and Jill brought hamburgers for our annual picnic, we brought potato salad.

Yes, this one sounds really stuffy, and you probably wouldn't use it because of its style—but it does make sense.

Now look at the second example:

Jamal wanted to go to the ball game, his friend Jason wanted to see the new movie.

You could rewrite it in this way:

Although Jamal wanted to go to the ball game, his friend Jason wanted to see the new movie.

or

While Jamal wanted to go to the ball game, his friend Jason wanted to see the new movie.

Note that in each of these examples the first part of the rewritten sentence (the part before the comma) could not stand alone as a sentence.

In closing, keep in mind that a sentence does not become a run-on merely because of its length. Take a look at this sentence:

At eleven-thirty one Saturday night not long ago, while young Sheila Anthren was absentmindedly driving her dilapidated 1953 gray-and-white Chrysler sedan down a lonely, one-lane gravel road that looked as if it had not been traversed in many a year, she suddenly glanced in the rearview mirror and was alarmed to see two blinking lights coming from what she supposed was a vehicle of some sort or another; instead of immediately panicking and screaming bloody murder, however, Sheila decided that perhaps this signaled a visit from someone from Outer Space, an alien who would be friendly and would take her to worlds that she had only dreamed of in all of the twenty years of her friendless life.

Although this paragraph is hardly the best-composed sentence in the world (at 119 words, it should be broken into several sentences) and is basically a nightmare to read, it is properly punctuated and it isn't a run-on. On either side of the semicolon there is just one complete thought.

Transitional Words and Phrases

Good writers rely on the use of transitional words and phrases (you might be more familiar with the terms *connecting words* or *parenthetical expressions*). Transitional words and phrases show your readers the association between thoughts, sentences, or paragraphs, and they help make your writing smoother.

Sometimes sentences and paragraphs have perfectly constructed grammar, punctuation, and usage, but they lack transitional words or phrases. Material written that way seems awkward and stiff, as in this example:

The blind date was a disaster. It was a complete debacle. I was intrigued by what my "friend" Sarah had told me about Bill; she had said that he was charming and was open to meeting someone new. He had recently seen me at a party and had wanted to meet me. Sarah said Bill was just my type. She said that he was an avid reader; we would have lots to talk about. He liked playing tennis; that was a plus for me. I had an earlier vow never to go out on another blind date. I agreed to meet Bill.

There's nothing wrong with the grammar, punctuation, or spelling in that paragraph, but it is choppy and boring. Now read the same paragraph after transitional words and phrases (underlined) have been added:

The blind date was <u>more than</u> a disaster. <u>In fact</u>, it was <u>clearly</u> a complete debacle. <u>At first</u>, I was <u>somewhat</u> intrigued by what my "friend" Sarah had told me about Bill; <u>namely</u>, she had said that he was <u>quite</u> charming and <u>also</u> was open to meeting someone new. <u>In fact</u>, he had recently seen me <u>in the distance</u> at a party and had wanted to meet me. <u>Besides</u>, Sarah said, Bill was just my type. She said that he was <u>quite</u> an avid reader <u>for one thing</u>; <u>therefore</u>, we would have lots to talk about. <u>In addition</u>, he liked playing tennis; that was <u>certainly</u> a plus for me. <u>So, in spite of</u> my earlier vow never to go out on another blind date, I <u>eventually</u> agreed to meet Bill <u>on Saturday</u>.

Much better, isn't it? By including the transitions, the movement from one idea to another is much smoother, and the language of the paragraph has some life in it.

As important as transitions are in sentences, they are equally important between paragraphs. (Do you see how that transition sentence connects the idea of the preceding paragraph with the idea of this one?) These transitions help you move smoothly from one major concept to the next one.

The following is an excerpt from a piece that compares an essay titled "Why Would You . . . ?" to a personal experience of the writer. Read the two paragraphs and pay particular attention to the first sentence of the second paragraph, the transitional sentence.

In Conrad Allen's essay "Why Would You . . . ?" the author recounts how he had been humiliated in elementary school. Allen had been infatuated with Mandy Grayson, a pretty, pigtailed little girl in his class. One Valentine's Day, Allen gave Mandy a card with Manndy *perfectly printed—if incorrectly spelled—on the envelope. After she tore open the card, Mandy glanced at it and, much to Conrad's dismay, let it drop on the floor. In a voice loud enough for all the class to hear, she said to Conrad, "Why would you give me a card? You're too dumb and ugly." Allen writes that he first felt his face turn red in embarrassment, and then he felt complete humiliation as the whole class turned around to stare at him to see his reaction. All he could do was stand frozen in front of Mandy, trying in vain to hold back his shame and his tears.*

Like Allen, I felt shame when I was young. When I was in the fifth grade, my family was undergoing some difficult times. At that age, I was close friends with a group of four other girls; in fact, we called ourselves the "Live Five." Because we all had the same teacher, we were able to spend recess and lunchtime together, and we frequently spent the night at each other's houses as well. At one of the sleepovers at my house, the Live Five vowed to stay up all night. Big mistake. In our efforts to keep each other awake, we disturbed my father. That night happened to be one of the many when he was drunk, and he came down to the basement and began cursing and screaming at all of my friends. Not only did he say horrible things to me, but he also yelled at each of my friends and called them terrible names. There was nothing that I could do to make him stop, and the shame of that night continues with me today whenever I see one of the Live Five.

Wow, get out the tissues! In reading these tearjerkers, you probably noticed that the sentence at the beginning of the second paragraph provides a connection between the ideas of the first paragraph and second paragraph. The first two words *(Like Allen)* signal that the main idea of the first paragraph will be continued and that a comparison will be made. Plus, the rest of the sentence *(I felt shame in school)* gives a clue about the topic of the second paragraph. If the transition sentence weren't there, and the second paragraph began *When I was in the fifth grade . . .* , the second paragraph would seem disjointed from the first, and the reader would be confused.

As you can see from these examples (that's another transitional phrase—but you knew that, didn't you?), you should add transitions whenever possible to provide necessary links between thoughts and between paragraphs. By using them, your writing becomes much more unified and articulate.

Remember that transitional phrases are usually enclosed in commas, unless they're necessary to the meaning of a sentence.

Classifying the Connectors

Transitional words and phrases can be divided into categories, grouped according to their use. The following should give you lots of ideas for adding transitional elements to your writing:

- **addition/sequence:** *additionally, afterward, again, also, and, and then, another . . . , besides, equally important, eventually, finally, first . . . second . . . third, further, furthermore, in addition, in the first place, initially, last, later, likewise, meanwhile, moreover, next, other, overall, second, still, third, too, what's more*
- **concession:** *admittedly, although it is true that, certainly, conceding that, granted that, in fact, it may appear that, naturally, no doubt, of course, surely, undoubtedly, without a doubt*
- **contrast:** *after all, alternatively, although, and yet, at the same time, but, conversely, despite, even so, even though, for all that, however, in contrast, in spite of, instead, nevertheless, nonetheless, nor, notwithstanding, on the contrary, on the other hand, or, otherwise, regardless, still, though, yet*
- **examples, clarification, emphasis:** *after all, an instance of this, as an illustration, by all means, certainly, clearly, definitely, e.g., even, for example, for instance, for one thing, i.e., importantly, indeed, in*

fact, in other words, in particular, in short, more than that, namely, of course, of major concern, once again, specifically, somewhat, such as, that is, that is to say, the following example, this can be seen in, thus, to clarify, to demonstrate, to illustrate, to repeat, to rephrase, to put another way, truly, undoubtedly, without a doubt

ESSENTIALS

Writers sometimes confuse the Latin abbreviations *e.g.* (*exempli gratia*, meaning *for example*) and *i.e.* (*id est*, meaning *that is* or *which is to say*). Use *e.g.* when you're giving one or more examples.Use *i.e.* when you need to explain or clarify a term or phrase.

- **place or direction:** *above, adjacent to, at that point, below, beyond, close by, closer to, elsewhere, far, farther on, here, in the back, in the distance, in the front, near, nearby, neighboring on, next to, on the other side, opposite to, overhead, there, to the left, to the right, to the side, under, underneath, wherever*
- **purpose/cause and effect:** *accordingly, as a consequence, as a result, because, consequently, due to, for that reason, for this purpose, hence, in order that, on account of, since, so, so that, then, therefore, thereupon, thus, to do this, to this end, with this in mind, with this objective*
- **qualification:** *almost, although, always, frequently, habitually, maybe, nearly, never, oftentimes, often, perhaps, probably, time and again*
- **result:** *accordingly, and so, as a result, as an outcome, consequently, hence, so, then, therefore, thereupon, thus*
- **similarity:** *again, also, and, as well as, besides, by the same token, for example, furthermore, in a like manner, in a similar way, in the same way, like, likewise, moreover, once more, similarly, so*
- **summary or conclusion:** *after all, all in all, as a result, as has been noted, as I have said, as we have seen, as mentioned earlier, as stated, clearly, finally, in any event, in brief, in conclusion, in other words, in particular, in short, in simpler terms, in summary, on the whole, that is, therefore, to conclude, to summarize*

- **time:** *after a bit, after a few days, after a while, afterward, again, also, and then, as long as, as soon as, at first, at last, at length, at that time, at the same time, before, during, earlier, eventually, finally, first, following, formerly, further, hence, initially, immediately, in a few days, in the first place, in the future, in the meantime, in the past, last, lately, later, meanwhile, next, now, on (a certain day), once, presently, previously, recently, second, shortly, simultaneously, since, so far, soon, still, subsequently, then, thereafter, this time, today, tomorrow, until, until now, when, whenever*

While transitional words and phrases are important to good writing, using them incorrectly can spoil your work. If you're not sure what words like *moreover, furthermore,* or *simultaneously* mean, look them up in the dictionary before you use them.

The Biggest Bugbears

Need a little advice (or should that be *advise?)* about when to use certain words? Are you feeling alright (or *all right?)* about your ability to distinguish between (or is that *among?) alumni, alumnae, alumnus,* and *alumna?* Do you feel as if you could use an angel (or an *angle?)* on your shoulder to give you some guidance? Are you anxious—or are you *eager?*—to become "unconfused" about when to use particular words?

Not to worry! This section contains an extensive list of words that are commonly misused or confused, along with an explanation of the differences between them. Also included are a number of mnemonics to help you remember the differences when this book isn't handy (although you know you *should* carry it with you at all times!).

Here are the words that cause some of the greatest amounts of perplexity and befuddlement:

a, an: *A* is used before words that begin with a consonant sound (*a* pig; *a* computer); *an* is used before words that begin with a vowel sound (*an* earring, *an* integer). The sound is what makes the difference. Write *a* *habit* because *habit* starts with the *h* sound after the article, but write *an honor* because the *h* in *honor* isn't pronounced (the first sound of *honor* is the vowel *o*).

What an honor and a privilege it is to meet a history expert like you.

a lot, alot, allot: Okay, let's begin with the fact that there is no such word as *alot*. If you mean a great number of people, use *a lot*. Here's a mnemonic for this: "a whole lot" is two whole words. If you mean *that allocate*, use *allot*. A mnemonic for *allot* is *allocate = allot*.

Tomorrow night, the mayor will allot a lot of money for various municipal projects.

accept, except: *Accept* has several meanings, including *believe*, *take on*, *endure*, and *consent*; *except* means *excluding*. If your sentence can keep its meaning if you substitute *excluding*, use *except*.

Except for food for the volunteers, Doris would not accept any donations.

adapt, adopt: To *adapt* is to change; to adopt is to take and make your own.

After the couple adopted the baby, they learned to adapt to having little sleep.

adverse, averse: *Adverse* means *unfavorable* or *unpleasant*; *averse* means *reluctant*. A mnemonic is to picture people who don't like to speak before a group; if they're called upon to recite a poem, they'd be *averse* to reciting *a verse* (get it?).

advice, advise: *Advise* is what you do when you give *advice*. Here's a mnemonic to help you remember: To adv*ise* you must be w*ise*. Good adv*ice* is to drive slowly on *ice*.

Grandpa tried to advise me when I was a youngster, but I wouldn't listen to his advice.

affect, effect: *Affect* is usually a verb (something that shows action), usually means *change* or *shape*, and—as a verb—has its accent on the first syllable. (There is a meaning of *affect* as a noun, but unless you are a psychologist you needn't worry about it.) *Effect* is almost always a noun meaning *result* or *outcome*, *appearance* or *impression* (*effect* has a rare use as a verb, when it means *to achieve* or *cause*). One mnemonic to help you remember is this: Cause and *effect* (that is, if you want the word that is to be used in this phrase, you want *effect*—the word that begins with the last letter of *cause*).

The effect of the announcement of impending war
will not affect Adam's decision to join the military.

aggravate, annoy: If you mean *pester* or *irritate*, you want *annoy*. Aggravate means *exaggerate* or *make worse*.

Steven was annoyed when his boss aggravated
the situation by talking to the press.

aid, aide: If you help, you *aid*; if you have a helper or supporter, you have an aid*e*.

The aid from my aide is invaluable.

aisle, isle, I'll: An *aisle* is in a theater; an *isle* is an island (a shortened form of the word); *I'll* is short for *I will*.

I'll walk down the aisle to meet my groom; then
we'll honeymoon on a desert isle.

all ready, already: If you mean all is ready, use *all ready*; if you mean in the past, use *already*.

I already told you we're all ready to go out to dinner!

all right, alright: Although you often see the incorrect spelling *alright*, *all right* is always two words. You wouldn't say something is *aleft* or *alwrong*, would you? (Please say you wouldn't!)

Is it all right with you if we eat in tonight?

all together, altogether: *All together* means *simultaneously* or *all at once*; *altogether* means *entirely* or *wholly*. If you can substitute *entirely* or *wholly* in the sentence and the meaning doesn't change, you need the form of the word that is entirely, wholly one word.

You're altogether wrong about the six friends going
all together to the dance; each is going separately.

allowed, aloud: If you mean *out loud* (as in you're saying something out loud), use a*loud*; if you mean you have permission, use *allowed*.

During the prayer, you're not allowed to speak aloud.

alumni, alumnae, alumnus, alumna: You can thank the Romans for this confusion; Latin had separate words for masculine, feminine, singular, and plural forms. Here's the rundown: One male graduate is an *alumnus*; one female graduate is an *alumna*; several female graduates are *alumnae*; and several male graduates or several male and female graduates are *alumni*. You can see why the short form *alum* is often used informally; when you use it, you don't have to look up the right form of the word.

Although Mary Jo and her sisters are alumnae from Wellesley, Mary Jo is the alumna who receives the most attention; her brothers Martin and Xavier are alumni of Harvard, but Martin is a more famous alumnus than Xavier.

FACTS

Here are other Latin singulars and plurals that are often confused:

<u>Singular</u>	<u>Plural</u>
criterion	criteria
datum	data
desideratum	desiderata
erratum	errata
larva	larvae/larvas
minutia	minutiae
phylum	phyla
septum	septa
stimulus	stimuli
syllabus	syllabuses/syllabi

Other Latin singulars and plurals are listed in Chapter 1.

allusion, illusion: An *allusion* is a reference; an *illusion* is a false impression. If you want a word that means mistaken idea, you want *illusion*.

Kay told Jerry that she was under the illusion he would be her Prince Charming; Jerry didn't understand the allusion.

altar, alter: If you change something, you alter it; you worship before an *altar*.

We'll alter the position of the altar so the congregation can see the new carvings.

among, between: Think division. If only two people are dividing something, use *between*; if more than two people are involved, use *among*. Here's a mnemonic: be*two*en for *two* and among for a group.

The money was divided between Sarah and Bob; the land was divided among Billy, Henry, and Janice.

angel, angle: An *angel* has wings; the degre*e* of an angl*e* is often studied.

The angel's wings are set at ninety-degree angles from its body.

anxious, eager: These two words are often confused. If you're *anxious*, you're nervous or concerned; if you're *eager*, you're enthusiastic.

I had been anxious about my medical test results, but when they proved negative I was eager to kick up my heels.

anybody, any body: *Anybody* means *any one person* (and is usually interchangeable with anyone). *Any body* refers (pardon the graphic reference) to one dead person.

Anybody can help to search for any body that might not have been found in the wreckage.

appraise, apprise: To ap*praise* is to give value to something (to see how much *praise* it needs); to apprise is to *in*form.

The auction house called to apprise our family as to how they would appraise various items for us.

bad, badly: When you're writing about how you feel, use *bad*. However, if you're writing about how you did something or performed or reacted to something, use *badly* (twisted your ankle *badly*; played *badly* in the game).

Gregg felt bad he had scored so badly on the test.

bazaar, bizarre: The first is a marketplace; the second means *strange, weird,* or *peculiar*.

The most bizarre purchase that came from the bazaar was a pair of sandals without any soles.

bear, bare: A b*ear* can t*ear* off your *ear*; if you're bar*e*, you're nud*e*.

The bare bathers were disturbed when the grizzly bear arrived.

besides, beside: If you want the one that means *in addition to*, you want the one that has an additional *s* (*besides*); *beside* means *by the side of*.

Besides her groom, the bride wanted her dad beside her in the photo.

breath, breathe: You take a *breath*; you inhal*e* and *e*xhal*e* when you breath*e*.

> *In the cold of the winter, it was hard for me to breathe*
> *when taking a breath outside.*

cavalry, Calvary: The *cavalry* refers to soldiers on horseback (and isn't capitalized unless it begins a sentence); Ca*l*vary is the hi*ll* where Christ was crucified (and is always capitalized).

> *The cavalry was not in attendance for the march up Calvary.*

can, may: If you *can* do something, you're physically able to do it. If you *may* do it, you have permission to do it.

> *You can use ain't in a sentence, but you may not.*

cannot, am not, is not, are not, and all other "nots": For some strange reason, *cannot* is written as one word. All other words that have *not* with them are written as two words. Go figure.

capital, capitol: The *capitol* is the building in which the legislative body meets. If you mean the one in Washington, D.C., use a capital *C;* if you mean the one in your state, use a lowercase *c.* Remember that the building (the one spelled with an *o*) usually has a dome. Use *capital* with all other meanings.

> *The capital spent by the legislators at the capitol is appalling.*

carat, caret, carrot, karat: A *carat* is a weight for a stone (a diamond, for instance); *carat* is also an alternate spelling of *karat*, which is a measurement of how much gold is in an alloy (as in the abbreviation 18k; the *k* is for *karat).* A *caret* is this proofreading mark: ^ (meaning that you should insert something at that point). Finally, a *carrot* is the orange vegetable your mother told you to eat.

> *Set in an eighteen-karat gold band, the five-carat*
> *diamond was shaped like a carrot.*

censor, censure: To censor is to take out the bad material; to *censure* is to place blame (don't cen*sure* someone unless you're *sure*).

> *The full Senate voted not to censure the senator for trying*
> *to censor the e-mail that came to other congressional employees.*

cite, sight, site: Your *sight* is your vision or a view (you use your *sight* to look at a beautiful *sight*); to cite is to make reference to a specific source; a *site* is a location, such as on the Internet.

The colors on the Web site you cited in your paper
were a sight to behold.

climactic, climatic: *Climactic* refers to a climax, a pinnacle; *climatic* is related to the weather (the climate).

Last year's weather featured many climatic oddities,
but the climactic point came when snow arrived in June.

coarse, course: If something is *coarse*, it's rough; *oars* are *coarse*. A *course* is a *route*, a class, or part of the idiomatic phrase "of course."

The racecourse led the runners over coarse terrain.

complement, compliment: If something completes another thing, it *complements* it (*complete* = *complement*). If you receive praise, you've gotten a *compliment* (*I* like to receive a compl*i*ment).

The jewelry will complement the outfit the star will wear,
and she will surely receive many compliments on her attire.

confidant, confident: If you're *entirely* sure of yourself, you're confid*ent*. If you have an *amigo* (a close friend), you have a confid*a*nt.

I'm so confident that my hairdresser is my confidant that
I share all my secrets with her.

conscience, conscious: Your *conscience* tells you whether something is right or wrong; if you're *conscious*, you're awake and aware.

Marie said she wasn't conscious of the fact that her conscience
told her not to take the ashtray from the hotel room.

continual, continuous: *Continuous* actions go on uninterrupted; *continual* actions are intermittent.

The continual rains lasted for ten days; because of that, the
Blacksons had a continuous problem with water in their basement.

core, corps, corpse: A *core* is a center or main section; a *corps* is a group or organization; a *corpse* is a dead body.

At the core of the Marine Corps lieutenant's sleeplessness was
his discovery of a corpse while on a training mission.

council, counsel: A *council* is an official group, a committee; to *counsel* is to give advice (the stock broker coun*sel*ed me to *sell*).

The town council decided to counsel the youth group on
the proper way to ask for funds.

desert, dessert: A *desert* is a dry, arid place or (usually used in the plural form) deserved reward or punishment *(just deserts)*. The verb that means *to leave* is also *desert*. The food that is *so* sweet is a dessert.

While lost in the desert, Rex craved a dessert of apple pie à la mode.

device, devise: A *device* is a machine or tool; to *devise* means *to invent* or *concoct something.*

To devise, you must be wise. Will this device work on ice?

discreet, discrete: *Discreet* means *cautious, careful,* or *guarded in conduct* (be discreet about whom you meet). *Discrete* means *separate* or *disconnected.*

The dancer's discreet movements were discrete from those performed by the rest of the chorus.

dual, duel: The first means *two* (*dual* purposes); the second is a fight or contest (the lover's jealousy was *fuel* for the *duel*).

There were dual reasons for the duel: revenge and money.

elicit, illicit: To *elicit* something is to *extract* it, to bring it out; something *illicit* is *illegal.*

The telephone scam artist engaged in the illicit practice of trying to elicit credit card numbers from the unwitting elderly.

emigrate, immigrate: To *emigrate* is to *exit* a country; to *immigrate* is to come *into* a country.

Ten people were trying to emigrate from the tyranny of their country and immigrate to the United States.

eminent, imminent: Someone well known is *eminent*; something that might take place *immediately* is *imminent.*

Our meeting with the eminent scientist is imminent.

ensure, insure: To *ensure* is to *make certain of something*; *insure* is used only for business purposes (to *insure* a car).

To ensure that we continue to insure your house and car, send payment immediately.

envelop, envelope: If you wrap something, you envelop it; the paper container that you use for your letter is an *envelope.*

The hidden purpose of the envelope was to envelop the two sticks of candy that were mailed to me.

everyday, every day: *Everyday* means *routine* or *daily* (*everyday* low cost); *every day* means *every single day* (low prices *every day*). Use *single* words if you mean every *single* day.

The everyday inexpensive prices of the store meant
that more shoppers came every day.

faze, phase: To *faze* is to *intimidate* or *disturb*. As a noun, a *phase* is *a period of time*; as a verb, it means *to establish gradually.*

I wasn't fazed by his wish to phase out our relationship.

fewer, less: Use *fewer* to describe plural words; use less to describe singular words.

The new product has fewer calories, but less fat.

figuratively, literally: *Literally* means *precisely as described*; *figuratively* means *in a symbolic or metaphoric way.*

When Pauline called, she asked if I was off my rocker; I thought she
meant the phrase figuratively and wondered why she thought I had
gone crazy. However, she intended to be taken literally, as she
wondered if I was still sitting outside in my rocker.

flaunt, flout: If you *flaunt* something, you show it off (*flaunt* your new jewelry); to *flout* is to jeer at someone or something in a contemptible way, or to intentionally disobey (*flout* the laws).

In an attempt to flaunt his new car to the girls on the other side of
the road, James decided to flout the law and not stop at the red light.

forego, forgo: If you mean something that has gone be*fore*, use *forego* (a *foregone* conclusion); if you want the word that means *to do without something*, use *forgo* (the one that is without the *e*).

It's a foregone conclusion that Meg and Marion will
forgo sweets when they're dieting.

foreword, forward: The word that means *the opening information in a book* is fore*word* (it comes be*fore* the first important *word* of the book); for any other meaning, use *forward.*

To gain insight into the author's intent, you should read the
foreword before you proceed forward in the book.

formal, former: An official occasion (or the clothes you might wear to one) is the word spelled formal; if you mean in earlier times, you want former.

The former Miss America was introduced at a
formal affair at the local country club.

foul, fowl: The animal is a *fowl*; the action on the basketball court is a *foul*; a bad odor smells *foul*.

The foul smell came from the fowl that had been slaughtered.

good, well: *Good* is an adjective; it does not mean in *a high-quality manner*, or *correctly*. If you want either of those meanings you need an adverb, so you want *well*.

You did well on the test; your grade should be good.

graduated, graduated from: A school *graduates* you; you *graduate from* a school.

The year Kathy graduated from college, the school
graduated 5,000 baccalaureate students.

grisly, grizzly: A horrible or gruesome sight is *grisly*; the North American bear is a *grizzly*.

A grisly scene was left after the attack by the grizzly bear.

hanged, hung: People are *hanged* (did they *hang* the entire *gang* of desperadoes?); artwork is *hung*.

The gruesome picture of the hanged man was hung on the wall.

heal, heel: The verb gives the trouble. *To heal* means *to cure* or *patch up* (to *heal* a wound); among other verb definitions, *to heel* is *to tilt to one side*, *to give money to*, or *to urge along*; a *well-heeled* person has a *considerable amount of money*.

You might need ointment to heal the blisters you get from
trying to right the sails when the ship heels in the wind.

hear, here: You h*ear* with your *ear*. *Here* is the opposite of *there*.

Did you hear that Aunt Lucy is here?

hopefully: If you mean *I hope*, or *it is hoped*; then that's what you should write. *Hopefully* means *confidently* or *with anticipation*.

The director waited hopefully for the Oscar
nominations to be announced.

imply, infer: Both of these have to do with words not said aloud. A speaker implies something; a listener infers something.

> *Rufus thought the boss had implied that she would be back*
> *for an inspection next week, but Ruth did not infer that.*

in, into: *In* means with*in*; *into* means from the outside *to* the *in*side.

> *Go into the house, go in my purse, and bring me money.*

its, it's: *It's* means only *it is* (before *it's* too late); *its* means *belonging to it* (I gave the dog *its* food and water).

> *It's a shame that the dog lost its bone.*

lay, lie: Now I *lay* my head on the pillow; last night I *laid* my head on the pillow; in the past I have *laid* my head on the pillow. If it helps to remember the difference, the forms of *lay* (meaning *to put or place*) are transitive (they take an object). Today I *lie* in the sun; yesterday I *lay* in the sun; in the past I have *lain* in the sun. The forms of *lie* (meaning *to rest or recline*) are intransitive (they take no object).

> *As I lay in bed, I wondered where I had laid my watch.*

lead, led: If you want the word that means *was in charge of* or *guided*, use *led*; otherwise, use *lead*.

> *The company, led by one of the richest people in the world,*
> *announced that its CEO was retiring; today a newcomer will lead it.*

loose, lose: *Loose* (which rhymes with *noose*) means *not tight*. *Lose* is the opposite of *find*.

> *Will I lose my belt if it's too loose?*

may of, might of, must of, should of, would of, could of: When we speak, we slur these phrases so that they all sound as if they end in *of*, but in fact all of them end in *have*. Their correct forms are *may have*, *might have*, *must have*, *should have*, *would have*, and *could have*.

> *I must have thought you would have been able to*
> *find the room without any directions.*

moral, morale: If something is *moral*, it is *right* or *ethical* (that's the adjective form); if something has a *moral*, it has a *message* or a *meaning* (that's the noun form). Your moral*e* is your *e*steem.

> *The moral high road that the politician took boosted*
> *the morale of the entire staff.*

myself, itself, yourself, himself, herself, themselves, ourselves, yourselves: None of these pronouns should ever be used without the antecedent that corresponds to it. You might write:

I myself would like to go for a drive.

But you wouldn't write, "Gene took Pat and myself for a drive."

nauseated, nauseous: *Nauseous* is often misused; it means *disgusting* or *sickening*; *nauseated* means *sick to your stomach* (you can get nause*ated* from something you *ate*).

The nauseous fumes caused the workers to become nauseated.

pacific, specific: *Pacific* means *peaceful*; *specific* means *precise or individualized.*

To be specific, the pacific view from Hickory Mountain is what calms me the most.

pair, pear: The first has to do with two (*pair* of pandas; to *pair* up for the dance); the second is a fruit (you *eat* a p*ear*).

The romantic pair bought a pear to share on the picnic.

passed, past: *Passed* is a verb; *past* is an adjective (p*ast* often means l*ast*) or noun meaning *the preceding time.*

In the past, twenty Easter parades have passed down this street.

peace, piece: *Peace* is the opposite of w*ar*; a *piece* is a part or portion (a *piece* of *pie*).

The father bargained with his small children, "Give me a half hour's peace, and I'll treat you to a piece of cake."

peak, peek, pique: A *peak* is a *high point*, like a mountain peak (think of the shape of the *A* in PE*A*K); to p*eek* at something is to try to *see* it; to *pique* is to *intrigue* or *stimulate.*

Dan tried to pique Lora's interest in climbing by telling her that she could peek through the telescope when they reached the mountain's peak.

persecute, prosecute: To *persecute* is to *oppress or bully*; to *prosecute* is to *bring legal action.*

We warned our neighbors that we would prosecute if they continued to persecute their dog.

pore, pour: If you *read something carefully*, you *pore* over it. If you make a liquid go *out* of a container, you p*our* it.

> *After Harry accidentally poured ink on the new floor, he pored over several books to find out how to clean the stain.*

prophecy, prophesy: You have a forecast or a prediction if you have a prophe*cy*. *Prophesy* is pronounced with the last syllable sounding like *sigh*, and you might sigh when you *prophesy* something dismal.

> *Last week the audience heard the medium prophesy about forthcoming bad weather; the prophecy has yet to come true.*

principle, principal: *Principle* means *law* or *belief*. *Principal* means *major* or *head*; it also means *money that earns interest in a bank*. The princi*pal* is the head person in a school; he or she is your *pal* and makes princi*pal* decisions.

> *That is the most important principle our principal believes.*

quiet, quite: *Quiet* is *calm* or *silence*; *quite* means *to a certain extent*. Be sure to check the ending of the word you use; that's where mistakes are made. You can think of being as qui*et* as an *E.T.* visiting Earth.

> *Are you quite sure that you were quiet in the library?*

real, really: *Real* means *actual* or *true*; *really* means *in truth* or *in reality*. Except in the most casual tone in writing, neither *real* nor *really* should be used in the sense of *very* (that's a *real* good song on the radio; I'm *really* glad that you tuned to that station).

> *When I realized I was really lost, the real importance of carrying a compass hit me.*

respectfully, respectively: If you're *full* of respect for someone and want to show it, you do it respect*fully*. *Respectively* means *in the order stated*.

> *Upon hearing the news, I respectfully called El, and Ty respectively.*

role, roll: A *role* is a *position or part* (in a production); a *roll* is a *piece of bread* on the dinner table; to *roll* is to *rotate*.

> *The role of the acrobat will be played by someone who can perform a backward roll.*

seam, seem: A *seam* joins parts of your clothing; to *seem* is to *appear or look* (how you *see* something is how it *seems*).

> *Does it seem that this seam is coming apart?*

set, sit: If you place something, you set it. If you're in an upright position (like in a chair), you sit. In addition, *set* is a transitive verb (it must have an object); *sit* is an intransitive verb (it doesn't have an object).

Please set the table before you sit down.

slow, slowly: *Slow* is an adjective, not an adverb. If you're using the word after *go*, *drive*, *walk*, or any other verb, use *slowly*.

I slowly walked. I walked at a slow pace.

sole, soul: *Sole* is an adjective meaning *only* or *special*; as a noun, a sole is the underside of a foot or a shoe, and it's also the name of a fish; your *soul* is associated with *your spiritual side*.

David's sole reason for going on the retreat was to examine his soul.

stalactite, stalagmite: Stalactites grow from the ceiling down; stalagmites grow from the ground up.

On a recent spelunking trip, I constantly worried about tripping over the stalagmites and bumping into the stalactites.

stationery, stationary: If you mean something that lacks any motion, use *stationary*; if you mean something you write a letter on, use stationery.

The stationery had a picture of people riding stationary bicycles.

supposed (to): Often the *-d* is incorrectly omitted from *supposed to* (meaning *expected to* or *designed to*).

In this job, you are supposed to be able to write clear and effective memos.

than, then: If you mean *next* or *therefore* or *at that time*, you want *then*. If you want the word that shows a comparison, use than.

For a while, Mary ran more quickly than I; then she dropped her pace.

that, which: For clauses that don't need commas (restrictive clauses), use *that*. For nonrestrictive clauses, which need commas, use *which*.

The local dog kennels, which are on my way to work, are the ones that have been featured in the news lately.

there, their, they're: If you want the opposite of *here*, use there; if you mean they are, you want they're; if you mean belonging to *them*, use *their*.

There are the employees who think they're going to get their ten percent raises tomorrow.

throne, thrown: If you can sit on it, it's a *throne* (you can sit on *one* thr*one*); if something has been tossed, it's been *thrown*.

When the king was deposed, his throne was thrown out the window.

to, too, two: If you mean something *additional*, it's the one with the *additional o (too)*; *two* is the *number after one*; *to* means *in the direction of something.*

Did our supervisor ask the two new employees to go to Detroit and Chicago, too?

troop, troupe: Both are groups of people, but *troupe* refers to actors only.

The troupe of actors performed for the troop of Brownies.

try and, try to: Almost always the mistake comes in writing *try and* when you need to use *try to.*

The lady said she would try to get the dress in my size; I hoped she would try and keep looking.

use to, used to: *Use to* means *employ for the purposes of; used to* (often misspelled without the *-d)* means *formerly* or *in the past.*

I used to like to listen to the excuses people would use to leave work early.

weather, whether: If you mean conditions of the climate, use *weather.* (Can you stand to *eat* in the h*eat* of this bad w*eat*her?) If you mean *which, whichever,* or *if it is true that,* use *whether.*

It's now mid-April, and the weather can't decide whether it's spring or winter.

when, where: If you're writing a definition, don't use either of these words. For instance, don't write "A charley horse is when you get a cramp in your leg"; instead, write something like: A charley horse is the result of a cramp in your leg.

A bank is a place in which you can make a deposit or withdrawal.

who, which, that: Don't use *which* when you're writing about people. Some style guides have the same restriction for *that* and some don't, so be sure to check with the guide used by your company or instructor.

The federal inspector, who gives the orders that we all must obey, said that the environmental protection law, which had never been enforced, would result in higher costs.

FACTS

No Such Puppy: These are considered nonstandard words and phrases (in other words, don't use them): anyways, can't hardly, can't help but, can't scarcely, everywheres, hisself, irregardless, nowheres, off of, theirselves, theirself—and the number one nonstandard word: ain't.

whose, who's: *Whose* means *belonging to whom*; *who's* is short for *who is* (the apostrophe means the *i* has been omitted).

After the sock hop, who's going to determine whose shoes these are?

woman, women: One *man*, two *men*. One wo*man*, two wo*men*. It's that simple.

> *The local woman asked the two visiting women if*
> *they'd like a tour of the town.*

your, you're: If you mean *belonging to you*, use *your* (this is *our* car; that is *your* car); if you mean *you are*, use *you're* (remember that the apostrophe means the *a* has been omitted).

If you're going to Florida, be sure to put some sunscreen on your face.

CHAPTER 13
In Plain English, Please

Clichés, redundancies, and wordiness can really clutter up your writing. They can be distracting and annoying to a reader and, perhaps worst of all, can completely obscure your message. Becoming more aware of their use in everyday life will make it easier for you to avoid them. The lists included in this chapter will also help.

Steering Clear of Clichés

A cliché is a worn-out expression, one you've heard over and over, or time and time again, or a thousand times before (do you get the picture?). It may have been clever or had a special meaning the first time you heard it, but by now you've come across it so many times that it's lost its pizzazz and so wouldn't add any spice to your writing.

As a rule, you should avoid using clichés because they're unoriginal, stale, and monotonous. Your readers won't think your work is the least bit creative if all they see is cliché-ridden writing.

You're most likely familiar with hundreds of clichés. If you read the first part of a phrase and you can fill in its ending, then your phrase is probably a cliché.

TAKE A LOOK AT THE FIRST PARTS OF THESE PHRASES:

put all your eggs_____	there's more there than meets _____
read the handwriting_____	costs an arm _____
every cloud has_____	that's the way the _____
take the bitter_____	see the light at _____
kill two birds_____	when in Rome, _____
practice what you_____	there's more than one way to _____

You can supply the ending for each of those, can't you? That's how you know they're clichés!

If English isn't your native language, you may not be familiar with these clichés.

HERE ARE THE COMPLETE PHRASES:

put all your eggs in one basket	there's more there than meets the eye
read the handwriting on the wall	costs an arm and a leg
every cloud has a silver lining	that's the way the cookie crumbles
take the bitter with the sweet	see the light at the end of the tunnel
kill two birds with one stone	when in Rome, do as the Romans do
practice what you preach	more than one way to skin a cat

FACTS

Many clichés are also similes (comparisons using *like* or *as*). You're probably familiar with the following expressions:

happy as a lark	*slippery as an eel*	*pretty as a picture*
fit as a fiddle	*blind as a bat*	*snug as a bug in a rug*
dumb as a post	*high as a kite*	*sharp as a tack*
sick as a dog	*smart as a whip*	*out like a light*
crazy like a fox	*pale as a ghost*	*growing like a weed*

When you're getting ideas or writing a first draft, sometimes you'll think of a cliché. Go ahead and write it down. But when you come back to revise your work, get your eraser out (or put your finger on the Delete key) pronto and get rid of that cliché.

If you can't think of an original way to reword your cliché, try "translating" it in a literal way. Say, for instance, that you've written:

It was plain as the nose on his face that Drew wouldn't stick his neck out for anybody else.

In that sentence, you're dealing with two clichés *(plain as the nose on his face* and *stick his neck out)*. To make the sentence cliché-free, you could change it to:

Plainly, Drew wouldn't take a risk for anybody else.

Is there any time that using a cliché is permissible? Sure. The style for using an occasional cliché is relaxed or casual (so keep in mind that clichés have no place in academic writing). But if your style allows you to use a cliché in a humorous way, it's okay to add one occasionally. For instance, you might be writing about nobility in Europe. With a casual tone, you might use this expanded cliché as your title: "Putting Up Your Dukes (and Earls)."

The trick is to let your reader know that you're using a cliché intentionally. If you're in a pinch (yes, that's a cliché), write something along the lines of "Even though I knew the cliché, 'Little pitchers have big ears,'. . . " and then go on to elaborate as to how the cliché fits in with your topic.

SSENTIALS If you're quoting someone who uses clichés, you must quote the dialogue exactly.

No Need to Repeat Yourself!

"I've said it before and I'll say it again."

"I've said it before, but now I'll reiterate."

"I've said it before and I'd like to repeat myself."

We've all heard words like these before—and, odds are, hearing people repeat themselves drives most of us crazy. When it comes to writing, using words or phrases that are redundant not only diminishes the value of the written work, it's also a waste of the reader's time.

Take a look at the following commonly seen or often heard redundant phrases and read the explanations about why they're redundant. (Get ready to smack yourself on the head as you mutter, "I should have thought of that"—but comfort yourself with the thought that you're certainly not alone in using these phrases!) Then get out your eraser or find your Delete key and start cutting your own redundancies.

FACTS In legal documents you'll often see redundant phrases like *cease and desist, will and testament,* and *goods and chattels.* The reason for these redundancies goes back almost a thousand years. Before William of Normandy conquered England in 1066, English law had commonly been written in Latin and Old English. When William took control of England, many in the legal profession began to use Norman French. Most people, however, were not fluent in all three languages. Since lawyers wanted to be certain that legal documents were understood by everyone, they developed phrases that incorporated words with synonyms in Latin, Old English, and Norman French. Many of these phrases survive today.

REDUNDANT PHRASE	EXPLANATION
absolutely certain	Certainty has no room for doubt, it's absolute.
advance planning	Planning must be done in advance.
A.M. in the morning	If occuring in the morning, it has to be A.M.
and also	Use one word or the other; not both.
and etc.	*Et cetera* is Latin for *and so forth*.
and plus	*Plus* means *and.* Use one or the other, but not both.
as an added bonus	If something is a bonus, it must be added.
ask the question	It's impossible to ask anything except a question.
assembled together	It's impossible to assemble apart. Delete *together.*
ATM machine	The *M* in *ATM* stands for *machine*, so you're saying an *Automated Teller Machine machine.*
autobiography of my life	I can't write an autobiography of someone else's life, can I?
basic essentials	If they're the essentials, they have to be basic.
basic fundamentals	It's the same as *basic essentials.*
biography of his life	*Biography* means *of someone's life.*
cash money	Is cash ever anything but money?
chili con carne with meat	*Con carne* means *with meat.* Delete *con carne.*
close proximity	You can't have far proximity, can you? Delete *close.*
close scrutiny	If it's scrutiny, it had better be close.
closed fist	A fist must be closed. Delete *closed.*
combined together	Things that are combined must be together. Delete *together.*
completely finish	It's impossible to partially finish something, isn't it? Delete *completely.*
completely unanimous	It's impossible for something to be partially unanimous. Delete *completely.*
consensus of opinion	Is there any other type of consensus?
continue on	Can you continue off? Delete *on.*
cooperate together	It would be hard to cooperate apart.
deadly killer	Can someone or something be deadly and not be a killer? Delete *killer.*

REDUNDANT PHRASE	EXPLANATION
each and every	The words mean the same thing; delete one.
each individual	*Each* and *individual* mean the same thing.
end result	Can you have a result that's not in the end?
estimated at about	*Estimated* means *about*. Delete *at about*.
exact replica	If something is a replica, it has to be exact.
exactly the same	If something is the same, it must be exact. Delete *the same*.
excised out	It's impossible to excise in, isn't it? Delete *out*.
fewer in number	As opposed to fewer in what else?
final conclusion	Is there a conclusion that's not final? Delete *final*.
finally ultimate	If something is the ultimate, it's final. Delete *finally*.
foreign imports	Material that's imported must be foreign.
free gift (free gratis)	If it's a gift or is gratis, by definition it's free.
future plans, prospects	Has anyone ever made past plans or had past prospects? Delete *future*.
green in color	As opposed to green in what?
HIV virus	The *V* in *HIV* stands for *virus*. Delete *virus*.
honest truth	If something isn't the truth, it isn't honest.
identical match	If things match, they're identical—or else they don't match. Delete *identical*.
important essentials	If items are essential, surely they're important.
large in size	The word *large* denotes size; use *large* only.
may possibly	If something may happen, it's possible to happen.
mix together	It's impossible to mix apart, isn't it?
month of May	Everybody knows that May is a month.
mutual cooperation	If you cooperate, it has to be mutual.
my own personal opinion	*My opinion* means it's your own and it's personal.
new innovation	By definition, an innovation must be new.
old adage	By definition, an adage has to be old.
ongoing evolution	If something is evolving, it must be ongoing.
overused cliché	If a cliché isn't overused, it's not a cliché.
past memory	It's impossible to have a future memory, isn't it?

REDUNDANT PHRASE	EXPLANATION
personal friend	Can someone have an impersonal friend?
PIN number	The *N* in *PIN* stands for *number*. Delete *number*.
please RSVP	The *P* in *RSVP* stands for *plaît*, the French word for *please*. Delete *please*.
P.M. at night	It's impossible for P.M. to be at any time except night. Delete *at night*.
possibly may	If I may do something, it's possible that I'll do it.
protest against	If you protest, you're against something.
raining outside	Even when the fire alarm turns on inside sprinklers, you don't say "raining inside." Delete *outside*.
rectangular in shape	If something is rectangular, that is its shape.
refer back	Hard to refer forward, isn't it? Delete *back*.
return back	Here again, it's hard to return forward. Delete *back*.
roast beef with au jus	The *au* means *with*; delete *with*.
rough estimate	An estimate can't be exact; it must be rough.
safe haven	A haven by definition is a safe place.
same identical	Something that's identical must be the same. Delete one word or the other.
strangle to death	A strangled person is dead; otherwise, the person is just choked. Delete *to death*.
sudden impulse	An impulse is sudden, or it's not an impulse.
sum total	If you have a sum, you have a total. Delete one word or the other.
surrounded on all sides	Something can't be surrounded on a few sides.
sworn affidavit	By definition, an affidavit is sworn. Delete *sworn*.
terrible tragedy	A tragedy must be terrible or it's not a tragedy.
totally monopolize	A monopoly is total, isn't it? Delete *totally*.
true fact	By definition, a fact must be true. Delete *true*.
unexpected surprise	It's rather hard for a surprise to be expected.
valuable asset	If something is an asset, then it has value.
VIN number	The *N* in *VIN* stands for *number*. Delete *number*.

When Less Is More

Wordiness is the first cousin of redundant writing. If you use six words when two will do, your writing becomes bloated and loses its effectiveness. Not only does wordiness (see what I mean?) take up your readers' valuable time, it also can make your writing seem pompous.

Still have your pencil handy or your finger on the Delete key? Take a look at the following list of common wordy expressions, then get to work putting your words on a diet. For even more common wordy expressions and their suggested substitutes, see Appendix D.

WORDY PHRASE	SUGGESTED SUBSTITUTE
a small number of	a few
being of the opinion that	I believe
cannot be avoided	must, should
due to the fact that	since, because
excessive number of	too many
for the purpose of	to, for
give consideration to	consider
has a tendency to	often
in a timely manner	promptly, on time
last but not least	finally
make an examination of	examine
none at all	none
on a daily (personal, regular) basis	daily, regularly
present time	present, now
reach a conclusion	conclude, end, finish
subsequent, subsequent to	after, later, next
the majority of	most
until such time as	until
with regard to	concerning, about

And the Survey Says . . .

In a recent informal survey, copyeditors and English teachers from around the world were asked about mistakes they frequently encounter in print or speech. This chapter includes some of the results of that survey. To start with, there is a list of commonly misused phrases (some of which are guaranteed to give you a good laugh). There is also a rundown of common grammatical and stylistic errors along with tips for avoiding them in your own writing. Don't feel as if you have to hang your head in shame if you see your own mistakes reported here; the point is to learn from them (and to promise yourself you'll never make them again!).

Close, but No Cigar: Misused Phrases

Sometimes people hear certain nifty or impressive phrases and then later use those same phrases in their own writing or speech. Problems arise when they either misheard the phrase or remembered it incorrectly. What they end up writing or saying is close to the original, but it's not quite right.

Sometimes the result is a humorous take on the correct phrase (like a "doggie-dog world" instead of a "dog-eat-dog world"), and sometimes it's just plain puzzling ("beckon call" instead of "beck and call").

Here are some of the more common mistakes of this variety as reported by copyeditors and teachers.

Do you see yourself in any of these? (Just nod silently. Now you'll know what to write next time.)

THE CORRECT PHRASE	WHAT YOU'LL SOMETIMES SEE OR HEAR
a bona fide certificate	a bonified certificate
a group of teetotalers	a group of tea toddlers
all it entails	all it in tails
all of a sudden	all of the sudden
amusing anecdotes	amusing antidotes

THE CORRECT PHRASE	WHAT YOU'LL SOMETIMES SEE OR HEAR
beck and call	beckon call
bated breath	baited breath
before you set foot in	before you step foot in
begging the question	bagging the question
beside the point	besides the point
by accident	on accident
can't fathom it	can't phantom it
diplomatic immunity	diplomatic impunity
down the pike	down the pipe
dyed in the wool	died in the wool
en route to a party	in route (or) in root to a party
for all intents and purposes	for all intensive purposes
free rein	free reign
get the lead out	get the led out
going off on a tangent	going off on a tandem
got my dander up	got my dandruff up
got his just deserts	got his just desserts
had the wherewithal	had the where with all
have to flesh that idea out	have to flush that idea out
he's just a go-fer	he's just a gopher
home in on	hone in on
humid, summery weather	humid, summary weather
I couldn't care less	I could care less
I hope to be at work tomorrow	hopefully, I'll be at work tomorrow
I'd just as soon (do something)	I'd just assume (do something)
in his sights	in his sites
in like Flynn	in like Flint
mind your p's and q's	mind your peas and cues
moot point	mute point
move in next door	move in next store
nip it in the bud	nip it in the butt
no prima donnas	no pre-Madonnas
nuclear power	nucular power
old wives' tale	old wise tale

THE CORRECT PHRASE	WHAT YOU'LL SOMETIMES SEE OR HEAR
one's surname	one's sir name
ongoing guerrilla warfare	ongoing gorilla war fair
out of whack	out of wack
pored over a document	poured over a document
prostate cancer	prostrate cancer
put on a pedestal	put on a pedestool
quashed an appeal	squashed an appeal
recent poll	recent pole
rein in	rain in, reign in
remains elusive	remains illusive
right-of-way	right away
rolling stone gathers no moss	rolling stone gathers no moths
scarce as hens' teeth	sharp as hens' teeth
shoo-in to win	shoe-in to win
singing "Auld Lang Syne"	singing "Old Lang Sign"
sold an objet d'art	sold an object d'art
spit and image	spittin' image
stay the course	stay on course
supposedly	supposably
take it for granted	take it for granite
taking the tack	taking the tact
tenets of their faith	tenants of their faith
the die is cast	the dye is cast
to the manner born	to the manor born
toe the line	towed the line
tongue in cheek	tongue and cheek
tough row to hoe	tough road to hoe
trials and tribulations	trails and tribulations
uncharted territory	unchartered territory
up and at 'em	up and adam
varicose veins	very close veins
visiting premier	visiting premiere
whet my appetite	wet my appetite
wind chill factor	windshield factor

Mirror, Mirror, on the Wall, Whose Mistakes Are Worst of All?

In their responses concerning blunders in written work, the copyeditors tended to focus on errors of grammar, spelling, and usage, while the teachers were inclined to concentrate on the specifics of writing. Following each "complaint" are some suggestions for eliminating these mistakes from your work.

Comments from the Copyeditors' Camp

Here is a list of errors frequently seen by copyeditors. (Do you see yourself in here anywhere?)

Simple misspellings. If you're working on a computer, be sure to send your material through a spell check. Your computer won't catch all of your mistakes (you have to do *some* work yourself), but you'll be surprised at the number of mistakes that it does find.

Omitted words or words put in the wrong place after cutting and pasting the text. If, through some great mystery, what you are certain that you've written is not what appears on the page, read, reread, and then (surprise!) reread your material—especially after you've cut and pasted. Use the techniques suggested in Chapter 15 for proofreading more effectively.

Use of passive construction when the active voice would be appropriate—and would read better, too. Look through your completed material for sentences written in the passive voice. Unless there's a particular need for the passive voice, rewrite the sentence to use the active voice.

Improper use of apostrophes (especially plural versus possessive). Review Chapter 3 on the use of apostrophes. Look at each one you've used in your work and ask yourself if it has a legitimate use in a contraction or in showing possession. Pay particular attention to apostrophes used with *yours, his, hers, theirs, ours, its* (only *it's* ever takes an apostrophe, and only when you mean *it is*).

Use of *they* to refer to a singular word (e.g., *the child . . . they/their*). Study each *they* in your material and determine which noun each one refers to (that is, look at each antecedent). If the noun (the antecedent) is singular, reword your sentence so that the noun is plural, or change *they* to a singular pronoun (*his* or *her*, *he* or *she*, *it*).

Gratuitous capitalization (sometimes dubbed "decorative capitalization"). Some writers seem to think something is given greater importance or specificity if it's capitalized, even if it isn't a proper noun. Anyone or anything that is referred to with some specificity in mind seems to get capitalized: job titles (Caseworker, Commissioner, Director), agencies (the Department, the College), or particular fields or programs (Child Welfare, Child Welfare System, Food Stamps, Welfare). If you see a lot of capital letters in your writing, take a look at each capitalized word and see if a particular rule applies to it. If not, use lowercase for the word.

Comma complaints. Here are a few of the transgressions that the copyeditors noted:

- Misplaced or omitted commas, often resulting in ambiguous sentences
- Commas inserted between a month and year (September, 2001)
- Commas dropped after parenthetical phrases (such as, "George Bush, president of the United States said he . . . ")
- Commas misused with restrictive and nonrestrictive clauses (no commas before which; commas before that used unnecessarily)
- Commas inserted between the subject and the verb (e.g., "The speeding car, was seen going through a red light")
- Commas used too frequently, even in positions that no style guide would accept

If these mistakes sound familiar, review the section on using commas (Chapter 3). Remember that commas are used for particular reasons, so make sure that you have a reason for each time you used a comma.

Number disagreements—either subject-predicate or antecedent-pronoun. Look for each verb and its subject (or each pronoun and its antecedent); then check to see if *both* of them are singular or *both* of them are plural. If you have a discrepancy, reword your sentence.

Use of *this* as a subject ("*This* can lead to confusion."). Identify what *this* refers to and then reword your sentences to eliminate *this* as a subject.

Lowercase *is* in a headline or title. *Is* is a verb, so capitalize it in a headline (or in a title).

Omission of a colon after the greeting in a business letter. If you're writing a business letter, put a colon after the greeting; if you're writing any other kind of letter, use a comma.

And the most common error: Mistakes in word choice. If you look through the following list of common mistakes and you recognize ones you often make, look up the correct usage and then develop mnemonics to help you remember. The most common mistakes in word choice are:

- Using *which* for *that* and vice versa
- Using *lead* for the past tense of *lead*
- Using *affect* for *effect* and vice versa
- Confusing *they're, their*, and *there*
- Confusing *your* with *you're*
- Overusing *utilize* (a made-up word for this phenomenon: *abutilize*)
- Using *between you and I* instead of *between you and me*
- Using *compare to* when *compare with* is correct
- Using *convince someone to* (rather than *persuade someone to*)
- Using *everyday* as one word, not attributively (e.g., *I ride the bus everyday* instead of the correct form *I ride the bus every day*)
- Using *additionally* when *in addition* is meant
- Using *its* for *it's* and vice versa (by far the most common mistake)

Testimony from Teachers in the Trenches

Here's what the English teachers identified as common problems:

Difficulty grasping the concept of a topic sentence. A topic sentence is the main sentence of the paragraph. All of the other sentences should support it or give examples to elaborate on it. Determine your paragraph's topic sentence; then read every other sentence separately and ask yourself if it elaborates on the topic sentence. If it doesn't, eighty-six it.

Trouble focusing on the subject at hand. Go back through your paper and read each sentence separately. Ask yourself if each sentence has to do with the topic sentence of its paragraph and also if each sentence relates to your thesis sentence. If you've strayed away from either your topic or your thesis, delete or reword the sentence.

No transition from paragraph to paragraph in language or thought. Review the section on transitional words and expressions (Chapter 12). As you reread your work, ask yourself where you move from one point to another or from one example to another; then use transitional words or phrases that are appropriate to make a meaningful connection.

Inconsistency in verb tense (especially present and past tense). Go back and determine which tense you've used. Unless you have a reason for a tense change, reword the sentences that change tense.

Reliance on the computer spell check for proofreading. Although spell checkers are often helpful, all they can do is offer suggestions about what you *may* have intended to spell. Using a dictionary, look at the suggested word's definition to be sure that what the checker suggests is in fact the word that you intended to write.

Comma splices. (For example: "I went to the store, I bought a jug of milk and a six-pack of cola.") Review each comma in your work.

Sentence fragments. Read each sentence separately and ask yourself if the words in that sentence make sense when you read them alone. If they don't, your "sentence" is a fragment. (Hint: To make a complete sentence, your fragment probably needs to be attached to the words immediately before or after it.)

Confusion of homophones. Homophones are words that sound alike but have different meanings and perhaps different spellings. Here are a few examples: *to, too, two; they're, their, there; here, hear*; and so on. If they are creeping into your writing, review the section on word usage in Chapter 12. Look up the correct usage of the homophones you often misuse, and then develop your own mnemonics to help remember them.

No sense of who the audience is. Be sure you're clear about who your intended audience is (that is, to whom or for whom you're writing). Then make sure that each sentence addresses that audience. Common problems arise in the tone used (for instance, don't use language or reasoning that insults people if you're trying to persuade them to your line of thinking) and in addressing someone who is not part of the audience (for instance, writing "When you take freshman English . . . " when the audience—in this case, the instructor—is not taking freshman English).

Colloquial usages that are inconsistent with the rest of the writing or inappropriate for the type of writing. Look through your writing for slang words or idiomatic phrases. Unless your work calls for a relaxed or conversational tone (and your instructor or supervisor agrees that tone is necessary), reword your piece and use more formal language.

No sentence variation (writing only noun-verb-complement sentences). Review the section on types of sentences in Chapter 8. Reword some of your sentences so that they begin with phrases or dependent clauses. Combine two related sentences into one to create less monotonous sentences.

Not following directions. Realize that you're not making up the rules for the assignment, and that—strange as it may seem—your teacher or supervisor probably has a reason for every direction that he or she has instructed. Keep the directions in mind as you write a rough draft, and then reread them after you've completed your assignment. If you've "violated" any of the directions, rewrite those parts.

Use of generalities, instead of specifics. Your paper must give details about what general statements you make. One way to generate details or supporting evidence is to ask *who? what? when? where? why?* and *how?* questions about your topic or thesis sentence.

Use of "non-sentences" that have lots of fluff but little substance. (For example, "Language is important to everyday life and society.") Look for generalizations, clichés, and platitudes in your work. Reword your sentences to be more specific, to give more details, or to be less hackneyed.

Point of view that changes (sometimes first person, sometimes third) or is inappropriate (usually second person). Check each sentence of your manuscript and determine its point of view. If you've changed from one point of view to another without a reason, reword your sentences. Also, check to see if using first or second point of view is permitted (third person is the only point of view allowed in many formats of academic writing).

CHAPTER 14
Putting Pen to Paper

If you're like lots of writers, you may find that getting your ideas on paper is one of the hardest parts of preparing your masterpiece for the eyes of the rest of the world. This chapter is meant to help you better contend with this often painful stage of the writing process by providing you with some ideas for organizing your thoughts.

Practical and Profitable Preliminaries

So at the "prewriting" stage of the game, how do you get ideas? Well, you could try the method used by one of the world's most prolific writers, Agatha Christie, who used to sit in her bathtub and munch on apples while plotting her bestsellers. What? You say apple eating doesn't appeal (pun intended) to you? Don't worry, there are plenty of other suggestions in this chapter.

Just remember that one method of prewriting may not work for you all the time. If it doesn't, try another one. Use whichever technique (or combination of techniques) that helps you think clearly and keep track of your ideas. And keep in mind that you're not being graded for the way you jot down your ideas; you can be as sloppy as you like, as long as you're able to decipher your scratches down the line.

No matter what genre you're writing in, you'll probably come up with a number of ideas that you'll eventually discard. That doesn't matter. What matters at first is getting your thoughts on paper. After you do that, you can go back and decide which ones are the keepers.

One way to organize your thoughts before you even begin the prewriting stage is to keep a journal. If you know for a while beforehand that you want to—or have to—write about a particular subject, try keeping a journal about your topic. Whenever ideas come to you, jot them down in your journal. Don't worry about writing in complete sentences; just write enough so that you'll know later what you meant. When the time comes for writing your first draft, you'll already have a number of ideas, so you can go back to them and decide which are the best to use.

A Free and Easy Format: Freewriting

Freewriting is one of the most effective methods of cultivating ideas. Begin by writing your topic at the top of the page. At this stage of the game, your topic may be so general that you might not even have a clear idea about what direction you want to take. That's not important right now. All you're going to do in freewriting is just (surprise!) write. Write anything related to your topic—words, phrases, or complete sentences, whatever scraps of thought come to mind. Give yourself a time limit of about ten minutes (you'd probably be wasting time with anything longer than that at this stage).

Because you've got only ten minutes, you should *not:*

- Be concerned with spelling or punctuation
- Go to the time or trouble of grouping your ideas
- Bother erasing anything
- Worry even if you digress from your topic
- Stop if you're in the middle of a thought and you can't think of a specific word (Just write *???* or *XXX* or some other shorthand; then go on and get the rest of the thought on paper. The same holds true if you have the first part of a good idea and you can't think of how to end it. Just use your "I'll-come-back-to-this-later" shorthand and forge ahead.)

If you're stumped for something to write, keep your pen moving on the paper or your fingers moving on the keyboard. You can even write something like "I don't know anything more about this topic. I don't think I can come up with another thought." Just keep writing and chances are, in spite of yourself, you'll come up with a new idea. At the end of your time allotment, stop. Look over your work. From the resulting splinters of writing, you'll see some good ideas and some that you're probably ready to toss. Decide what best fits with the direction that your work takes, and cross out what doesn't. Then go back to the ideas that seem workable and underline the key parts of them.

Now, you've got a start. You can repeat the process to expand on the ideas that you like. Since you're working in ten-minute sessions, the assignment may not seem as overwhelming as it first did. Also, you won't suffer from "brain strain" and you might find that you're quite productive when you use these short segments.

Making a List and Checking It Twice: Brainstorming

In brainstorming—a first cousin to freewriting—you also make a list of whatever comes to mind about your topic, you jot down words or phrases as they pop into your head, and you don't worry about spelling, punctuation, usage, or grouping ideas.

Unlike freewriting, though, you have no time restrictions. If you're interrupted in your list making, you just return to it later. In fact, sometimes there's an advantage to brainstorming in short shifts (maybe your brain can take just so many storms at a time?). Whatever length of time you have, use each stint of your brainstorming sessions to write as much as you can think of about your topic.

Here's an example: Suppose that a writer is angry with a company and wants to write a complaint letter to its customer relations department. His or her brainstorming list may look something like this:

TELEMARKETERS
rude questions
IMPUDENCE!
2hrs. = three unasked-for calls
why treat potential customers like this
put me on don't call list imediately
is this indication of way company feels about customers????
told caller wasn't interested all three times he called
caller said in smart-aleck way they'd call back and get information
asked about way I pay bills—none of their business—invasion of priv'cy
won't do business with company now, even though I was considering switching to it

As you can see, the thoughts are random, jotted down as they popped into the writer's head. There's no order as yet, and the writer didn't bother with spelling, punctuation, or writing style. (Can you tell that the writer was still very angry about the calls?)

Nevertheless, this brainstormed list gives a good start. The ideas are there; and with some organization and some surface corrections, the letter will be ready for the mail.

If you find that you don't have much luck making a written list while brainstorming, you might want to consider using a tape recorder to act as your pen and paper. Just switch it on and begin talking about your topic, saying anything that comes into your mind. Since your mind often works faster than you can write, you may get more ideas recorded this way. After you've gotten your ideas on tape, then go back and transcribe them so that you can begin to get them organized.

If you don't have a mechanical tape recorder handy, turn to one of the human kind. As you talk to a friend, an instructor, or a supervisor, have him or her jot down what you're saying. Your human "recorder" might ask some questions that send you in a different direction or might prod you into giving explanations or details that you hadn't realized were needed.

Just Pretend You're Jimmy Olsen: Questioning

Get out your press card, your stubby pencil, and your pocket notebook—you've just become an ace reporter. Asking the reporter's fundamental six *w* and *h* questions *(who? what? when? where? why? how?)* is another method to help you develop ideas. The twist is that you are interviewing yourself.

Suppose you've been given a very general topic like "relate a terrible dining experience you once had." In thinking back to a particularly horrible experience, you could ask yourself questions like these:

Who was involved?
(you and your date Pat)

What happened at first?
(you were on a first date with someone you barely knew)

What happened before the horrible part of the evening?
(since you didn't know each other well, you were just trying to find things to talk about)

What started the "horrible" part of the evening?
(you both became sick while still sitting at the table)

What happened next?

(the manager of the restaurant noticed that you were ill and came to the table to offer to help)

When did this happen?

(on a summer evening in 2001)

Where did this happen?

(at Sally's Scrumptious Shrimp Shack, in Seattle)

Why did this happen?

(you had eaten seafood that hadn't been cooked long enough)

How did this happen?

(you both felt yourselves turning green and having upset stomachs)

How did the evening end at the restaurant?

(the manager gave you a complimentary dinner and a gift certificate to return another time)

How did the evening end after leaving the restaurant?

(you both wound up in the emergency room at the hospital)

What could you have done differently?

(you could have been more suspicious when you thought the food smelled bad)

What lessons did you learn?

(if it smells funny, don't put it in your mouth)

Who was at fault?

(mostly it was the restaurant's fault for serving ill-prepared food)

How could the night have been any better?

(in almost every way, with no bad food and no trip to the hospital)

What was the silver lining in the experience?

(you did get to become good friends with your date)

Because you expanded on the basic *who? what? when? where? why? how?* questions, you've compiled lots of details to give your readers a more descriptive picture of what happened that night.

You might also ask questions to help you broaden the way you look at your topic by approaching it from various points of view. For instance, if you're writing about a recent concert you attended, write down your own reflections and then put yourself in the place of the performers you heard. What might have been their reaction to the goings-on that night? What about the stagehands? the parking attendants? the ushers? Thinking about the experiences that others had often will take your mind in a separate direction and will help you generate new ideas.

Lines and Circles and Words, Oh My!

Still stumped at getting started? Maybe your brain works better with drawings than with just words alone. If you think this may be the case, try the prewriting strategy called "clustering" (also known as "mapping"). In clustering, you use circles and lines to connect your thoughts. You can use clustering to begin your writing, or you can use it to help generate ideas for any subsections that have you stumped. Begin by drawing a circle in the middle of your paper and writing your topic inside it.

Then start thinking of random words or phrases associated with your topic. As you think of something, write it in a separate circle and connect it to the main idea with a line.

As you think of ideas that are offshoots of the new circles, draw other circles, write the new information in them, and then connect them.

Don't worry about your clusters being messy or unartistic, and don't be concerned if you can't think of anything associated with some of the circles. (If you get stumped, you might try asking yourself one of the *who? what? when? where? why? how?* questions.)

As with other techniques for getting ideas, with clustering you'll probably end up with some material that you won't include in your final paper. That's fine. At this point, you're just getting ideas down.

HERE IS AN EXAMPLE OF CLUSTERING:

```
                          ┌──────────┐
                          │ first job │
                          └──────────┘
                    ┌───────────┐  ┌─────────────┐
                    │ absolute  │  │ needed money │
                    │  terror   │  └─────────────┘
                    └───────────┘
        ┌──────────┐  ┌──────────┐  ┌──────────┐  ┌──────────┐
        │boss seemed│  │was the only│ │needed to save│ │wanted to │
        │intimidating│ │young person│ │ for college  │ │buy a car │
        └──────────┘  └──────────┘  └──────────┘  └──────────┘
   ┌──────────┐  ┌──────────┐       ┌──────────┐  ┌──────────┐
   │  never   │  │talked only│       │hoped to start│ │had my eye on│
   │welcomed me or│ │about getting│  │college in one year,│ │a late-model│
   │even smiled │ │orders right │    │if had enough│ │convertible │
   └──────────┘  └──────────┘       │money saved │  └──────────┘
                                     └──────────┘
```

Out in the Open: The Outline

You might find that your work becomes easier if you create an outline, a kind of blueprint that helps you organize your thoughts in a logical pattern, and see the relationships between your main ideas and supporting ideas. You can use outlining as a prewriting method in itself, or you can use it as a way of organizing the ideas you generated in freewriting, brainstorming, questioning, clustering, or any other technique.

There are two types of outline: a formal and an informal outline. If you write a formal outline, you must use a prescribed style. You must:

- Designate your main points with Roman numerals
- Designate your subordinate points with capital letters, Arabic numerals, and lowercase letters
- Alternate between using numbers and letters

- Have at least two entries in each category (that is, you must have at least two Roman numerals, two capital letters under each Roman numeral, and so on)
- Maintain a parallel grammatical structure in your entries (for instance, if the first Roman numeral is a noun, the other Roman numerals must be nouns)

Is all of this confusing? It won't be when you examine the sample of the formal outline that follows, which compares and contrasts watching a movie in a theater and watching a movie at home.

If the formal outline style seems a bit overwhelming, think of it this way: After you write down your main points, then you just fill in the subcategories with details or examples.

Contrast and Compare Watching a Movie in a Theater and at Home
A number of differences and similarities exist between watching a movie in a theater and watching a movie at home.

    I. Differences
        A. Home
            1. Greater freedom
                a. More comfort
                    (1) Can watch wearing pajamas, if I choose
                    (2) Have choice of seating at home
                        (a) Can sit in favorite easy chair
                        (b) Can lie on floor or couch
                b. More choice of times to watch
                    (1) Can stop to talk if phone rings
                    (2) Can stop for bathroom breaks
                    (3) Can stop if want to get food or drink
                    (4) Can finish watching movie another
                        time
            2. Fewer restrictions about food or drink
                a. Less expensive at home
                b. Open choice of food or drink
        B. Movie theater

1. Much larger screen at movies
2. Better popcorn at movies
3. Earlier date for availability to be seen
4. Better sound system
5. Larger seating capacity, if needed for large group of friends
6. Better "maid service" (someone else picks up the discarded candy wrappers, etc.)

II. Similarities

A. (Follow the same format to fill in details about the similarities between watching a movie at a theater and at home)

   1.

      a.

         (1)

         (2)

           (a)

           (b)

      b.

   2.

B.

Looking at the organization in this formal outline, you'll see that each main entry begins with a Roman numeral. Then come the indented capital-letter entries (*Home* and *Movie Theater*) under each Roman numeral, and both are written in a parallel way (in this case, as nouns). Then come indented entries written with Arabic numbers; each of these begins with a comparative adjective (*Greater, Fewer, Larger, Better, Earlier*). As you can see, the entries go on—lowercase letters, then numbers inside parentheses, then lowercase letters inside parentheses—and each subcategory has a parallel grammatical layout.

If you're writing an informal outline, begin by writing your topic (or main idea) and your thesis statement (the main point you are trying to make about your topic) at the top of your paper. These give you a good reference and help you keep your work focused. If you're outlining from a list or cluster you've already created, take a look at what seem to be your major points. Fill these in as the main categories of your outline, being sure to leave a number of lines in between them. After that, go back and fill in details or examples about each of the main points. If you have additional points about the examples or details, write them under the appropriate category (again, make sure you indent a little with each new subcategory). If you indent the same amount each time you write a subcategory, you'll be able to see the various sections more easily.

SSENTIALS

Some writers find it helpful to create an outline after they've finished their first draft. In looking over the outline, they can see how well—or not so well—their ideas connect.

Delineating the Details of Your First Draft

After you have your ideas in some form (an outline or a cluster or a list—whichever kind of prewriting you chose), it's time to take those ideas and write your first draft. (Did you notice the adjective *first?*) The object of this next stage of writing is not to have something that's ready to turn in to your teacher, your supervisor, or your editor, but just to get all of your ideas down on paper in complete sentences. Even if you're writing a personal journal, the piece you develop in this stage probably won't be in its final form. All of that will come later.

Start by taking a look at your ideas—whether they're complete sentences or just random words and phrases—and organize them into groups. Decide which ideas are more important than others and which give details or examples of the main ideas. Keep in mind that you might not use all of your initial ideas. If something in your original list or cluster seems superfluous or if it goes in a separate direction from the rest of your piece, just cross it out; you can always include it later if you change your mind.

Once you get your information organized, begin writing in complete sentences and paragraphs.

In this phase, some writers prefer to begin thinking about mechanics, usage, and spelling, and others prefer to worry about the fine-tuning later.

Do whatever works for you. Right now your main concerns are (1) your purpose in writing, (2) the audience for whom you're writing, and (3) the format or type of writing that's required.

And Your Point Is? Defining Your Purpose

Almost all writing tries to prove a point, answer a question, give instructions, provide reflection, or present entertainment. Before you begin writing, decide what your particular purpose for this piece is (this may have been decided for you by your teacher or supervisor) and keep this purpose in mind as you write.

> **IS THIS PIECE ONE OF THE FOLLOWING:**
> Narrative (telling a story)
> Expository (explaining or giving information)
> Descriptive (providing a written picture of someone, someplace, or something)
> Informative or explanatory (giving data or some other type of information)
> Expressive (detailing your thoughts or emotions)
> Persuasive or argumentative (attempting to influence others to come around to your way of thinking)
> Analytical (examining material presented to you)

Remember that you can improve most academic-related nonfiction (such as descriptive, narrative, expository, persuasive, or analytical writing) by using lots of specific examples or supporting details. Take a look at this sentence, written for an essay about an ideal vacation spot:

> *England is a good place to visit.*

That sentence doesn't exactly make you want to pack your bags, does it? However, with a few details added, it becomes a workable sentence:

> *From the jam-packed boulevards of cosmopolitan London, to the barely wide enough cobblestone paths of ancient York, to the right-for-rambling lanes of Lake District villages, olde England crooks its finger and beckons me.*

Now, you have examples of why England is so enticing (the three regions) as well as specific details about those areas—all of which gives readers a much clearer picture of why the author wants to travel there.

Not only is it important that you know your purpose, you must also communicate it to your reader—preferably in your first few sentences. For example, if you had read the revised sentence about visiting England, you'd expect that the rest of the work would be about what a fascinating place England is to visit. In other words, from reading the first sentence you'd expect that the author's purpose was to inform you about England's various charms or to persuade you to visit England on your next vacation.

This sentence would be called your thesis sentence or thesis statement. If you use a thesis statement, your readers should be able to easily identify it. Also, they should know just from reading it what's in store in the rest of the piece.

If your writing format requires a thesis statement, here's an additional point to keep in mind: Every sentence of your work has to be connected to the thesis statement in some way. Writers, especially student writers, often find themselves drifting away from the thesis when they're giving examples. After you've finished, look at each separate sentence or idea and ask yourself if it is somehow related to your thesis statement. If it isn't, cross it out.

It might help to keep a large copy of your thesis statement on a piece of paper close to your desk. Referring to this copy will help you stay focused on your purpose and stick to your main idea.

Even for writing that doesn't require a thesis statement, you might find that writing a one-sentence statement of your purpose helps you center your thoughts. You won't necessarily include this in the final version of your work, but referring to it will keep you from straying from your main point(s).

Playing to the House: Anticipating Your Audience

Picture a group of comedians performing in a retirement village. Then picture the same group appearing on late-night TV. Because of the difference in the two audiences, the comedians would probably use different material and they'd probably present it in a different way.

What's that got to do with you? Just like a performer, you need to be aware of your audience, the person or group for whom you're writing. If the piece is for yourself, then you can approach your subject matter any way you want. However, if it's for a specific person or group, you should keep certain things in mind, like the tone, vocabulary level, and style that's appropriate for your audience.

If you're writing a letter of complaint, for instance, you might use a far more aggressive tone (and maybe even a different level of vocabulary) than if you're writing for yourself, your business, or your instructor. Also, depending on what you're writing, your style could be formal, informal, or very casual. A good idea is to put yourself in your reader's place and ask yourself what style of writing you'd expect to read.

In considering your audience, think about these questions:

- Are there age considerations that would mean you should write on a particular level? (Usually there aren't, unless you're writing for children.)
- Will your audience expect extra information in your work, like quotations, citations, tables, or graphs? (These might be needed in an academic or business paper.)
- Are you writing for people from a specific location? If so, are there geographic considerations or cultural differences that you need to explain?
- Are your readers people of a specific gender, or do they have a particular political or religious preference? If this is the case, be sure to keep it in mind and don't step on toes—unless, of course, your purpose is to be argumentative.
- What's the occupation of your audience? For instance, are you writing for your teacher, your supervisor, the readers of the local newspaper, the quality control department of your company?
- What need does your audience have for what you're writing? Will the information clarify the purpose of a particular meeting, help you get a good grade, decrease civic problems, track a lost package?
- What information does your audience already have? (There's no use in defining terms that your audience should be familiar with.)

- What might your audience not be aware of? For example, they may not be aware of the plot of a literary work that you're critiquing, may not know the names of participants at a work meeting, may not be informed about why the city would be wasting money on a proposed project, may not know when a package was ordered and to whom it was to be shipped.

As you write, keep in mind that you don't want to insult your audience either by using inappropriate humor or by being patronizing or pretentious, so adjust your tone and your vocabulary accordingly.

Remember that conveying sarcasm and irony in writing is very difficult in any situation, and neither of those has a place in most academic or business writing.

Writing à la Mode: Adhering to a Particular Style

The next part of your work is deciding the style or format to use. If you have an assignment from school or work, the style may have been decided for you. For example, for school you might be assigned to write a three-page essay critiquing a recent tax proposal, or at your business you may need to write a summary of the main points of a meeting you attended.

If a particular style is required, make sure that you adhere to it. Generally speaking, teachers and supervisors don't appreciate it if you create a style on your own; they expect you to present material in the way they have directed. If you're not certain about how to write in a particular style or format, look at successful past material and model your work after it.

If, for instance, you're told to write the definitive essay about the pros and cons of front-wheel drive, and the format you're to use is a five-paragraph essay, your essay should not exceed five paragraphs, even if you find it next to impossible to squeeze in all your ideas. Or if your boss says that your analysis of a new product should contain bulleted lists rather than complete sentences, use the bulleted lists, odd as you may think they look.

Also, don't forget the minor details of a mandatory format. For instance, check to see if you're required to use a title, page numbers, headings, citations and other references, and a table of contents. If these are required, you should find out if they must be written in certain positions or in a specific way.

Even if you don't like the format that's required or if you don't think it allows you to express yourself in the best way, use it anyway. Later on, you'll have plenty of time to write the way you want to—when a grade or salary isn't at stake.

Relax, Pat Yourself on the Back, and Leave Your Writing Alone—For Now

After you've finished writing your first draft you can relax—for a while. You'll have plenty of time to improve your material, so don't worry about it being perfect at this stage of the game. In the next step you'll polish your work by editing and revising, but right now you should just take a moment to enjoy the fact that you've made it to this stage!

ESSENTIALS

Remember that you don't have to write in sequence. Lots of writers find it easier to compose the middle part of their work, then go back and write the beginning and ending. Begin by writing whatever part seems easiest; then go back and fill in the hard parts.

CHAPTER 15

The Final Dress Rehearsal

Now, it's time to fine-tune your work by revising it. This chapter will help you with this process by specifying a variety of organizational, grammatical, and content-related issues to check in your draft. Here are pointers that will help you get the most out of the time you invest.

Rereading, Revising, and Rewriting

Revising is much more than just looking for misspelled words and an errant comma or two. Rather, it entails looking at the big picture (organization, purpose, vocabulary, tone, and so on) as well as the little brush strokes of punctuation, usage, and spelling. Keep in mind that making these improvements takes time, and you can usually count on writing more than one revision. In fact, in most cases it's a good idea to allow time for four or five revisions. I hope you haven't passed out from the shock of that idea, but the truth is, if you want your writing to be the best it can be, you need to devote a lot of time to the editing process. If it helps, give yourself breaks of a day or two in between your various revisions (if you can afford the extra time).

Looking at the Big Picture

A good place to begin is by looking back at your subject and your purpose in writing. What were you supposed to do in this piece? For instance, if you were supposed to argue against capital punishment, did you maintain that argument throughout your paper or did you slip into an "on the other hand" approach and start giving arguments for the opposing side? If you wrote a summary of a meeting that took place in your job, did you emphasize all the points of the meeting or did you insert a recommendation for something that wasn't discussed? If you wrote a letter to the editor of a newspaper, did you stick to the one point of your letter and make sure that you made your point in an understandable and forceful manner?

ESSENTIALS

If you find your writing has a tendency to wander, try this trick: circle the main idea of each paragraph, and then go back and ask yourself if each sentence relates to that idea.

How about your introduction: Is it clear enough? Does it contain enough information to lead your readers to your main points? Is your conclusion effective? Does it stray from the topic or your thesis statement? One helpful trick is to read your introduction and your conclusion (skipping the parts in between), and ask yourself if both are saying the same thing. If not, you need to revise.

If your piece of writing required a thesis, did you state it clearly? Did you make sure that each of your supporting points relates to your thesis? Are you certain that each of your other sentences is focused on your thesis? Have you checked that each sentence relates to the point of the individual paragraph it's in?

Have you presented all of your information coherently? Have you given enough examples, facts, or details to support each of your points? If you gave examples in your work, did you explain why each example is significant? Do your examples follow each other in a logical order? Would rearranging them (for example, in chronological or emphatic order) make them clearer or more forceful? Would adding anything strengthen your work? Will your audience be familiar with all the terms you used? If not, you may need to add extra explanatory information.

Take a look at the organization of your paragraphs. Would your points be more emphatic if your paragraphs were organized differently? If you moved or eliminated any of them, would your work be easier to understand? If you think there may be a problem with the way your material flows, try cutting and pasting paragraphs into different positions.

Consider the tone you've used throughout the piece. Is it suitable for your audience? Have you gone overboard and ended up presenting your material in a manner that's too personal or too emotional? Have you used any language that's inappropriate either for your audience or the genre of writing?

Have you adhered to the formatting or style that was mandated? Do you have the prescribed margin sizes? font style? point size? spacing requirements? Must you use a particular style to identify yourself, your class, your department, or your company? Are your pages numbered in the right places? in the right way?

If your paper is about a literary work, have you stated the author's first and last names and the title of the work? After you cited the author the first time, have you used only his or her last name in later references? Have you used the proper citation or documentation methods required for your paper? Have you checked to see that any paraphrasing you included was in fact paraphrasing and not a direct quote?

If you're using citations, make sure that your quotes, periods, and commas appear in the right places and that you have followed the assigned order for listing author, publisher, publication date and location, and other necessary material. Instructors often say that a major problem in formal papers is students not being meticulous about following the assigned rules for citations.

If you have included any tables or graphs, have you labeled them well enough that your readers will have no problem interpreting them? Do any of them need information in addition to captions? Have you included a title that communicates the concepts of your paper?

Particulars to Ponder in the Perusal of Your Piece

How do your sentences look? Have you varied your sentence structure and the length of your sentences? Look to see if you've begun a number of sentences in the same way (for example, look for several sentences that start with "The company . . . " or "The main character . . . "). Check to see if a number of your sentences are composed in a subject-verb-complement format. If you do have too much repetition, vary your sentence structure—create more compound or compound-complex sentences; change your sentence length; alter the rhythm of your words. Do whatever it takes to keep your writing from being monotonous. Finally, look to see if several of your sentences have nearly the same number of words; if so, try combining some of them.

Do you need to put any of your sentences on a diet? Have you overexplained anything? Look for wording that can be more concise. If you can use fewer words and convey the same meaning, by all means do so. (See Chapter 13.) Look at each sentence and ask yourself if your wording could be more precise, more vivid, or more explanatory.

What types of pronouns have you used in your paper? Have you used any first- or second-person pronouns *(I, we, you, us)?* Is using them in writing acceptable in your class or workplace? Is it appropriate? While you're looking at pronouns, check to see that you have maintained a consistent point of view with them.

Have you used transitional words and phrases to your best advantage? (See Chapter 12.) Have you used enough transitions so that your work reads smoothly? Do your transitions guide your readers from one thought to the next? from one paragraph to the next? Have you used them in the correct way? Do you see any related thoughts or sentences that would become stronger if you used a transitional word or phrase between them?

What about the voice you used? Except for certain scientific material, you should write using the active voice (see Chapter 11) whenever possible. If you have a number of sentences that contain *be* verbs (*is, are, was, were,* and so on), change the structure of your sentence. For instance, you could change:

The downtown area is enhanced by the new streetlights. (passive voice)

to

The new streetlights enhance the downtown area. (active voice)

Along the same lines, look for sentences that begin with expletives like *it, this,* or *there*; these sentences can often become more forceful when you reword them. If you've written, for instance:

There are six changes that should be made in the method of production of the widget.

Change the sentence to:

Six changes should be made in the production method of the widget.

Are there synonyms that you could use to make your meaning clearer or to make your work read more smoothly? Don't hesitate to consult a dictionary or thesaurus. (If you're using a word processor, you probably have quick access to a built-in thesaurus.) Substitute synonyms for repeated words or phrases if you can.

Has any slang or jargon crept into your work? Ask yourself if using either is appropriate and reword as necessary. Also look for any clichés that you've used and change them to more original thoughts.

Some instructors (and perhaps some companies) dictate that certain words not be used (generally these are overused words like *great* and *very*). If that applies to you, have you checked through to see if you have deleted those particular words or phrases? Note that the Find function on word processing software can show you if any taboo words or phrases appear in your work. The thesaurus can help you to find replacements.

Jettisoning Gender-Based Generalities

One hot spot that you want to make sure you avoid in your written work is the use of sexist language. If you've mentioned particular jobs by name, for example, make sure your wording is not exclusively all-male or all-female. The following list of substitutions might help you to avoid sexist language:

SEXIST TERM	SUBSTITUTION
chairman/chairwoman	chair, chairperson, presiding officer, coordinator, moderator
coed	student
congressman/congresswoman	congressional representative, legislator
forefathers	ancestors
foreman	supervisor
layman	layperson, nonspecialist
man/men	person/people, individual(s)
man hours	work hours
mankind	men and women, humankind, the human race, humanity
man-made	synthetic, manufactured
manpower	workforce
one-man show	one-person show
policeman	police officer
saleslady/salesman/saleswoman	sales clerk, salesperson, sales representative

In years gone by, the rule was to use the masculine pronouns *he*, *him*, or *his* to refer to any noun that could be masculine or feminine. ("Every employee must check his voice mail.") Thankfully, today that rule is obsolete; the generally accepted rule is to use both the masculine and feminine forms. ("Every employee must check his or her voice mail.")

In an effort to avoid sexist language, however, you may find yourself using too many dual constructions (*he or she*, *his or hers*, and *him or her*), which can make your writing boring and cumbersome. To avoid having to use too many of these constructions, you might:

- Change your wording to plural pronouns

Original: Every day, each supervisor should greet all of his or her employees by name.
Revised: Every day, supervisors should greet all their employees by name.

- Substitute a noun

Original: Tell him to change the sexist language.
Revised: Tell the writer to change the sexist language.

- Alternate using a male and a female pronoun in long constructions where you must use a singular form
- Reword your sentences to use the first or second person (providing this is permitted)

Original: If a driver loses a number of points on his license, he must attend driving school.
Revised: If you lose a number of points on your license, you must attend driving school.
Alternate revised: If we lose a number of points on our license, we must attend driving school.

After you've checked your paper for all these points, you'll probably need to rewrite parts of it. Just jump right in and do it. Then reread the revision section and apply it to your rewritten version. (Remember that warning that more than one revision would be necessary?)

If you're writing on a computer, be sure to use a spell checker to catch mistakes that your eye doesn't see. Remember, though, that a spell checker won't catch words that are spelled correctly but that aren't the words you intended. To get around that problem, you need to use your own eagle eye for checking (more about that in the proofreading section).

A computer's grammar checker is another story—use it with a grain of salt. If you send your manuscript through a grammar checker, be aware that you may disagree with what the computer tells you—and you may be right. If you're unsure about a grammar question, consult the corresponding section of this book or other grammar handbooks.

The Proof Is in the Reading

Hurray! You're almost home free. You've checked your content, your organization, and your sentence structure, and you're satisfied that everything you've written is brilliant (you are sure about that, aren't you?). Now, you're ready to do some serious proofreading to help you find those little nitpicky errors that can change a masterpiece into a laughter piece (spell check wouldn't have caught that mistake).

The hints that follow will help to slow down your eyes so that they don't go faster than your brain. In other words, you read what you *actually* wrote rather than what you *think* you wrote. These strategies should help you to find mistakes more easily:

FACTS

Some writers find it helpful to do separate "read-throughs" of their paper—one looking at spelling, one at punctuation, one at tense, and so on.

To begin with, try reading your paper out loud. Reading aloud may help you to catch any word you out. (Oops! Reread the preceding sentence. Did you read it correctly the first time?) When you read silently, you often read what you *think* you've written. When you read out loud, however, you must read more slowly, so you'll often catch grammatical and spelling mistakes that you'd miss in silent reading. Also, reading out loud helps you to hear the rhythm of your words. In revising your paper, you looked for sentences that have similar construction, but by reading your work out loud you may hear similarities that your eye didn't catch. If you have time, tape-record yourself as you read your paper, then listen to the tape the next day to see if your thoughts flow smoothly.

As you read your paper, touch each word with a pencil. (An added bonus of this tip is that you'll already have your pencil in hand if you find a mistake.) Try using a ruler or piece of paper to cover the lines below what you're reading. This helps you to focus on each line. If you're pressed for time and you have to edit and proofread before you print, pretend you're back in primary school. Move your finger across the screen as you read each word separately.

Read backward. Start at the end and read the last sentence, then the sentence before that, and so on until you reach the beginning. When you read out of order, you'll more easily spot errors.

Think about errors that you're prone to make, and take extra time to look for them. For instance, if you have trouble with sentence fragments, go back through your work and closely examine each sentence. Read each one as a separate thought and ask yourself if it makes sense by itself, without the sentences on either side of it. If you often make mistakes with comma usage, check each comma to make sure you know the reason why you've used it. Remember that a comma splice (that is, putting a comma where you need a stronger punctuation mark) is a frequent mistake. If each thought on either side of a comma could be a separate sentence, then change your comma to a semicolon or break down the sentence into two separate sentences.

Use the Search or Find function on your computer to look for spelling errors that you tend to make. For instance, if you often misuse *its* and *it's*, search for each usage of the words. Keep this book open to the page that explains *it's* and *its* (see p. 204) and then check each word separately to be sure you've used it correctly.

Even though you've put your work through a spell checker, be aware that you also need to check for spelling yourself. You know that a spell checker will detect only words that are not in the dictionary. If you intended to type *not* and instead you typed *nor*, the spell checker won't know the difference. A good idea is to make one pass through your copy looking for spelling errors alone. Pay particular attention to words that you frequently mistype and for words that are common spelling errors, like *to*, *two*, and *too*, and *their*, *they're*, and *there*.

Check your tense usage. If you began your piece using the past tense, for example, make sure that you wrote the rest in the past tense (not including any quoted material, of course). Instructors say that unnecessary tense change is one of the most common problems in papers.

If you have time, let your paper get "cold." Give yourself an hour or two—or overnight, if possible—and then come back to it. Odds are you'll see what you wrote in a fresh light and you'll make further revisions.

Let someone else—more than one person, if possible—proofread and respond to your paper (this is known as peer editing). Ask the other readers to be as critical as possible and to look for any kind of error—in spelling, punctuation, usage, mechanics, organization, clarity, even in the value of your ideas. Although you may not agree with the other person's editing suggestions, chances are if he or she had trouble reading or understanding your material, you should do some extra revision. Repeat your editing and proofreading process as many times as necessary.

In your revision, remember five important rules of writing from George Orwell from "Politics and the English Language":

1. *Never use a metaphor, simile, or other figure of speech [that] you're used to seeing in print.*
2. *Never use a long word where a short one will do.*
3. *If it is possible to cut a word out, always cut it out.*
4. *Never use the passive where you can use the active.*
5. *Never use a foreign phrase, a scientific word or a jargon word if you can think of an everyday English equivalent.*

When Really Bad Is Really Good

You've been working so hard on your drafting, revising, and proofreading that you're probably just about due for a good laugh. Collected here are some examples of really bad writing culled from the Bulwer-Lytton Fiction Contest, which challenges writers to compose the *worst* possible opening sentence. The contest, which began in 1982, was named for Victorian novelist Edward George Earle Bulwer-Lytton (that's Baron Lytton of Knebworth to you), who used one of the most famous (infamous?) lines in the English language to begin his novel *Paul Clifford:* "It was a dark and stormy night."

If you'd like to read more about the contest, see the "Lyttony" of winners at *www.bulwer-lytton.com/lyttony.htm*.

Recent winning entries have included the following:

The heather-encrusted Headlands, veiled in fog as thick as smoke in a crowded pub, hunched precariously over the moors, their rocky elbows slipping off land's end, their bulbous, craggy noses thrust into the thick foam of the North Sea like bearded old men falling asleep in their pints.

—Gary Dahl, Los Gatos, California (2000 Winner)

Through the gathering gloom of a late-October afternoon, along the greasy, cracked paving-stones slick from the sputum of the sky, Stanley Ruddlethorp wearily trudged up the hill from the cemetery where his wife, sister, brother, and three children were all buried, and forced open the door of his decaying house, blissfully unaware of the catastrophe that was soon to devastate his life.

—Dr. David Chuter, Kingston, Surrey, England (1999 Winner)

The corpse exuded the irresistible aroma of a piquant, ancho chili glaze enticingly enhanced with a hint of fresh cilantro as it lay before him, coyly garnished by a garland of variegated radicchio and caramelized onions, and impishly drizzled with glistening rivulets of vintage balsamic vinegar and roasted garlic oil; yes, as he surveyed the body of the slain food critic slumped on the floor of the cozy, but nearly empty, bistro, a quick inventory of his senses told corpulent Inspector Moreau that this was, in all likelihood, an inside job.

—Bob Perry, Milton, Massachusetts (1998 Winner)

The moment he laid eyes on the lifeless body of the nude socialite sprawled across the bathroom floor, Detective Leary knew she had committed suicide by grasping the cap on the tamper-proof bottle, pushing down and twisting while she kept her thumb firmly pressed against the spot the arrow pointed to, until she hit the exact spot where the tab clicks into place, allowing her to remove the cap and swallow the entire contents of the bottle, thus ending her life.

—Artie Kalemeris, Fairfax, Virginia (1997 Winner)

"Ace, watch your head!" hissed Wanda urgently, yet somehow provocatively, through red, full, sensuous lips, but he couldn't you know, since nobody can actually watch more than part of his nose or a little cheek or lips if he really tries, but he appreciated her warning.

—Janice Estey, Aspen, Colorado (1996 Winner)

CHAPTER 16

Maximizing Your Means of Expression

I f you're confused about a style of writing that you've been assigned—whether for a class or for work—or if you just want to try your hand at different styles, take a look at the various types of writing in this chapter. You'll find descriptions of a number of styles—from short essays to abstracts and process papers.

Short Takes

Let's start out with the short papers. You may be asked to condense all your knowledge on a subject into a pithy essay or abstract, or even into a single paragraph. It's okay. Take a deep breath. You can do it, and here's how.

All in One: A Single Paragraph

Let's start out small. If you find yourself in a position where you must get your thoughts across in only a single paragraph, you should pay attention to the central thought of your paragraph and the details that support that thought. The most important part of a single paragraph is its topic sentence, which contains the paragraph's main idea. The topic sentence is often (but not always) the first sentence. All the other sentences in the paragraph should support the topic sentence in some way. If they don't, cut them.

Some one-paragraph compositions also end with a summary sentence that restates, reviews, or emphasizes the main idea of the paragraph (using different words, of course).

 **SSENTIALS**

Some writers who have been confused about the organization of a single paragraph have found this military analogy helpful:

A paragraph has a topic sentence as its general; all the rest of the sentences "report to" the topic sentence. If some sentence goes AWOL (if it strays from the main idea of the paragraph), it should be court-martialed (or crossed out).

Some writers have trouble understanding how to show support of a main idea. If you're one of them, think about ways that you can:

- *Elaborate* on your topic sentence
- *Explain* or *clarify* your topic sentence
- *Give details* about your topic sentence

- *Provide factual information or proof* about your topic sentence
- *Help define* your topic sentence

A good topic sentence lets your readers know what to expect from the rest of the paragraph. Read this topic sentence:

While April is the favorite time of year of many people, I dread it because my allergies are aggravated by blooming plants, I'm under a lot of tension to get my taxes finished by the fifteenth, and I have to attend seven birthday parties for various family members.

After you read this topic sentence, you know that the rest of the paragraph will give you more details about the allergies, the tax-related tension, and the birthday parties.

Don't forget to use transitional words or phrases within your paragraph. These help show your reader the connection between the various ideas you state or points you make.

Room for Expansion: The Five-Paragraph Essay

After single paragraphs, beginning writers often proceed to five-paragraph essays. These works follow a prescribed form (could you guess that it has five paragraphs?) of an introductory paragraph, three body paragraphs, and a concluding paragraph.

Just as a topic sentence is the main focus of a single paragraph, five-paragraph essays are centered around a thesis statement (or thesis sentence), the central view or argument of the whole essay. Your thesis statement may be either argumentative or informative, depending on the direction you take in your body paragraphs, and it should be a summary of what the rest of your essay will contain. By reading your thesis statement alone, readers should know either the direction of the rest of your essay or the individual points you'll make. Make sure that your thesis statement is narrow enough to cover a five-paragraph essay. For example:

The United States needs to increase its aid to Jamaica, Bosnia, and Namibia.

This statement is much too broad because you'd need far more than five paragraphs (maybe five books?) to explain why additional aid is needed for those countries.

Your introductory paragraph should contain your thesis and also give a clear indication about what your body paragraphs will be about. Some instructors or style guides mandate that your thesis statement be the first or last sentence of your introductory paragraph; some will allow it to be in any position in your first paragraph. Whichever format you follow, be sure that your first paragraph contains more than just your thesis statement; it should also include sentences that develop on or build up to your thesis statement.

Your body paragraphs give more elaborate support for your thesis statement. Each of your body paragraphs should contain a topic sentence (a sentence that tells what that particular paragraph is about) and must be directly related to your thesis statement. In other words, one subtopic (one individual point) can be developed in each of your three body paragraphs. Some writers find that they stay more focused if they list these three subtopics in their thesis statement. Read this example:

I will no longer fly Zebra airlines because their online reservation system is not reliable, their support staff is not helpful, and their departures and landings are rarely on time.

From the thesis statement alone, readers know the first body paragraph will elaborate on the complaint about the reservation system, the second body paragraph will elaborate on the problems with the support staff, and the third body paragraph will elaborate on the unreliability of the schedules.

If you arrange the information in your body paragraphs in chronological order, be sure that you word your thesis statement chronologically. Or if you arrange your body paragraphs so that the most important or emphatic reason or example comes last, word your thesis statement in the same way. Some instructors or style guides specify that you write a certain minimum number of sentences in each paragraph of the essay; some leave this up to the individual writer. Be sure you're aware of any requirements that apply to your essay.

As with every kind of writing, it's extremely important that you include transitions in the five-paragraph essay. Each of your body paragraphs should have some sort of word or phrase that ties together what you said in the preceding paragraph with the subtopic you're beginning in that paragraph.

One common problem in essays is body paragraphs that don't pertain to the thesis statement. To remedy this problem, many writers find it helpful to (1) reread their thesis statement, then (2) read each body paragraph separately, and then (3) ask themselves if what they've written in each paragraph directly relates to their thesis statement. If the paragraph doesn't relate, then they know they've veered away from their focus and they need to revise that paragraph.

Your concluding paragraph is a summary of what you've stated in your body paragraphs (of course, with different wording). The information in your concluding paragraph gives you the opportunity to recap what you stated in the preceding paragraphs and give additional emphasis to your individual points. You should be careful not to introduce any new material in your concluding paragraph.

Some writers find that restating (again, in different words) their thesis statement is a straightforward way to begin their concluding paragraph. If you are having trouble writing your concluding paragraph, try start out with the phrase *In conclusion* or *To summarize.* Don't keep the phrase after you finish your paragraph (some instructors find phrases like these to be trite). But using one of the phrases in writing your first draft may be enough to help you get started.

Some writers find that it is easier for them to compose a five-paragraph essay when they see an outline for it and then fill in the parts.

OUTLINE OF A FIVE-PARAGRAPH ESSAY

1. *INTRODUCTORY PARAGRAPH*

Has the thesis sentence (check if it must be in a specific place in this paragraph)

Has sentences that follow or lead up to the thesis sentence

2. *BODY PARAGRAPH #1*

Has a transitional word or phrase connecting the preceding paragraph and this one

Begins with a topic sentence

Has other sentences that support, elaborate on, or give specific evidence for the topic sentence

Has transitional words or phrases throughout the paragraph

3. *BODY PARAGRAPH #2*

Has a transitional word or phrase connecting the preceding paragraph and this one

Begins with a topic sentence

Has other sentences that support, elaborate on, or give specific evidence for the topic sentence

Has transitional words or phrases throughout the paragraph

4. *BODY PARAGRAPH #3*

Has a transitional word or phrase connecting the preceding paragraph and this one

Begins with a topic sentence

Has other sentences that support, elaborate on, or give specific evidence for the topic sentence

Has transitional words or phrases throughout the paragraph

5. *CONCLUSION*

Has several sentences

Has transitional words or phrases

Might contain a summary

Might contain general closing remarks

Might restate the idea of the thesis sentence

Summing It All Up: The Abstract

Don't worry—there's actually nothing at all abstract about writing an abstract. In an abstract (usually written in just one paragraph), you summarize the methodology, essential sections, and main points (or conclusion) of research or a manuscript. By examining your abstract alone, readers should be able to determine what information the complete manuscript contains.

Different instructors, publications, and companies use different styles, so ask about particular requirements. Here are some general points concerning abstracts:

- The purpose of an abstract is to summarize a longer work (which commonly is a literary, scientific, or historic work, although it might be in some other field) and any methods the work described or conclusions it reached.
- If you have a specific word limit, be sure to write as close as possible to that limit without going over it. Abstracts that exceed a specified word limit will often be rejected because they can't fit in certain databases or summary formats.
- Be sure you emphasize the primary discoveries and major conclusions of the work and include the key words of the research or work (that is what will be used in databases).
- Your wording should be as concise as possible and all irrelevant details should be omitted.

Taking a Stand: The Argument Essay

An argument is an essay in which you take a stance on a particular issue and expand on your point of view with supporting evidence. To construct an argument, it would be a good idea to begin by asking yourself what your main point is, then deciding why that particular point is important. For instance, would a segment of society benefit if your stance were taken? Would certain problems be eradicated? Would money be saved?

Keep in mind that you must pursue some line of thought that's open to question—or else it's not an argument. In other words, you wouldn't write something like:

Cotton candy is mostly made out of sugar.

That's because it's a simple statement of fact—there's nothing to argue. However, if you wrote that people should eat more cotton candy, you'd have the basis for debate. Then you could proceed with an argument.

It will help you to give a lot of thought to the evidence you can give to support your point. If you can't think of several reasons your point is important (or if you can't find reasons through research), then you should abandon that particular idea because you won't be able to support it well enough in your essay.

Note that the strength of an argument essay lies not only in the evidence provided by the writer to support his or her point, but in the writer's ability to anticipate opposing arguments and to objectively disprove them.

Remember that requirements for an argument vary with individual instructors, with various academic disciplines, and with publications. Be sure that you understand specific requirements with regard to the format you must use and the type or amount of support or proof you must give.

FACTS

According to Aristotle, three types of appeal exist in argument:

Ethos—the appeal of the character and credibility of the speaker or writer (establish your credentials or the credentials of those whose research you cite).

Pathos—the appeal to the emotion of your audience (ask yourself what feelings you want your audience to have).

Logos—the logical appeal through facts or reasons (present enough supporting evidence so that your readers will be convinced yours is the only sound conclusion).

Just the Facts, Ma'am: Business and Technical Writing

Because they cover such wide fields, business and technical writing often have many individual fine points. The business you're writing for probably has particular styles that you're expected to use. In general, however, in business and technical writing, you should concentrate on five areas: audience, clarity, conciseness, tone, and correctness. First, keep in mind who's going to receive your information (who your audience is). If you're writing for the general public, you'll probably need to take a different slant than if you're writing to a business associate. Your audience may also determine the tone that you'll use. Sometimes—for instance, when you're conveying technical information to beginners—you'll need to use a basic, "here-are-the-instructions" tone. Other times—for example, in business dealings—you'll need to be more formal (but not so formal that you offend your audience by seeming pompous or cold).

Whether you're selling services or conveying information to your audience, you want your message to have an impact. To that end, make sure that your writing is clear and concise. Use vocabulary that your audience will be familiar with. Now isn't the time to impress readers with twenty-dollar words; they'll simply turn away from the piece (or, worse, they'll toss it in the trash). If you must introduce a word or concept that's unfamiliar to your audience, be sure to explain it in plain language.

After you've written your piece as clearly as possible, go back through it and see if there are any places you can shorten it. Your audience will read and remember a short piece more easily than they will a long one.

Flowery descriptions and bloated language simply don't have a place in business and technical writing. Be as succinct as possible in getting your point across. For instance, look at this sentence:

Please be advised that your shipment will arrive on October 16.

You could eliminate the first four words and say the same thing. The same holds true of this example:

I am writing this letter to advise you that we are pleased to announce that we would like to pursue negotiations with your company.

Cut out the beginning nine words and you've saved time for both you and your readers.

Let's say you've written a perfect piece. You know your audience, and you can tell that you've picked the right words to convey your message. You've checked to be sure that you've written as clearly and concisely as possible. What could possibly go wrong?

Know madder how good you're peace is if it ain't spelled an punctuated proper oar if you yews words wrong youll loose your readers. After you've written your piece, be sure to check—and recheck and recheck—your spelling, punctuation, and word usage. You sure don't want something you wrote to be the latest joke around the water cooler.

If X, Then Y: The Cause-and-Effect Essay

In a cause-and-effect essay, you examine the relationships between how certain events bring about or lead to other events. Depending on the depth of your topic, you need to determine if there are several causes that you need to explore, some causes may have more importance than others, or some causes have more immediate or long-term effects than others.

For instance, if you're looking at the causes of U.S. involvement in World War II, you'd write about the immediate cause (the bombing of Pearl Harbor) as well as causes that had been building up for some time (growing hostilities between the United States and Germany and the United States and Japan, increasing bonds between the United States and the Allies, and so on).

In a cause-and-effect essay, some writers find it helpful to think in terms of the following:

- If *X* happens, why does *Y* occur?
- Because *X* happened, why did *Y* occur?
- If *Y* happens, what will *X* have done?
- When *Y* happened, what *X* was a cause?

Be sure that there is actually a relationship between *X* and *Y*. For instance, suppose you buy a new car and then two days later the dealership lowers the price on the model you bought. The dealership's sale had nothing to do with your previous purchase of the car, so there was no cause-and-effect relationship.

The following transition words and phrases can come in handy when writing a cause-and-effect essay: *accordingly, as a consequence, as a result, because, consequently, for this purpose, for that reason, hence, in order that, so, so that, then, therefore, thereupon, thus, to do this, to this end, with this in mind, with this objective.*

Learning to Look Beyond the Obvious

In a comparison-and-contrast paper, you record the similarities and the differences of people, places, events, and so on. Be sure that you omit any statements of the obvious (e.g., Mercury and Mars are both planets that revolve around the sun), because they will undermine the effectiveness of your paper.

Comparing and contrasting two people—or places or works—that have many similarities makes for an interesting or informative piece only if you look beyond what's readily apparent and describe or examine similarities and differences that your readers may not have been aware of or have thought about.

If an assignment calls only for comparison, make sure that you don't contrast—or vice versa. On the other hand, if the assignment calls for both, be sure that you do in fact include both and give each approximately the same amount of space.

The following transition words and phrases of contrast can be useful when you're writing your paper: *after all, alternatively, although, and yet, at the same time, but, conversely, despite, even so, even though, for all that, however, in contrast, in spite of, instead, nevertheless, nonetheless, nor, notwithstanding, on the contrary, on the other hand, otherwise, regardless, still, though,* and *yet.*

Transition words and phrases of similarity include *again, also, and, as well as, besides, by the same token, for example, furthermore, in a like manner, in a similar way, in the same way, like, likewise, moreover, once more, similarly,* and *so.*

Advancing an Assessment: The Critical Analysis

In a critical analysis, you examine and assess a work from a number of points of view. Requirements often vary by instructor or company as to what you should include in this type of work, but you should always include the following:

- Enough background information to familiarize your reader with the piece you're analyzing (including the name of the author or artist)
- A description of the way the piece was written
- The general thesis behind the piece or a synopsis of the work

Since details and the proper use of quotations and citations are important in a critical analysis, you should take care to follow classroom or company directions explicitly.

Considering the following list of questions may be helpful when composing a critical analysis.

- What biographical data about the author or artist is important?
- What are the purpose, tone, and format of the piece?
- How can the work be interpreted? (Note that you're not writing a summary of the work but rather an interpretation of its meaning.)
- Is there any information in the work that's inaccurate or incomplete?
- In what ways was the piece successful?
- How did the author or artist achieve the success?
- In what ways did the author or artist fail?
- What could the author or artist have done to be more successful?
- Is the piece fair (the piece you're analyzing, not the piece you're writing)? If not, what is your evidence that it's biased or subjective?
- Are there historical, psychological, geographical, gender, racial, cultural, or religious considerations that have an impact on the work?

If you're writing a critical analysis of a literary work, you need to consider points such as theme, symbolism, imagery, figurative language, setting, and characterization. Remember to avoid using the first-person point of view in a critical analysis unless your teacher, editor, or employer has specified that you may. In most instances, your personal like or dislike of a work would not be considered a suitable subject (but I bet you'd already figured that out). In order to get the ball rolling, you might begin a sentence this way:

> *I think that the Larkin Busby piece "Trials of a Country Farmer" succeeds on a number of levels.*

But when you're revising, cross out "I think that" and then begin your sentence.

Dear Diary: The Journal

The material you write in a journal might be very personal or very detached—or anything in between. You might wish to use a journal just to record snippets of thoughts about work, or quotations that you find appealing or inspirational, or even the foods you eat every day—or you may choose to write about more personal experiences of your private life.

If you must keep a journal for a class, you might be given specific topics to reflect upon. In this case, be sure you understand whether your journal entries will be shared with others, and don't write anything that you feel is too personal (after all, you don't want the whole world to know your personal business!).

Painting Word Pictures: The Essay of Description

An essay of description relies on imagery to be successful. Your readers are dependent on your words alone in order to see, hear, smell, taste, or feel your subject. For example:

> *The unexpected spring storm sent sharp pellets of rain onto my face, forcing me to swallow the droplets as I panicked and screamed for help.*

In this sentence, the reader can see, feel, and taste the rain, can hear the scream, and can therefore get a good picture of the narrator's predicament.

FACTS

Onomatopoetic words often help convey imagery and impact. The murmur of the wind helps readers hear the specific sound the wind makes; the swish of the basketball helps readers see and hear the excitement of the game; the splatter of the raindrops as they hit the ground shows readers their sound and sight.

Description is used for a number of reasons. In a short story or novel, description of a setting helps readers feel closer to the characters or the plot because they can see and appreciate the characters' environment. In a nonfiction work, description helps readers know how a finished product should look (or feel, taste, smell, or sound).

In writing a description, ask yourself what the dominant impressions are that you want to convey. Do you want your readers to appreciate the beauty and scent of the spring flowers that you saw on a recent walk? Or do you want to convey the various smells and tastes that you remember from your grandmother's kitchen when you arrived for Thanksgiving dinner? Or perhaps you want to express the unsightliness and rancid smell of a local landfill you've visited.

In these examples, you're conveying images that are subjective, so you're allowed to use words that may otherwise be seen as biased. However, if you're describing something objectively (such as a particular building, giving its height, occupancy, rental rates, history, and so on), you shouldn't use words that give a particular connotation or bias to your subject.

Works of description rely on details, so be generous with them. Since description relates to as many of the senses as possible, use adjectives and adverbs liberally. In addition, take a look at the verbs you use and see if you can substitute ones that are more descriptive or precise. Instead of writing, "The man walked into the room," for example, give the reader a better look at how the man entered. Did he tiptoe into the room? bound? slink? prance? Each of those verbs gives a better picture of what happened. Now add adjectives and adverbs. Did the well-dressed man scurry into the room breathlessly? Did the seedy-looking man slink into the room furtively? Did the always-late man tiptoe into the room hesitantly?

While you should choose your descriptive words carefully, be careful not to overdo them. Keep in mind that every noun doesn't need an adjective (much less two or three) and every verb doesn't need an adverb.

The Autobiographical Narrative

If you're writing an autobiographical narrative (sometimes called a personal narrative), you're telling a story about a noteworthy experience in your life. This type of story (usually written in the first person) revolves around an incident that made an impact in your life or taught you an important lesson, one that you can convey to your readers. You should pay particular attention to your characters, plot, setting, and climax. In addition, be sure to include descriptions of the tension—the events that create the interest in your work.

Be sure to focus on a story that is not only important to you but also is valuable enough to be shared. The story of your exhilaration the first time you were behind the wheel of a car may be something you'd like to remember, but it alone would be boring for your readers. However, if you learned some valuable lesson that your readers can relate to (such as how you learned not to try to talk your way out of a speeding ticket) or an amusing anecdote that readers can be entertained by (such as how you met your favorite movie star by accidentally crashing into his or her car on the freeway), then you have an incident that you can develop into an autobiographical narrative.

Be sure to add concrete details to explain and enhance your plot, setting, and characters. These will help you re-create the incident so your readers will stay involved in your story.

The Abridged Version: The Précis

Although you may already have had some type of experience with several of the writing styles mentioned thus far, you may not be at all familiar with the précis (pray-*cee*, from the French word for *precise*). A précis is a clear and logical summary or abridgement of another author's work. Your précis should include the substance or general ideas put forth in the original work, but you must use your own words.

In writing a précis, you must:

- Identify the author's tone and point of view
- Include the key words and major points of the original work
- Include any valuable data that illustrates or supports the original work
- Disregard any introductory or supplementary information
- Use your own voice (you don't have to copy the original author's tone or voice)
- Not give your opinion of the author, the work, or the ideas presented.

Still confused? Think of a newspaper headline; it's a type of précis in that it summarizes the content, focus, and tone of a longer piece.

In general, your précis should be no more than one-third the length of the original work you're summarizing. Remember that requirements (both of length and of format) vary with instructors, publishers, and companies, so be sure to check with them about what they specify.

An Exercise in Explication: The Process Paper

A process paper is a kind of how-to or explanation paper that explains a particular process by giving step-by-step directions or by describing certain changes or operations. Remember that a process paper is written in chronological order; if it's written out of sequence, you defeat the purpose of your paper.

When you begin a process paper, you should be able to define your audience, because they'll determine what kind of language you'll use and how much detail you'll go into. For instance, in a process paper about how to change a tire, you'd write in a less detailed manner for an audience of mechanics than you would for a group of beginning drivers.

If you're writing for a general audience, you need to explain anything that they might find confusing or unfamiliar. Think about how you would explain the process to children. Then reread your material and add a simple explanation of any words or concepts that children wouldn't be familiar with (without being patronizing in the process!). In addition, be sure to be precise when you give measurements. While you may be comfortable in writing "Use a little compost in the mixture," your readers may think that "a little" is a tablespoon, when you actually meant a gallon.

Your readers will have an easier time following your directions if you explain the "whys" behind the directions. So, instead of writing:

When pots are on top of the stove, turn their handles to the side.

Elaborate by giving the reason:

When your pots are on top of the stove, turn their handles to the side so that you'll be less likely to accidentally bump into them, knock them over, and burn yourself.

Remember that transition words and phrases help your reader see the chronological flow of the steps *(next, after that, finally)* as well as the placement of materials *(above, beside that, to the right)*.

Instead of just picturing the activity as they're writing about it, many writers actually perform the activity and tape-record the various steps of what they're doing. This helps them record all the steps correctly, completely, and chronologically.

Be sure to check with your instructor, publisher, or company about any mandates regarding:

- Point of view (usually a process paper is written in second person)
- Use of bulleted lists (for instance, in listing the materials to have on hand before beginning)
- Use of illustrations, diagrams, or photos (if they're allowed, be sure to include any that enhance the written part of your work—and therefore make your instructions easier to understand)

Digging Up the Details: The Research Paper

In a research paper you investigate a topic (often one that's been approved by an instructor or publisher) through consulting various sources, interpreting what the sources relate, developing ideas or conclusions, and citing the sources in your paper. A research paper might be one of the longest and (dare I say it?) most work-intensive pieces you'll ever have to write.

Research papers fall into one of two categories: analytical papers, which provide evidence that investigates and evaluates issues, or argumentative papers, which provide evidence to support your point of view and convince your readers that you're right. Research papers can be written in many formats, and entire books are available to detail various styles. Before you jump into your topic, be sure that you know whether you're supposed to use a specific documentation style. The two most popular are the Modern Language Association (MLA) style, which is detailed in the *MLA Handbook for Writers of Research Papers*, and the American Psychological Association (APA) style, which is detailed in the *Publication Manual of the American Psychological Association.* Other books that you may be directed to use include:

- *The American Medical Association Manual of Style: A Guide for Authors and Editors*, by C. L. Iverson, A. Flanagin, P. B. Fontanarosa, et al. (Baltimore, MD: Williams & Wilkins, 1998.)

- *The Chicago Manual of Style: The Essential Guide for Writers, Editors, and Publishers*, John Grossman (preface). (Chicago, IL: University of Chicago Press, 1993.)
- *Effective Writing: Improving Scientific, Technical, and Business Communication*, by Christopher Turk and John Kirkman. (New York, NY: E. & F.N. Spon, 1989.)
- *Form and Style: Research Papers, Reports, Theses*, by Carole Slade. (Boston, MA: Houghton Mifflin Company, 1999.)
- *Good Style: Writing for Science and Technology*, by John Kirkman. (New York, NY: Chapman & Hall, 1992.)
- *A Manual for Writers of Term Papers, Theses, and Dissertations*, by Kate L. Turabian. (Chicago, IL: University of Chicago Press, 1966.)
- *Scientific Style and Format: The CBE Manual for Authors, Editors, and Publishers*, by Edward J. Huth. (New York, NY: Cambridge University Pres, 1994.)

HERE ARE A FEW PROBLEMS COMMON TO RESEARCH PAPERS TO AVOID:

Topics that are too broad (for instance, "Jupiter: The Fifth Planet" or "Why Americans Enjoy the Cinema")

Papers that don't adhere to specified page limits or word limits

Papers that don't follow the directions about font size, font style, spacing, and margin size

Papers that contain material that is plagiarized

Citations that aren't written in the prescribed manner. In checking your references and citations, make sure you have:

    Included all the information that is necessary

    Correctly placed the information

    Correctly punctuated the information

Often, there's more to a research paper than meets the eye. Be sure you're aware of any timelines about material you must turn in before your actual paper is due. Some instructors give grades on different phases of writing a research paper, such as:

- Identification of your topic
- A preliminary proposal of your paper
- Your notes (sometimes required to be on cards of a specific size)

- An outline of your paper
- Various drafts of your paper
- Identification of bibliographic information and footnote style

An Opportune Occasion to Offer an Opinion

While there are many ways to write a review, every way has this in common: you give your opinion about something and you also support or explain your opinion. Whether you're reviewing a scholarly book, a recent movie, or your tour of the Great Coral Reef, making a statement like "It was cool" without giving your reader any information as to why it was cool sure doesn't give him or her any reason to read further. Because you're writing a critical evaluation, not only do you have to mention both the noteworthy and the flawed aspects of your subject, you also have to explain what made them receive high or low marks in your review.

In writing a review—as with any other kind of writing—keep your audience in mind. If you're reviewing a new restaurant, for instance, would your audience be familiar with the type of food you ordered or menu the restaurant specialized in? You'd probably need to give more explanation to a general newspaper audience than you would to the readers of *Great Gourmet Goodies in America* magazine.

Your instructor, your company, or the publication you're writing for may mandate specific issues for you to address in your review. If that's the case, take some time to read other reviews from magazines, newspapers, or scholarly papers that are written in a style and format similar to what you must use. As you read, note the various features that the writer addressed, and be sure to include those features in your work.

If a rating system is allowed, be sure that you create one that's both clever and applicable to your subject matter (a number of Venetian blinds, for example, to rate a new film noir, or a calendar to show how long readers should wait—or not wait—to read a particular book).

APPENDIX A
Related Web Sites

Adjectives

A number of interactive quizzes on adjectives may be found at these links:

  ✍ *http://members.home.net/englishzone/grammar/1adjectives.html*
  ✍ *http://members.home.net/englishzone/grammar/1compare.html*
  ✍ *www.gsu.edu.tr/Digerwebler/bidem/GsuBdem/gramlib1/gr85.htm*
  ✍ *http://ccc.commnet.edu/grammar/quizzes/adjectives_quiz2.htm*

Adverbs

For an interactive quiz on adverbs, see these Internet sites:

  ✍ *http://ccc.commnet.edu/cgi-shl/quiz.pl/adverbs_quiz.htm*
  ✍ *http://members.home.net/englishzone/grammar/1compare.html*
  ✍ *www.gsu.edu.tr/Digerwebler/bidem/GsuBdem/gramlib1/gr85.htm*

Apostrophes

For an interactive quiz on apostrophes, see this Internet site:

  ✍ *http://webster.commnet.edu/grammar/quizzes/apostrophe_quiz2.htm*

Clauses

For interactive quizzes on clauses, see these Internet sites:

  ✍ *www.uottawa.ca/academic/arts/writcent/hypergrammar/rvnaacls.html*
  ✍ *http://cctc2.commnet.edu/grammar/quizzes/clause_quiz.htm*

For interactive quizzes on independent clauses, see these Internet sites:

  ✍ *http://cctc2.commnet.edu/grammar/quizzes/indep_clause_quiz.htm*
  ✍ *http://cctc2.commnet.edu/cgi-shl/quiz.pl/indep_clause_quiz2.htm*
  ✍ *http://cctc2.commnet.edu/grammar/quizzes/niu/niu4.htm*

For an interactive quiz on distinguishing phrases from clauses, see this Internet site:

  ✍ *www.uottawa.ca/academic/arts/writcent/hypergrammar/rvclause.html*

Colons

For an interactive quiz on colons, see this Internet site:

  ✍ *http://webster.commnet.edu/grammar/quizzes/nova/nova5.htm*

Commas

For an interactive quiz on all uses of commas, see these Internet sites:
- *http://ccc.commnet.edu/grammar/quizzes/comma_quiz.htm*
- *http://webster.commnet.edu/grammar/quizzes/commas_fillin.htm*

For an interactive quiz on commas with introductory phrases, see this Internet site:
- *http://webster.commnet.edu/grammar/quizzes/nova/nova2.htm*

Misused Words

For an interactive quiz on *lay* and *lie*, see this Internet site:
- *www.chompchomp.com/tense6/tense6.htm*

Nouns

A number of interactive quizzes for nouns can be found at these links:
- *http://members.home.net/englishzone/grammar/1nouns.html*
- *http://ccc.commnet.edu/grammar/quizzes/nouns_quiz1.htm*

For an interactive crossword puzzle on count and noncount nouns, see this Internet site:
- *http://ccc.commnet.edu/grammar/quizzes/cross/nouns_cross.htm*

For an interactive quiz on count and noncount nouns, see this Internet site:
- *http://ccc.commnet.edu/cgi-shl/par_numberless_quiz.pl/nouns_quiz.htm*

Outlining

To see a formal outline of ideas for the topic "Why You Should Outline," take a look at this Internet site:
- *http://web.odu.edu/al/writing_tutorial_serv/outline.htm*

Parallelism

If you'd like to try an interactive quiz on parallelism, see this site:
- *www.es.cc.va.us/DEPTS/ENG/grammar/quizzes/parallelismquiz.htm*

Phrases

For an interactive quiz on distinguishing phrases from clauses, see this Internet site:

✐ *www.uottawa.ca/academic/arts/writcent/hypergrammar/rvclause.html*

Prepositions

To take interactive quizzes to check how well you use prepositions, see the sites at:

✐ *http://members.home.net/eng-zone/preps/index.html*

✐ *http://ccc.commnet.edu/grammar/quizzes/preposition_quiz2.htm*

For crossword puzzles using prepositions, see these Internet sites:

✐ *http://ccc.commnet.edu/grammar/quizzes/cross/cross_prep.htm*

✐ *http://ccc.commnet.edu/grammar/quizzes/cross/cross_prep2.htm*

✐ *http://ccc.commnet.edu/grammar/quizzes/cross/cross_prep3.htm*

Pronouns

For interactive quizzes on pronouns, see these Internet sites:

✐ *http://webster.commnet.edu/cgi-shl/quiz.pl/consistency_quiz.htm*

✐ *http://webster.commnet.edu/cgi-shl/quiz.pl/pronoun_quiz.htm*

✐ *http://webster.commnet.edu/grammar/quizzes/pron2_quiz.htm*

✐ *http://webster.commnet.edu/grammar/quizzes/niu/niu8.htm*

✐ *http://webster.commnet.edu/grammar/quizzes/which_quiz.htm*

✐ *http://webster.commnet.edu/cgi-shl/quiz.pl/pronouns_add1.htm*

✐ *http://webster.commnet.edu/cgi-shl/quiz.pl/pronouns_add2.htm*

✐ *http://webster.commnet.edu/cgi-shl/par_quiz.pl/pronouns_add4.htm*

You can test your skills with reflexive pronouns by taking an interactive quiz at:

✐ *http://members.home.net/englishzone/grammar/reflex01.html*

For an interactive quiz on *who*, *whom*, *that*, and *which*, see this Internet site:

✐ *http://webster.commnet.edu/grammar/quizzes/which_quiz.htm*

Question Marks

A number of interactive quizzes on question marks can be found at:
http://members.home.net/englishzone/grammar/1questions.html

Redundancies and Wordiness

If you'd like to take some interactive quizzes about redundancies and wordiness, try these Internet sites:
http://webster.commnet.edu/grammar/quizzes/wordy_quiz.htm
http://webster.commnet.edu/grammar/quizzes/nova/nova8.htm
http://webster.commnet.edu/grammar/quizzes/nova/nova11.htm

Run-on Sentences

For an interactive quiz on run-on sentences, see this Internet site:
http://webster.commnet.edu/grammar/quizzes/runons_quiz.htm
For interactive quizzes on comma splices, see these Internet sites:
http://webster.commnet.edu/grammar/quizzes/nova/nova4.htm
http://webster.commnet.edu/grammar/quizzes/nova/nova3.htm
For interactive quizzes on comma splices and fused sentences, see these Internet sites:
www.chompchomp.com/csfs1/csfs1.htm
www.chompchomp.com/csfs2/csfs2.htm
www.chompchomp.com/csfs3/csfs3.htm
www.chompchomp.com/csfs4/csfs4.htm
www.chompchomp.com/csfs5/csfs5.htm

Sentence Fragments

For interactive quizzes on sentence fragments, see these Internet sites:
http://webster.commnet.edu/grammar/quizzes/fragment_fixing.htm
http://webster.commnet.edu/cgi-shl/quiz.pl/fragments_add1.htm
http://webster.commnet.edu/cgi-shl/quiz.pl/fragments_add2.htm
http://webster.commnet.edu/cgi-shl/quiz.pl/fragments_add3.htm

Sentence Types

For an interactive quiz on sentence types, see this Internet site:

http://cctc2.commnet.edu/cgi-shl/quiz.pl/sentence_types_quiz.htm

Spelling

Try the interactive spelling tests at:

www.funbrain.com/spell/index.html (Click on either the easy or hard test and see how you do with twenty words.)

Then go to:

http://members.home.net/englishzone/spelling/1misc.html

Click on the links for the various tests. Finally, for a quiz of fifty of the trickiest words in the language, go to:

www.sentex.net/~mmcadams/spelling.html

Here are a few helpful sites for spelling rules. These sites range from very elementary to quite detailed.

Susan Jones' Spelling Rules: *www.gsu.edu/~wwwesl/egw/susan.htm*

Prof. Charles Darling's site:

http://webster.commnet.edu/grammar/spelling.htm

The Dictionary of English Usage:

www.lineone.net/dictionaryof/englishusage/d0082823.html

Reading from Scratch: *www.dyslexia.org/spelling_rules.shtml*

To test yourself with homonyms (you remember—words that sound alike but are spelled differently and have different meanings), try the online test at:

www.ambleside.schoolzone.co.uk/ambleweb/quizes/spell2.htm

(Keep in mind that this test originated in the United Kingdom, so you'll probably notice some British spellings.)

Subject-Verb Agreement

For interactive quizzes to check your knowledge of subject-verb agreement, see these Internet sites:

http://members.home.net/englishzone/verbs/1agreement.html

http://webster.commnet.edu/cgi-shl/quiz.pl/sv_agr_quiz.htm

http://webster.commnet.edu/grammar/quizzes/svagr2.htm

✐ *http://webster.commnet.edu/grammar/quizzes/svagr3.html*

✐ *www.cityu.edu.hk/elc/quiz/subverb1.htm*

✐ *http://gabiscott.com/bigdog/agrsv_exercise.htm*

Tenses

To test yourself on correct forms of the simple present tense, try the interactive quiz at:

✐ *http://members.home.net/englishzone/verbs/habit.html*

To test yourself on correct forms of the simple present tense versus simple past tense, try the interactive quiz at:

✐ *http://members.home.net/englishzone/verbs/pres-past.html*

To test yourself on correct forms of the simple present tense versus the present progressive tense, try the interactive quiz at:

✐ *http://members.home.net/englishzone/verbs/pres-pprg.html*

To test yourself on correct forms of the past progressive tense, try the interactive quiz at:

✐ *http://members.home.net/englishzone/verbs/pst-pprg.html*

To test yourself on correct forms of the present perfect tense, try the interactive quizzes at:

✐ *http://members.home.net/englishzone/verbs/prsperf1.html*

✐ *http://members.home.net/englishzone/verbs/prsperf2.html*

✐ *http://members.home.net/englishzone/verbs/prsperf3.html*

To test yourself on using the present perfect tense versus the simple past tense, try the interactive quiz at:

✐ *http://members.home.net/englishzone/verbs/prsperf4.html*

To see if you understand the difference between past perfect and simple past, use the interactive quizzes at:

✐ *http://members.home.net/englishzone/verbs/pstperf1.html*

✐ *http://members.home.net/englishzone/verbs/pstperf2.html*

Use these quizzes to check yourself on the past versus the perfect tenses:

✐ *http://members.home.net/englishzone/verbs/1tenses.html*

✐ *http://members.home.net/englishzone/verbs/pasttenses2.html*

You can check your skills with the past perfect progressive forms with an interactive quiz at:

✐ *http://members.home.net/englishzone/verbs/pstprfprg1.html*

Verbals

See how well you can identify gerunds and infinitives by taking these interactive quizzes:

    ✍ *http://members.home.net/englishzone/grammar/ger-inf01.html*
    ✍ *http://members.home.net/englishzone/grammar/ger-inf02.html*
    ✍ *http://members.home.net/englishzone/grammar/ger-inf03.html*
    ✍ *http://members.home.net/englishzone/grammar/ger-inf04.html*
    ✍ *http://members.home.net/englishzone/grammar/ger-inf05.html*
    ✍ *http://members.home.net/englishzone/grammar/ger-inf06.html*

Verbs

If you'd like to take an interactive quiz on "be" verbs, go to:

    ✍ *http://webnz.com/checkers/GramVerbs.html*

To be sure you're using verb forms correctly, you can test yourself with interactive quizzes at these Internet sites:

    ✍ *www.chompchomp.com/tense1/tense1.1.htm*
    ✍ *www.chompchomp.com/tense2/tense2.htm*
    ✍ *www.chompchomp.com/tense3/tense3.htm*
    ✍ *www.chompchomp.com/tense4/tense4.htm*
    ✍ *www.chompchomp.com/tense5/tense5.htm*
    ✍ *www.es.cc.va.us/DEPTS/ENG/grammar/quizzes/verbquiz.htm*

For an interactive quiz on the subjunctive mood, see this Internet site:

    ✍ *http://webster.commnet.edu/cgi-shl/quiz.pl/subjunctive_quiz.htm*

APPENDIX B

999 of the Most Commonly Misspelled Words

1. abdicate
2. absence
3. academically
4. accelerator
5. accessible
6. acclaim
7. acclimated
8. accommodate
9. accompanied
10. accomplish
11. accordion
12. accumulate
13. achievement
14. acknowledge
15. acoustics
16. acquaintance
17. acquitted
18. acute
19. adequately
20. adjacent
21. adjective
22. admission
23. admittance
24. adolescent
25. adultery
26. advantageous
27. adverb
28. advertisement
29. aerial
30. aerobic
31. aggravate
32. algebraic
33. alleged
34. allegiance
35. alliance
36. alliteration
37. allotting
38. almanac
39. already
40. altogether
41. amateur
42. ambassador
43. among
44. analogy
45. analysis
46. analyze
47. anecdote
48. angle
49. annihilate
50. annual
51. annul
52. antagonist
53. antithesis
54. apartheid
55. apartment
56. apologetically
57. apparatus
58. apparent
59. appearance
60. appositive
61. aptitude
62. arguing
63. argument
64. arrangement
65. ascend
66. aspirin
67. assessment
68. associative
69. assonance
70. asterisk
71. atheist
72. athletics
73. attendance
74. attitude
75. autumn
76. auxiliary
77. awfully
78. bachelor
79. balance
80. ballet
81. balloon
82. bankruptcy
83. barbarian
84. barbaric
85. barbecue
86. barbiturate
87. bargain
88. basically
89. battalion
90. bazaar
91. beautiful
92. beggar
93. beginning
94. behavior
95. beneficial
96. benefited
97. bilingual
98. biography
99. biscuit
100. bisect
101. bizarre
102. blasphemy
103. bologna
104. bookkeeper
105. bouillon
106. boulevard
107. boundary
108. boycott
109. bracelet
110. brackets
111. buffet
112. buoyant
113. bureaucrat
114. burial
115. calculation
116. camouflage
117. candidate
118. cantaloupe
119. caramel
120. caravan
121. carburetor
122. caricature
123. caring
124. cartographer
125. catalyst
126. catapult
127. catastrophe
128. category
129. cellar
130. centimeters
131. chagrined
132. challenge
133. changeable
134. changing
135. character
136. characteristic
137. chassis
138. chastise
139. chocolate
140. chord
141. chrome
142. chromosome
143. chunky
144. cigarette
145. cinquain
146. circumference
147. circumstantial
148. citizen
149. cliché
150. climbed
151. cliques
152. coefficient
153. coherence
154. coincide
155. collectible
156. colonel
157. colony
158. colossal
159. column
160. coming
161. commingle
162. commission
163. commitment
164. committed
165. committee
166. communication
167. commutative
168. comparative
169. compatible
170. compelled
171. competent
172. competition
173. complementary
174. completely
175. complexion
176. composite
177. concede
178. conceit
179. conceivable
180. conceive
181. condemn
182. condescend
183. conferred
184. congratulations
185. congruent
186. conjunction
187. connoisseur
188. conscience
189. conscientious
190. conscious
191. consensus
192. consequences
193. consistency
194. consolidator
195. consonance
196. constitution
197. consumer
198. continuous
199. contraction
200. controlled
201. controller
202. controversial
203. controversy
204. convection
205. convenient
206. coolly
207. coordinates
208. corollary
209. corporation
210. correlate
211. correspondence
212. counselor
213. courteous
214. courtesy
215. criticism
216. criticize
217. crowded
218. crucifixion
219. cruelty
220. curriculum
221. curtail
222. cyclical
223. cylinder
224. dachshund
225. daughter
226. debacle
227. decadent
228. decagon
229. deceit
230. deep-seated
231. deferential
232. deferred
233. definitely
234. dependent
235. depose
236. descend
237. describe
238. description
239. desirable
240. despair
241. desperate
242. detrimental
243. devastation
244. develop
245. development
246. diagonal
247. diameter
248. dictionary
249. difference
250. dilettante
251. diligence
252. dimension
253. dining
254. disappearance
255. disappoint
256. disastrous
257. discipline
258. discrimination
259. disdainfully
260. disguise
261. dispel
262. dispensable
263. dissatisfied
264. disservice
265. distinguish
266. diversified
267. dormitory
268. drugged
269. drunkenness
270. easily

271. economy
272. ecosystem
273. ecstasy
274. efficiency
275. eighth
276. either
277. electrolyte
278. electromagnet
279. elegy
280. elevation
281. eligible
282. eliminate
283. ellipsis
284. embarrass
285. emigrate
286. eminent
287. emperor
288. emphasize
289. empire
290. employee
291. empty
292. enamel
293. encouragement
294. encouraging
295. endeavor
296. enemy
297. enormous
298. enthusiastically
299. entirely
300. entrance
301. equality
302. equator
303. equipped
304. espionage
305. espresso
306. essential
307. exaggerate
308. excellence
309. excess
310. exercise
311. exhaustion
312. exhibition
313. exhilarate
314. expansion
315. experience
316. experiment
317. exponent
318. expression
319. extinct
320. extraneous
321. extremely
322. extrovert
323. exuberance
324. factor

325. fallacious
326. fallacy
327. familiarize
328. fantasy
329. fascinate
330. fascination
331. fascism
332. favorite
333. feasible
334. federation
335. feisty
336. felicity
337. feminine
338. fiction
339. fictitious
340. financially
341. financier
342. fiscal
343. fission
344. fluent
345. forcibly
346. foreign
347. foresee
348. foreshadowing
349. forfeit
350. formula
351. forty
352. fourth
353. frantically
354. frequency
355. fudge
356. fulfill
357. fundamentally
358. galaxy
359. gauge
360. genius
361. geography
362. government
363. governor
364. grammatically
365. grandeur
366. graphic
367. grievous
368. grizzly
369. grocery
370. guarantee
371. guerrilla
372. guidance
373. gyration
374. handicapped
375. happily
376. harass
377. heinous
378. heist

379. hemorrhage
380. heredity
381. heritage
382. heroes
383. hesitancy
384. hexagon
385. hierarchy
386. hieroglyphics
387. hoping
388. horizontal
389. hospital
390. humorous
391. hygiene
392. hyperbole
393. hypocrisy
394. hypocrite
395. hypotenuse
396. hypothesis
397. ideally
398. idiom
399. idiomatic
400. idiosyncrasy
401. ignorance
402. illogical
403. imaginary
404. imitate
405. immediately
406. immigration
407. immortal
408. implement
409. inaudible
410. incidentally
411. incredible
412. indicted
413. indispensable
414. individually
415. inequality
416. inevitable
417. influential
418. information
419. ingenious
420. initially
421. initiative
422. innocent
423. innocuous
424. inoculate
425. instantaneous
426. institution
427. insurance
428. insurgency
429. intellectual
430. intelligence
431. intercede
432. interesting

433. interfered
434. interference
435. interjection
436. interminable
437. intermittent
438. interrogate
439. interrupt
440. intricate
441. introduce
442. introvert
443. invertebrate
444. irony
445. irrelevant
446. irresistible
447. irritable
448. isosceles
449. isthmus
450. jealousy
451. jewelry
452. journalism
453. judicial
454. jugular
455. kaleidoscope
456. kerosene
457. kindergarten
458. kinetic
459. laboratory
460. laborious
461. lapse
462. larynx
463. latitude
464. legitimate
465. length
466. lenient
467. liaison
468. library
469. license
470. lieutenant
471. lightning
472. likelihood
473. likely
474. limerick
475. lineage
476. liquefy
477. literature
478. llama
479. longitude
480. lose
481. lounge
482. lovely
483. luxury
484. lyric
485. magistrate
486. magnificence

487. mainland
488. maintain
489. malicious
490. manageable
491. manufacture
492. mariner
493. martyrdom
494. mass
495. mauve
496. meadow
497. mean
498. meanness
499. median
500. medieval
501. mediocre
502. melancholy
503. melodious
504. metallic
505. metaphor
506. mien
507. migratory
508. mileage
509. millennium
510. millionaire
511. miniature
512. minute
513. mischievous
514. misnomer
515. missile
516. misspelled
517. monarchy
518. mosquitoes
519. mundane
520. municipal
521. murmur
522. muscle
523. myriad
524. mysterious
525. myth
526. mythology
527. naïve
528. narcissism
529. narrative
530. nationalism
531. naturally
532. necessary
533. necessity
534. neighbor
535. neurotic
536. neutral
537. neutron
538. nineteen
539. ninety
540. ninth

541. nonpareil
542. noticeable
543. novelist
544. nowadays
545. nuclear
546. nucleus
547. nuisance
548. nutrition
549. nutritious
550. oasis
551. obedience
552. obsolete
553. obstacle
554. obtuse
555. occasionally
556. occurred
557. occurrence
558. octagon
559. official
560. omission
561. omitted
562. onomatopoeia
563. opaque
564. opinion
565. opossum
566. opponent
567. opportunity
568. oppose
569. opposition
570. oppression
571. optimism
572. optimistic
573. orchestra
574. orchid
575. ordinarily
576. origin
577. originate
578. outrageous
579. overrun
580. oxymoron
581. pageant
582. pamphlet
583. panicky
584. panorama
585. paradox
586. paralysis
587. paralyze
588. parenting
589. parliament
590. particular
591. pastime
592. patronage
593. pavilion
594. peaceable

595. peasant
596. pedestal
597. peers
598. penetrate
599. penicillin
600. peninsula
601. pentagon
602. perceive
603. performance
604. perimeter
605. permanent
606. permissible
607. permitted
608. permutation
609. perpendicular
610. perseverance
611. persistence
612. personal
613. personality
614. personification
615. personnel
616. perspiration
617. persuasion
618. pessimistic
619. pharaoh
620. pharmaceutical
621. phenomenon
622. Philippines
623. philosophy
624. physical
625. physician
626. picnicking
627. pilgrimage
628. pitiful
629. pixie
630. pizzazz
631. placebo
632. plagiarism
633. plagiarize
634. plague
635. planning
636. plausible
637. playwright
638. pleasant
639. pneumonia
640. politician
641. polygon
642. polyhedron
643. portray
644. Portuguese
645. possession
646. possessive
647. possibility
648. postscript

649. potato
650. potatoes
651. power
652. practically
653. prairie
654. precede
655. precedence
656. precipitation
657. precision
658. predation
659. predicate
660. preference
661. preferred
662. prefix
663. prehistoric
664. premier
665. premiere
666. preparation
667. preposition
668. prescription
669. presence
670. prestige
671. presumption
672. prevalent
673. prime
674. primitive
675. prism
676. privilege
677. probability
678. probably
679. probation
680. procedure
681. proceed
682. professor
683. prognosis
684. prominent
685. pronounce
686. pronunciation
687. propaganda
688. propagate
689. protagonist
690. protein
691. proximity
692. psalm
693. psychoanalysis
694. psychology
695. publicly
696. pumpkin
697. pursue
698. puzzling
699. pyramid
700. pyrotechnics
701. quadrant
702. quadrilateral

703. quadruple
704. qualify
705. qualms
706. quandary
707. quantity
708. quarantine
709. quell
710. quench
711. querulous
712. query
713. quest
714. questionnaire
715. queue
716. quibble
717. quiescent
718. quinine
719. quintessentially
720. quipster
721. quizzes
722. quorum
723. quotation
724. quotient
725. radioactive
726. rampage
727. rampant
728. rampart
729. rarefy
730. ratio
731. realistically
732. realize
733. realtor
734. rebellion
735. recede
736. receipt
737. receive
738. receiving
739. reception
740. recession
741. reciprocals
742. recognize
743. recommend
744. rectify
745. reference
746. referred
747. referring
748. reflections
749. refraction
750. regiment
751. rehearsal
752. reign
753. reimburse
754. reincarnation
755. relieve
756. relieving

757. religious
758. remembrance
759. reminiscence
760. remittance
761. repetition
762. representative
763. repugnant
764. resemblance
765. reservoir
766. resistance
767. resources
768. responsibility
769. responsibly
770. restaurant
771. restoration
772. resume
773. retaliate
774. retrospect
775. reveal
776. rheumatism
777. rhombus
778. rhyme
779. rhythm
780. rhythmical
781. ridiculous
782. rotary
783. rotations
784. sacrifice
785. sacrilegious
786. safari
787. safety
788. salami
789. salary
790. sanitize
791. sarcasm
792. satellite
793. satire
794. saturate
795. scalene
796. scenery
797. schedule
798. scholastic
799. scrimmage
800. secede
801. sediment
802. segregate
803. segue
804. seismic
805. seismograph
806. seize
807. sensitive
808. sensory
809. sentry
810. sequence

811. sergeant
812. serpent
813. severely
814. shady
815. shameful
816. shanghai
817. shepherd
818. sherbet
819. sheriff
820. shining
821. shish kebab
822. shrewd
823. siege
824. significance
825. simian
826. similar
827. simile
828. siphon
829. situation
830. skeptical
831. skimp
832. skinned
833. soliloquy
834. sophomore
835. souvenir
836. spasmodic
837. specifically
838. specimen
839. sphere
840. sponsor
841. spontaneous
842. stalemate
843. stamen
844. statistic
845. statistics
846. statue
847. stimulus
848. stopped
849. straitjacket
850. strategy
851. strength
852. strenuous
853. stretch
854. stubbornness
855. studying
856. stupefy
857. subcontinent
858. submersible
859. subordinate
860. succeed
861. success
862. succession
863. sufficient
864. summary

865. summed
866. superintendent
867. supersede
868. supervisor
869. supplementary
870. supposed
871. supposition
872. suppress
873. surround
874. surroundings
875. susceptible
876. suspicious
877. sustenance
878. Swedish
879. swelter
880. syllable
881. symbolic
882. symmetrical
883. sympathy
884. symphonic
885. synchronize
886. syncopation
887. synonymous
888. synopsis
889. synthesize
890. syringe
891. tachometer
892. taciturn
893. talkative
894. tangent
895. tangible
896. tapestry
897. tariff
898. technical
899. technique
900. technology
901. temperamental
902. temperature
903. tenant
904. tendency
905. terminator
906. terrain
907. tertiary
908. themselves
909. theology
910. theoretical
911. theories
912. therefore
913. thermal
914. thermodynamic
915. thesaurus
916. thorough
917. though
918. thought

919. through
920. tolerance
921. tomorrow
922. tortoise
923. tournament
924. tourniquet
925. traffic
926. tragedy
927. transcend
928. transferring
929. transitory
930. transparent
931. trapezoid
932. tried
933. trough
934. trousers
935. truly
936. twelfth
937. tyranny
938. ukulele
939. unanimous
940. undoubtedly
941. universal
942. unmistakable
943. unnatural
944. unnecessary
945. unscrupulous
946. usually
947. utopian
948. vaccine
949. vacuum
950. vagabond
951. valedictory
952. valuable
953. variation
954. vaudeville
955. vehicle
956. vendor
957. veneer
958. vengeance
959. ventriloquist
960. venue
961. veracity
962. versatile
963. vestige
964. village
965. vinegar
966. violence
967. visage
968. visible
969. warrant
970. warring
971. warrior
972. watt

973. weather
974. welcome
975. wherever
976. whether
977. whisper
978. whistle
979. whittling
980. wholesome
981. withhold
982. woman
983. women
984. writing
985. written
986. wrongful
987. wrung
988. xylophone
989. yacht
990. yawn
991. yea
992. yeah
993. yuppie
994. zenith
995. zephyr
996. zinnia
997. zodiac
998. zoological
999. zoology

Root Words, Prefixes, and Suffixes

ROOT WORDS

Word	Definition	Examples
arch	ancient	archetype, archaic, archaeology
aster/astra	star	astronomy, astronaut
audi	hear	inaudible, auditorium, audio
bio	life	biology, biosphere, biography
brev	short	abbreviation, breviary, brevity
chron	time	synchronize, chronicle, chronic, chronological
cog	think	cognition, cogitate, precognition, cognizant, recognize, unrecognizable
cred, credit	belief, faith, confidence	creditable, credit card
curr	run	current
cycle	wheel, circle	motorcycle, bicycle, tricycle, cyclical
derm	skin	dermatologist, dermatitis
dic, dict	speak	benediction, dictionary, dictator, diction, edict, dictatorial, prediction, dictation, interdiction
fer	bring	ferry, infer, refer, conference, reference, inference, transference
fix	fasten	fix, suffix, affix, fixation, fixative, transfix, prefix
geo	earth	geography, geology, geometry, geophysics, geothermal
graph	write/draw	graphic, photography, paragraph, telegraph
grat	free, thanks	ingratiate, gratuitous, gratification, gratify, ingrate, congratulatory, ingratitude
hydro	water	hydroelectric, hydropower, hydrate
illus	draw, show	illusory, illustration, illustrative, disillusion
legis, leg	law, write	legislature, illegible, illegal, legacy, legend, legality, illegitimacy
log, logue	word, thought	monologue, illogical, dialogue, prologue, logician, logistic, logbook
meter, metr	measure	metric, thermometer, meter, geometry, pedometer, centimeter
nega	deny	negative, negate
op, oper	work	cooperation, operator, inoperable, operational
path	feeling	pathetic, sympathy, empathy, psychopath
ped	feet	pedal, impediment, pedestal, pedestrian, centipede, quadruped, peddler, pedicure, pedometer
phil	love	philosophy, Anglophile, philanthropic
phon	voice, sound	telephone, phonology, phonetic, phonograph
phys	body, nature	physics, physiology, physicality, physically, physiologically
port	move	transport, report, import, export, portable, transportation, deportation, portal, portfolio, portage
psych	soul, mind	psyche, psychological, psychiatric, psychic
quar	four	quart, quarter, quarto
quint	five	quintet, quintuplet, quinquennial
science	knowledge	conscience, conscientiousness
scrib, script	write	scribble, manuscript, transcript, inscription, prescription, superscript, prescribe, subscription
sex	six	sextet, sextuplet

tact	touch	intact, tactile
tele	far off, distant	telephone, telegraph, telegram, telecommute, television
ten	to hold	tenure, tenant
ter, terr	earth	extraterrestrial, terrain, terrace, terrier, territorialize
term	end	terminate, termination, terminator, interminable, terminally
urb	city	urban, urbane
vac	empty	vacant, vacuum, vacate, vacuous, vacancy, evacuation, vacationing
val	true	valid, invalidate, valuation, validation, invaluable, revalidation
verb	word	verbal, verbose, adverb, reverberate, reverberation
vid, vis	see	video, television, envision, revise, invisibility, envisage, supervisory

PREFIXES

WORD	DEFINITION	EXAMPLES
a-, an-	without, not	asocial, anarchy, anachronism
ab-	away, away from	abnormal, abstract, abductor
ad-	to, toward, near	adhere, adductor muscle
aero-, aer-, aeri-	air, mist, wind	aeronautics, aerobiology, aerosol
agri-, agrio-	fields	agriculture, agribusiness
ambi-, amb-	on both sides, around, about	ambidextrous, ambiguous, ambient, ambivalent
ambul-	walk, move around	ambulatory, ambulance
ami-, amic-	friend	amicable, amity
amor-	love, loving, fondness for	amorous, amoretto, amorist, amoral
amphi-	round, both sides	amphitheater, amphibian
anima-, anim-	life, breath, soul, mind	animate, animal
anni-, annu-	year, yearly	annual, annuity
ante-	before, prior to	antedate, antecedent, anteroom, antebellum
anthro-	man	anthropology, anthropomorphic
anti-	against	antipathy, anti-Semitic, anticlimax
aqua-	water	aquarium, aqueous
auto-	self, directed from within	automatic, automaton, automated
bi-	two, double	bipartisan, biennial, biceps, bivalve
biblio-	book	bibliography, bibliophile
cardio-	pertaining to the heart	cardiologist, cardiogram
carni-	flesh, meat	carnivorous, carnivore
centi-, cent-	hundred	centigrade, cent, centipede
chrom-	color	chromatic, chromaticity, chrominance
cinema-	set in motion, movement	cinematography, cinematic
circum-	around, surrounding	circumference, circumvent, circumnavigate, circumstantial, circumspect
co-	with, together, jointly	cohabitate, cooperate, coworker, co-owner
contra-, counter-	opposed, against	contradict, contrary, counterintelligence, contravene
corp-, corpus-	body	corpse, corporeal, corporation
cour-	heart	courage, courageous
cur-	heal, cure	curative, curable
curr-, curs-	run, go	curriculum, cursive

Prefix/Root	Meaning	Examples
de-	away from, downward	dethrone, demystify, decelerate, depart
deca-	ten	decimal, decade, decathlon
dei-, div-	God	deity, divine
demos-	people	democracy, demographic
dent-	teeth	denture, dentist
di-	two, double	dimorphism, dichotomy, digress
dia-	across, through	diagonal, dialectic, dialogue, diagnosis
dis-	not, apart, reversal	disrespect, disinherit, disenfranchise, disappear
do-, don-	gift	donation, donate, donor
dominus-	lord	dominant, dominion
dorm-, dormi-	sleeping	dormitory, dormant
duo-, du-	two, a number	duodecimal, duplicate, duologue
dyna-, dyn-	power, strength, force	dynamite, dynamic
dys-	bad, harsh, disordered, abnormal	dysfunction, dysentery, dyslexia, dystrophy
eco-	house, household affairs	ecology
ego-	I, self	ego, egomaniac, egocentric
en-, em-	in, into, to cover or contain	endoskeleton, encipher, embody
epi-	upon, above, over	epidermis, epidemic, epigram, epitaph
ergo-, erg-	work	ergometer, ergonomics
etym-	truth, true meaning, real	etymology, etymologist
eu-	good, well, normal, happy	euphoria, euphemism, Eucharist, eugenic, eulogy
ex-	out of, former	exterior, extemporaneous, extract
extra-	beyond, outside, external	extracurricular, extramural
fac-, feas-	make, do, build, cause, produce	factitious, facsimile, feasible
fidel-	believe, belief, trust, faith	fidelity
fin-	end, last, limit, boundary, border	finality, finish, infinity
flagr-	fire, burn, blaze	flagrant
fluct-	flow, wave	fluctuation, fluctuant
fortu-, fortun-	chance, fate, luck	fortune, fortunate
frater-	brother	fraternity, fraternal, fratricide
grad-	walk, step, move around	grade, graduate, gradual
grav-, griev-	heavy, weighty	gravity, grief, grievous
gymno-, gymn-	naked, uncovered, unclad	gymnasium, gymnastics
helio-, heli-	sun	heliocentric, heliostat, heliographic
hem-, hemo-	blood	hemoglobin, hemophilia, hemorrhage
hemi-	half	hemisphere, hemistich
hetero-	mixed, different, unlike	heterogeneous, heteronym, heterosexual
hippo-, hipp-	horse	hippodrome, hippogriff, hippopotamus
homo-	same, alike	homonym, homogeneous, homogenized
hyper-	above, over, excessive	hyperventilate, hypercritical
hypo-	under, below, less than	hypoglycemia, hypoallergenic, hypothesis
icon-	likeness, sacred or holy image	iconology, iconoclast
ideo-	idea	ideology, ideal
idios-	one's own	idiom, idiosyncrasy, idiot
ign-, igni-	fire, burn	ignite, ignition
il-	not, in, into, within	illogical, illiterate, illicit, illegal
im-	not	impossible, imperceptible, immoral
in-	in	incorporate, induction, indigenous, intrude
inter-	between, among	interact, intercollegiate, interpret, interrupt, Internet
intra-	within, inside	intramural, intravenous, intrapersonal, intrastate
is-, iso-	equal	isometric, isosceles
jet-	throw, send, fling, cast, spurt	jettison, jetsam, jetty

junct-	join, unite, yoke	juncture, junction
kilo-, kil-	one thousand	kilobar, kilobyte, kilogram, kilometer
kine-	move, set in motion	kinematics, kinesis, kinesthetic
lav-, lava-	wash, bathe	lavage, lavatory
lexis-	word	lexicon, lexicography
liber-	free, book	liberty, library, liberal
linguo-, lingu-, lingua-	tongue, language	linguistic, lingual
loc-	talk, speak, speech	locution
lumin-, lum-	shine	luminescence, luminaries
luna-	moon, light, shine	lunar, luna moth, lunatic
macro-	large, great, enlarged	macroeconomics, macroscopic, macrobiotics
magni-, magn-	large, big, great	magnificence, magnify
mal-	bad, ill, wrong, abnormal	maladjusted, malodorous, malfeasance
medio-, medi-	middle	median, mediocre, mediate
mega-	large, great, big, powerful	megavitamin, megalomania, megalopolis
micro-	small, tiny	microscope, micrometer, microfiche
migr-, migrat-	wander, moving	migrant, migratory
milli-	thousand	millimeter, millisecond, milligram
mini-, minut-, minu-	small, little	minuscule, miniature, miniskirt, minimal
mis-	bad, badly	mistake, mistrust, misspell, miscast, misapply
miso-, mis-	hate, hater, hatred	misogamy, misogyny
miss-	send, let go, throw, hurl, cast	missile, mission
mne-, mnem-	memory, to remember	mnemonic
mono-	one, alone	monocle, monopoly, monogamy, monologue, monarchy
mor-, mori-	death, dead	mortician, mortuary, morbid
multi-	many, much	multinational, multitalented, multiply, multicolored
neo-, ne-	new, recent, current	neoclassical, Neolithic, neophyte
nom-	name	nomenclature, nominal, nominative, nomination
non-	not	nonessential, nonworking, nondescript, nonfiction
novo-, nov-, novi-	new, recent	novel, novice, nova
oligo-, olig-	few, abnormally small	oligarchy, oligopoly
omni-, omn-	all, every	omnipresent, omniscience, omnipotent, omnivorous
onoma-	name, word	onomatopoeia, onomastic
ortho-, orth-	right, straight, correct, true	orthodox, orthodontics
oste-, osteo-	bone	osteoporosis, osteal, osteopath
pac-	calm, peaceful	pacify, pacific
pachy-, pach-	thick, dense, large, massive	pachyderm, pachysandra, pachytene
pan-	all, every, completely	pantheistic, panorama, pan-American
pater-	father	paternal, paternity, patricide
patho-	feeling, perception, suffering	pathetic, pathos, pathologist
peri-	around, about, near	peripatetic, periscope
petro-	stone, rock	petrography, petroleum, petrodollar
photo-	light	photosynthesis, photon, photoelectric
pneum-	lung	pneumograph, pneumonia, pneumatic
poly-	many, much, excessive	polygamy, polygon, polymorphous
post-	after	postscript, postgraduate, posterior
pre-	before	pregame, premier, preview, prenuptial, preclude
pro-	before, in favor of, forward	project, prognosis, projectile, pronoun
pyro-, pyr-	fire, burn	pyromania, pyrotechnics
re-	restore, back, again	reassemble, rearrange, redirect, revoke, return
retro-	backward, behind, back	retrospective, retroactive, retrofit, retrogress
rupt-	break, tear, rend, burst	rupture
sana-, sani-, san-	healthy, whole	sanitary, sanitarium

sed-	sit	sedate, sedentary
seismo-	shake, earthquake	seismograph, seismic
semi-	twice, half	semiannual, semicircle, semiconductor, semicolon
senso-, sens-	feeling, discern by the senses	sensory, sensual, extrasensory
sol-	sun	solar, solarium, solar system
soli-, sol-	one, alone, only	solitary, solo
sono-, son-, sona-	sound	sonar, sonogram, sonic, supersonic
spec-	see, look, appear, examine	spectator, spectacles
stell-	star	stellar, stellate, stelliform
stereo-, stere	solid, firm, three-dimensional	stereograph, stereophonic, stereoscope
sub-	under, beneath	subterranean, subterfuge, subway, subordinate
super-, supra-, sur-	above, over, excessive	supermodel, supranational, surcharge, surname
syn-, sym-	together, with, along with	synchronize, symmetry
tacho-, tach-	fast, swift, rapid acceleration	tachometer, tachyarrthythmia
techno-, techn-	art, skill, craft	technology, technique
tempo-, tempor-	time, occasion	temporary, temporal
theo-, the-	God, god, deity, divine	theology, theocracy
therap-	heal, cure, treatment	therapy, therapeutic
thermo-, therm-	heat	thermometer, thermal, thermodynamics, thermostat
toxi-, tox-	poison	toxic, toxicant
trans-	across, on the other side	transport, transcend, transatlantic
ultra-	extreme, beyond	ultraconservative, ultrachic, ultralight
un-	not	unsanctioned, unhappy, unorthodox
uni-	one, single	union, unity, unicorn, unicycle
vice-	in place of	vice-president, viceroy, vice versa
xeno-, xen-	foreign, strange	xenophobia, xenobiotic, xenolith
xero-, xer-	dry	xeroderma, xerography, xerophyte
zoo-	animal, living being, life	zoo, zoology, zoolatry

SUFFIXES

Suffix	Definition	Examples
-able, -ible	able, likely, can do	capable, changeable, visible
-ade	act, action	blockade, renegade
-al	characterized by, pertaining to	national, fictional, directional
-an, -ian	native of, pertaining to	American, Martian, Kentuckian
-ance	quality or state of being	protuberance, parlance
-ancy	action, process, condition	hesitancy, infancy
-ant	someone who or something that	observant, servant, savant
-ar	resembling	circular, avuncular, cellular
-arch	ruler, chief	monarch, patriarch, matriarch
-ary	related to, connected with	budgetary, planetary
-ate	cause, make	liquidate, agitate, populate
-ation	action, result	syncopation, navigation
-cian	possessing a particular skill	musician, physician
-cide	kill	homicide, herbicide, pesticide, genocide
-cracy	rule	democracy, theocracy, technocracy
-cy	action, condition, function	occupancy, hesitancy, prophecy, normalcy
-dom	state of being, realm, office	freedom, dukedom, wisdom
-ee	one who receives action	employee, nominee, refugee
-eer	worker, one who does	auctioneer, pamphleteer, profiteer

-en	made of, resembling, become	maiden, harden, earthen, quicken
-ence, -ency	action, condition, quality	reference, presidency, difference, despondency
-er, -or	one who, that which	weaver, actor, carpenter, miner, agitator, dictator
-ery	skill	bravery, midwifery, millinery, embroidery
-escent	in the process of, becoming	adolescent, obsolescent, quiescent
-ese	a native of	Chinese, Portuguese, Sudanese
-esque	in the manner of, resembling	picturesque, Romanesque, statuesque, humoresque
-ess	female	waitress, goddess, actress
-et, -ette	small one, group	cigarette, midget, islet, majorette
-fic	making, causing	terrific, scientific
-ful	full of, characterized by	cheerful, beautiful, bountiful, wonderful
-fy	make, cause	glorify, simplify, modify, exemplify
-hood	order, quality, state of being	falsehood, neighborhood, brotherhood
-ial	characterized, pertaining to	presidential, manorial, commercial, industrial
-ic	like, having the nature or form of	gigantic, futuristic, diagnostic, agnostic, automatic
-ify	make, cause	purify, electrify, vilify
-ine	relating to, characteristic of	opaline, masculine, medicine
-ish	origin, suggesting, resembling	Spanish, foolish, childish, selfish
-ism	condition, manner	feminism, capitalism, nationalism
-ist	one who, believer, does	pianist, elitist, socialist, biologist
-ite	native, descendant, follower	Brooklynite, Jacobite, Israelite
-itis	inflammation, burning sensation	bursitis, tendonitis, phlebitis
-ity, -ty	state of, quality	captivity, civility, adaptability
-ize	to make or cause to be	emphasize, sterilize
-less	without	groundless, mindless, helpless, penniless
-ly	like	gradually, happily, friendly
-ment	act of, result, means	disappointment, amendment, statement
-ness	quality, degree, state of	forgiveness, goodness, happiness
-ology	study of	psychology, anthropology, ideology, theology, biology
-ory	about, place for	priory, contributory, lavatory
-osis	action, process, condition	hypnosis, osmosis, tuberculosis, halitosis
-ous	marked by, having quality of	courteous, judicious, fibrous
-phobia	fear of	claustrophobia, xenophobia, agoraphobia
-ship	state, quality	relationship, internship, craftsmanship, dictatorship
-tude	quality, state	gratitude, fortitude, servitude, aptitude
-ure	act, office	exposure, legislature
-ward	in the direction of	homeward, leeward, windward, downward, backward
-wise	in the direction of	clockwise, crosswise
-y	full of	blossomy, dirty, muddy

APPENDIX D

Suggested Substitutes for Wordy Phrases

WORDY PHRASE	SUGGESTED SUBSTITUTE
a considerable number of	many
a number of	some, several
absolutely essential	essential
according to our data	we find
adequate number of	enough
adjacent to	next to, near, by, beside, close to
adverse impact on	hurt, set back
affords the opportunity of	allows, lets
ahead of schedule	early
along the lines of	like
already exist	exist
am of the opinion	think
an estimated	about, nearly, almost
are in receipt of	have
are of the same opinion	agree
arrived at the conclusion	concluded
as a consequence	because
as a matter of fact	in fact
as a means of	to
as long as	if, since
as prescribed by	in, under
as regards	about
as to	about, on
as to whether	whether
as well as	and, also
ascertain the location of	find
at all times	always
at the conclusion of	after
at the end of	after
at the present time	currently, now, today
at the same time that	while, when
at this point in time	now
attached herewith	here's, here are
based on the fact that	because
be aware of the fact that	know
both of these	both
brief in duration	brief
by means of, by virtue of	by, with
by the use of	using
came to a realization	realized
cancel out	cancel
center around	concern, revolve around
come to an agreement	agree
comply with	follow, obey
concerning the matter of	about, regarding
conduct an investigation (or) experiment	investigate, experiment
considering the fact that	because, since
costs a total of, costs the sum of	costs
course of	during, while, in
desirous of	want, desire

WORDY PHRASE	SUGGESTED SUBSTITUTE
despite the fact that	although, though
did not succeed	failed
draw to your attention	to show, point out
during such time	during, while, when
during the time that	when
each and every one	each, all
enclosed herewith please find	enclosed is
except when	unless
exhibits the ability to	can
extend an invitation to	invite
for a period of	for
for the reason that	because, since, why
give an account of	describe
give an indication of	show
give and take	compromise, discussion
happens to be	is
has a requirement for	requires, needs
has the ability to, has the capacity for	can
hold a conference (a meeting)	confer, meet
if conditions are such that	if
in a position to	can, may, will
in accordance with	by, following
in accordance with your request	as you requested
in addition to	besides, beyond, and, plus
in advance of	before
in all cases	always
in all likelihood (or) probability	likely, probably
in an effort to	to
in case	if
in close proximity to	near, close, about
in conjunction with	with
in connection with	about, regarding, concerning
in excess of	more than
in large measure	largely
in lieu of	for, instead of
in light of the fact that	since, because
in many cases, in many instances	often, usually
in my own personal opinion	I believe, in my opinion
in no case	never
in order to	to
in possession of	have
in reference to, in relation to, in regard to	about, regarding, for
in relation to, in respect to	about
in respect of	for
in some cases	sometimes
in spite of the fact that	although, despite
in terms of	in, with, for, about
in the absence of	without
in the amount of	for
in the context of	in, about

WORDY PHRASE	SUGGESTED SUBSTITUTE
in the course of	during, while, in, at
in the event of (or) that	if
in the field of	in
in the final analysis	finally
in the form of	as
in the light of	considering
in the majority of instances	usually
in the midst of	during, amid
in the near future (or) in the not too distant future	soon
in the neighborhood of	near, close, about
in the very near future	soon
in the vicinity of	in, near, close to, about
in this day and age	currently, now, today
in today's society	today
in view of the fact that	because, since
in view of the foregoing circumstances	therefore
inasmuch as	since, because
incumbent upon	must
interface with	meet
is able to	can
is aware of the fact that	knows
is capable of	can
is in a position to	can
is in conflict with	conflicts with
it could happen that	perhaps
it has come to my attention that we must, should	I have learned that it is crucial that (or) important that we
it is generally believed	many think
it is imperative that we	we must
it is interesting to note that	note that
it is my understanding	I understand
it is often the case that	often
it is possible that	perhaps
it is recommended that	we recommend
it is worth pointing out that	please note that
it would appear that	apparently
lacked the ability to	could not
limited number	few
made a statement	said
maintain cost control	control costs
make a decision	decide
make a purchase	buy
make an application	apply
make an assumption	assume
make an inquiry regarding	ask about, inquire about
make contact with	meet, call
make preparations for	prepare
make reference to	refer to
manner in which	how
not in a position to	unable to, cannot
not later than	by

WORDY PHRASE	SUGGESTED SUBSTITUTE
notwithstanding the fact that	although
off of	off
on account of the fact that	because
on behalf of	for
on most occasions	usually
on no occasion	never
on numerous occasions	often
on the basis of	because, since, based on
on the grounds that	because, since, why
on the occasion of	on
on the order of	about, approximately, roughly
on the part of	by, for
one of the	a, an, one
owing to the fact that	because, since, why
per diem	daily, daily allowance
period of time	period, time
place a major emphasis on	stress
predicated upon the fact that	based on
previous to, prior to	before
provided that	if
pursuant to your request	as you requested
put an end to	end
range all the way from	range from
realize a savings of	save
refer to as	call, name, term
relating to	about, on
some of the	some
spell out	explain, specify, illustrate, describe, detail
study in depth	study
sufficient number of	enough
take action	act
take into consideration	consider
take the place of	substitute
that being the case	therefore
the fact that	that
the overall plan	the plan
the possibility exists for	may, might, could
the reason for	because, since, why
through the use of	through, by, with
to a certain degree	somewhat
to the extent that	as much as
to the fullest extent possible	fully
to whatever extent	however
under circumstances in which	when
under the provisions of	under
use up	use
utmost perfection	perfection
with a view to	to, so that
with reference to the fact that	concerning, about
with the exception of	except for

Index

The EVERYTHING Series!

BUSINESS

Everything® Business Planning Book
Everything® Coaching and Mentoring Book
Everything® Fundraising Book
Everything® Home-Based Business Book
Everything® Landlording Book
Everything® Leadership Book
Everything® Managing People Book
Everything® Negotiating Book
Everything® Network Marketing Book
Everything® Online Business Book
Everything® Project Management Book
Everything® Robert's Rules Book,
    $7.95($11.95 CAN)
Everything® Selling Book
Everything® Start Your Own Business Book
Everything® Time Management Book

COMPUTERS

Everything® Build Your Own Home Page Book
Everything® Computer Book

COOKBOOKS

Everything® Barbecue Cookbook
Everything® Bartender's Book, $9.95
    ($15.95 CAN)
Everything® Chinese Cookbook
Everything® Chocolate Cookbook
Everything® Cookbook
Everything® Dessert Cookbook
Everything® Diabetes Cookbook
Everything® Fondue Cookbook
Everything® Grilling Cookbook
Everything® Holiday Cookbook
Everything® Indian Cookbook
Everything® Low-Carb Cookbook
Everything® Low-Fat High-Flavor Cookbook
Everything® Low-Salt Cookbook
Everything® Mediterranean Cookbook
Everything® Mexican Cookbook
Everything® One-Pot Cookbook

Everything® Pasta Cookbook
Everything® Quick Meals Cookbook
Everything® Slow Cooker Cookbook
Everything® Soup Cookbook
Everything® Thai Cookbook
Everything® Vegetarian Cookbook
Everything® Wine Book

HEALTH

Everything® Alzheimer's Book
Everything® Anti-Aging Book
Everything® Diabetes Book
Everything® Dieting Book
Everything® Hypnosis Book
Everything® Low Cholesterol Book
Everything® Massage Book
Everything® Menopause Book
Everything® Nutrition Book
Everything® Reflexology Book
Everything® Reiki Book
Everything® Stress Management Book
Everything® Vitamins, Minerals, and
    Nutritional Supplements Book

HISTORY

Everything® American Government Book
Everything® American History Book
Everything® Civil War Book
Everything® Irish History & Heritage Book
Everything® Mafia Book
Everything® Middle East Book

HOBBIES & GAMES

Everything® Bridge Book
Everything® Candlemaking Book
Everything® Card Games Book
Everything® Cartooning Book
Everything® Casino Gambling Book, 2nd Ed.
Everything® Chess Basics Book
Everything® Collectibles Book
Everything® Crossword and Puzzle Book

Everything® Crossword Challenge Book
Everything® Drawing Book
Everything® Digital Photography Book
Everything® Easy Crosswords Book
Everything® Family Tree Book
Everything® Games Book
Everything® Knitting Book
Everything® Magic Book
Everything® Motorcycle Book
Everything® Online Genealogy Book
Everything® Photography Book
Everything® Poker Strategy Book
Everything® Pool & Billiards Book
Everything® Quilting Book
Everything® Scrapbooking Book
Everything® Sewing Book
Everything® Soapmaking Book

HOME IMPROVEMENT

Everything® Feng Shui Book
Everything® Feng Shui Decluttering Book,
    $9.95 ($15.95 CAN)
Everything® Fix-It Book
Everything® Homebuilding Book
Everything® Home Decorating Book
Everything® Landscaping Book
Everything® Lawn Care Book
Everything® Organize Your Home Book

EVERYTHING® KIDS' BOOKS

All titles are $6.95 ($10.95 Canada)
unless otherwise noted
Everything® Kids' Baseball Book, 3rd Ed.
Everything® Kids' Bible Trivia Book
Everything® Kids' Bugs Book
Everything® Kids' Christmas Puzzle
    & Activity Book
Everything® Kids' Cookbook
Everything® Kids' Halloween Puzzle
    & Activity Book ($9.95 CAN)

All Everything® books are priced at $12.95 or $14.95, unless otherwise stated. Prices subject to change without notice.
Canadian prices range from $11.95–$31.95, and are subject to change without notice.

Everything® Kids' Hidden Pictures Book
($9.95 CAN)
Everything® Kids' Joke Book
Everything® Kids' Knock Knock Book
($9.95 CAN)
Everything® Kids' Math Puzzles Book
Everything® Kids' Mazes Book
Everything® Kids' Money Book ($11.95 CAN)
Everything® Kids' Monsters Book
Everything® Kids' Nature Book ($11.95 CAN)
Everything® Kids' Puzzle Book
Everything® Kids' Riddles & Brain Teasers Book
Everything® Kids' Science Experiments Book
Everything® Kids' Soccer Book
Everything® Kids' Travel Activity Book

KIDS' STORY BOOKS

Everything® Bedtime Story Book
Everything® Bible Stories Book
Everything® Fairy Tales Book
Everything® Mother Goose Book

LANGUAGE

Everything® Conversational Japanese Book
(with CD), $19.95 ($31.95 CAN)
Everything® Inglés Book
Everything® French Phrase Book, $9.95
($15.95 CAN)
Everything® Learning French Book
Everything® Learning German Book
Everything® Learning Italian Book
Everything® Learning Latin Book
Everything® Learning Spanish Book
Everything® Sign Language Book
Everything® Spanish Phrase Book,
$9.95 ($15.95 CAN)
Everything® Spanish Verb Book,
$9.95 ($15.95 CAN)

MUSIC

Everything® Drums Book (with CD),
$19.95 ($31.95 CAN)
Everything® Guitar Book
Everything® Home Recording Book
Everything® Playing Piano and Keyboards Book
Everything® Rock & Blues Guitar Book
(with CD), $19.95 ($31.95 CAN)
Everything® Songwriting Book

NEW AGE

Everything® Astrology Book
Everything® Divining the Future Book
Everything® Dreams Book
Everything® Ghost Book
Everything® Love Signs Book,
$9.95 ($15.95 CAN)
Everything® Meditation Book
Everything® Numerology Book
Everything® Paganism Book
Everything® Palmistry Book
Everything® Psychic Book
Everything® Spells & Charms Book
Everything® Tarot Book
Everything® Wicca and Witchcraft Book

PARENTING

Everything® Baby Names Book
Everything® Baby Shower Book
Everything® Baby's First Food Book
Everything® Baby's First Year Book
Everything® Birthing Book
Everything® Breastfeeding Book
Everything® Father-to-Be Book
Everything® Get Ready for Baby Book
Everything® Getting Pregnant Book
Everything® Homeschooling Book
Everything® Parent's Guide to Children
with Asperger's Syndrome
Everything® Parent's Guide to Children
with Autism
Everything® Parent's Guide to Children
with Dyslexia
Everything® Parent's Guide to Positive Discipline
Everything® Parent's Guide to Raising a
Successful Child
Everything® Parenting a Teenager Book
Everything® Potty Training Book,
$9.95 ($15.95 CAN)
Everything® Pregnancy Book, 2nd Ed.
Everything® Pregnancy Fitness Book
Everything® Pregnancy Nutrition Book
Everything® Pregnancy Organizer,
$15.00 ($22.95 CAN)
Everything® Toddler Book
Everything® Tween Book

PERSONAL FINANCE

Everything® Budgeting Book
Everything® Get Out of Debt Book

Everything® Get Rich Book
Everything® Homebuying Book, 2nd Ed.
Everything® Homeselling Book
Everything® Investing Book
Everything® Money Book
Everything® Mutual Funds Book
Everything® Online Business Book
Everything® Personal Finance Book
Everything® Personal Finance in Your
20s & 30s Book
Everything® Real Estate Investing Book
Everything® Wills & Estate Planning Book

PETS

Everything® Cat Book
Everything® Dog Book
Everything® Dog Training and Tricks Book
Everything® Golden Retriever Book
Everything® Horse Book
Everything® Labrador Retriever Book
Everything® Poodle Book
Everything® Puppy Book
Everything® Rottweiler Book
Everything® Tropical Fish Book

REFERENCE

Everything® Astronomy Book
Everything® Car Care Book
Everything® Christmas Book,
$15.00 ($21.95 CAN)
Everything® Classical Mythology Book
Everything® Einstein Book
Everything® Etiquette Book
Everything® Great Thinkers Book
Everything® Philosophy Book
Everything® Psychology Book
Everything® Shakespeare Book
Everything® Tall Tales, Legends, & Other
Outrageous Lies Book
Everything® Toasts Book
Everything® Trivia Book
Everything® Weather Book

RELIGION

Everything® Angels Book
Everything® Bible Book
Everything® Buddhism Book
Everything® Catholicism Book
Everything® Christianity Book
Everything® Jewish History & Heritage Book

All Everything® books are priced at $12.95 or $14.95, unless otherwise stated. Prices subject to change without notice.
Canadian prices range from $11.95–$31.95, and are subject to change without notice.

Everything® Judaism Book
Everything® Koran Book
Everything® Prayer Book
Everything® Saints Book
Everything® Understanding Islam Book
Everything® World's Religions Book
Everything® Zen Book

SCHOOL & CAREERS

Everything® After College Book
Everything® Alternative Careers Book
Everything® College Survival Book
Everything® Cover Letter Book
Everything® Get-a-Job Book
Everything® Hot Careers Book
Everything® Job Interview Book
Everything® New Teacher Book
Everything® Online Job Search Book
Everything® Personal Finance Book
Everything® Practice Interview Book
Everything® Resume Book, 2nd Ed.
Everything® Study Book

SELF-HELP/ RELATIONSHIPS

Everything® Dating Book
Everything® Divorce Book
Everything® Great Marriage Book
Everything® Great Sex Book
Everything® Kama Sutra Book
Everything® Romance Book
Everything® Self-Esteem Book
Everything® Success Book

SPORTS & FITNESS

Everything® Body Shaping Book
Everything® Fishing Book
Everything® Fly-Fishing Book
Everything® Golf Book
Everything® Golf Instruction Book
Everything® Knots Book
Everything® Pilates Book
Everything® Running Book
Everything® Sailing Book, 2nd Ed.
Everything® T'ai Chi and QiGong Book
Everything® Total Fitness Book
Everything® Weight Training Book
Everything® Yoga Book

TRAVEL

Everything® Family Guide to Hawaii
Everything® Family Guide to New York City, 2nd Ed.
Everything® Family Guide to Washington D.C., 2nd Ed.
Everything® Family Guide to the Walt Disney World Resort®, Universal Studios®, and Greater Orlando, 4th Ed.
Everything® Guide to Las Vegas
Everything® Guide to New England
Everything® Travel Guide to the Disneyland Resort®, California Adventure®, Universal Studios®, and the Anaheim Area

WEDDINGS

Everything® Bachelorette Party Book, $9.95 ($15.95 CAN)

Everything® Bridesmaid Book, $9.95 ($15.95 CAN)
Everything® Creative Wedding Ideas Book
Everything® Elopement Book, $9.95 ($15.95 CAN)
Everything® Father of the Bride Book, $9.95 ($15.95 CAN)
Everything® Groom Book, $9.95 ($15.95 CAN)
Everything® Jewish Wedding Book
Everything® Mother of the Bride Book, $9.95 ($15.95)
Everything® Wedding Book, 3rd Ed.
Everything® Wedding Checklist, $7.95 ($12.95 CAN)
Everything® Wedding Etiquette Book, $7.95 ($12.95 CAN)
Everything® Wedding Organizer, $15.00 ($22.95 CAN)
Everything® Wedding Shower Book, $7.95 ($12.95 CAN)
Everything® Wedding Vows Book, $7.95 ($12.95 CAN)
Everything® Weddings on a Budget Book, $9.95 ($15.95 CAN)

WRITING

Everything® Creative Writing Book
Everything® Get Published Book
Everything® Grammar and Style Book
Everything® Grant Writing Book
Everything® Guide to Writing a Novel
Everything® Guide to Writing Children's Books
Everything® Screenwriting Book
Everything® Writing Well Book

· ·

Introducing an exceptional new line of beginner craft books from the Everything® series!

All titles are $14.95 ($22.95 CAN)

Everything® Crafts—Create Your Own Greeting Cards
1-59337-226-4
Everything® Crafts—Polymer Clay for Beginners
1-59337-230-2

Everything® Crafts—Rubberstamping Made Easy
1-59337-229-9
Everything® Crafts—Wedding Decorations and Keepsakes
1-59337-227-2

Available wherever books are sold!
To order, call 800-872-5627, or visit us at *www.everything.com*
Everything® and everything.com® are registered trademarks of F+W Publications, Inc.